Time and Temporality in Organisations

Kätlin Pulk

Time and Temporality in Organisations

Theory and Development

Kätlin Pulk
Estonian Business School
Tallinn, Estonia

ISBN 978-3-030-90695-5   ISBN 978-3-030-90696-2 (eBook)
https://doi.org/10.1007/978-3-030-90696-2

© The Editor(s) (if applicable) and The Author(s), under exclusive licence to Springer Nature Switzerland AG 2022
This work is subject to copyright. All rights are solely and exclusively licensed by the Publisher, whether the whole or part of the material is concerned, specifically the rights of translation, reprinting, reuse of illustrations, recitation, broadcasting, reproduction on microfilms or in any other physical way, and transmission or information storage and retrieval, electronic adaptation, computer software, or by similar or dissimilar methodology now known or hereafter developed.
The use of general descriptive names, registered names, trademarks, service marks, etc. in this publication does not imply, even in the absence of a specific statement, that such names are exempt from the relevant protective laws and regulations and therefore free for general use.
The publisher, the authors and the editors are safe to assume that the advice and information in this book are believed to be true and accurate at the date of publication. Neither the publisher nor the authors or the editors give a warranty, expressed or implied, with respect to the material contained herein or for any errors or omissions that may have been made. The publisher remains neutral with regard to jurisdictional claims in published maps and institutional affiliations.

This Palgrave Macmillan imprint is published by the registered company Springer Nature Switzerland AG.
The registered company address is: Gewerbestrasse 11, 6330 Cham, Switzerland

*Dedicated to the memory of my parents
Jaan Pulk (deceased May 2020)
Maris Nettan (deceased October 2020)*

Foreword

This book contains an impressive array of insights and ideas. Kätlin Pulk extracts insights into time from a broad range of works in different scientific disciplines, which she then uses to enrich our understanding of time in relation to organizational research. Her book reveals first and foremost how time notions used in organizational research have tended towards the simplistic and reductionist, whereas time may be used to reveal important nuances in organizational life. Because nuances there are, we can let go of the mainstream notions of time and embrace more diverse understandings. A strength of this book is the interrelating of time concepts across levels, between contexts, and between ontologies. Kätlin Pulk problematizes underlying assumptions about, for instance, clock time and event time. She also pursues the ontological origins of such time notions to deconstruct their assumed differences. I see it as a book that problematizes rather than develops solutions. It reveals understandings of time and suggests important areas of connections and disconnections. The dynamics of time is seen from multiple angles and nuances are discussed in the light of multiple scientific disciplines. This is also what makes the book a useful contribution towards broadening organizational research to take on challenges in the world that we inhabit and even more so in the world that we are moving towards. Hopefully, in the years to come, organizational scholars will embrace increasingly complex models of time and temporality. To do that, they will need to draw upon resources, such as this book, which discuss the broad range of ideas and insights related to time and temporality that exist in various scientific disciplines. Models and concepts have accumulated over the years, and scholars increasingly need to be informed of what exists as they develop useful theories for the emerging future. By showing us and discussing the diversity of time theories available to us, this book fulfils such a need. It is now up to scholars to extend these insights into organizational research that takes on the future that lies in front of us.

Copenhagen Business School Tor Hernes
Copenhagen, Denmark
University of South-Eastern Norway
Notodden, Norway

Preface

Having been asked once, "what is my research interest," and after replying that I am interested in time and temporality, I received the comment, "oh, you know, I don't worry about time and temporality. I just follow the approach from physics, that there is no such thing as time" I was surprised, not so much that time and temporality could be considered uninteresting and irrelevant, but that there is no time in physics. I was convinced that time is addressed in physics and occupies a pretty central position in theoretical physics. However, after checking some sources, it turned out that theoretical physics could manage with very little time and even without time at all. To my comfort, I found that despite time's non-prominent role in theoretical physics, several authors from the field do highlight the special role of time in social affairs and human life.

This book is about time and temporality as manifested in organizations in their different forms. To some extent, the structure of this book reflects my journey in discovering different layers and dimensions of time and temporality. It is not exhaustive, and some topics, such as, organization-individual temporal fit, temporal anchoring, mono- and polychronicity, among others, are not covered in detail. These topics left uncovered are not somehow unimportant or irrelevant, but for some reason, they did not become central in my journey. However, I try to show the path through some of the main classifications of time and temporality and indicate where we are dealing with antonyms. This book does not attempt to create a new theory about organizational time. Instead, considering that the relationships human beings have with time are simultaneously geographical and historical, physical and biological, technical and psychological, individually and socially constructed, it tries to synthesize different fields and explain social time, including organizational time, as heterogeneous and multi-layered phenomena. The approach taken in this book is like peeling an onion—uncovering, layer by layer, various related aspects of time and temporality, each allowing more profound further research. Although not exhaustive, the references used are quite extensive and include both recent publications and several seminal works that have endured time and function as anchors towards a gradual development of the field. In that respect, if the reader is interested in joining the ongoing debates related to topics concerning time and temporality and the development of the field, this book may serve as an initial introduction. I hope sincerely that this book offers some interesting food for thought.

Tallinn, Estonia Kätlin Pulk
31 July 2021

Acknowledgements

I want to express my gratitude to several people who have had a direct or an indirect role in helping this book to its completion.

First, I would like to thank Jessica Harrison, who, at EGOS 2019 in Edinburgh, at the time she was an editor at Palgrave Macmillan, invited me to write a book proposal. I am grateful to Jessica for recognizing the potential, offering this possibility, believing in me, and encourage me to write a monograph. I am also thankful to Jessica for her patience and encouragement because I had no experience in writing monographs, so I had my doubts and hesitations. Thank you, Jess!

I am thankful to two reviewers who gave the green light to my book proposal on top of valuable comments and suggestions.

I want to express my gratitude to my colleague at Estonian Business School, Riina Koris. She was the one who read the first drafts of all the chapters except Chap. 4, gave her feedback, and constantly asked for more examples. Therefore, whenever you feel the need for example(s), and there are none, you can be sure that I have probably ignored Riina's request for examples without any solid reason. Riina's support during the writing process was invaluable.

I am thankful to Michael Haagensen for editing the manuscript despite the sweltering summer we experienced in Estonia.

I thank Ruby Panigrahi, Srishti Gupta, Alec Selwyn, and Anette Weisse from the Springer Nature/Palgrave Macmillan production team for the pleasant cooperation and smooth production process. I am especially grateful to Ruby Panigrahi for answering my numerous questions related to the manuscript preparation.

I am grateful to the Center of Organizational Time at Copenhagen Business School, led by Tor Hernes, for organizing regular seminars and inviting scholars to present their recently published work on time and temporality. During the restrictions imposed due to COVID-19, these webinars served as valuable connections to the network of this specific research community.

I express my gratitude to the organizers of the EGOS standing working group on time and temporality 2019–2021 and all the participants who have participated in the fruitful discussions. I gained a lot from these discussions, and I hope that these exciting discussions will continue in the future.

I am thankful to the PROS conference organized by Haridimos Tsoukas, Ann Langley, and Sophia Tzagaraki for creating an exceptional atmosphere for exciting and thought-provoking debates and discussions, including on time and temporality.

I am deeply grateful to all the scholars who have contributed to the study of time and temporality, whether recently or long ago. Although I did not start writing this book as a complete novice in the field, I learned tremendously throughout the writing process, from more recent publications and work published years, decades, and even centuries ago.

My wholehearted gratitude goes to my family, who have tolerated me becoming one with the sofa corner while barricading my position with piles of printouts, journals, and books. Their systematic cheering in the style of "you can do it!" managed to carry me through the last year and a half.

About This Book

This book serves as an introduction to different understandings of time and temporality in organizations. Considering the humans' relationship to time is simultaneously geographical, historical, physical, biological, technical, psychological, instrumental, existential, and individually and socially constructed, this book tries to synthesize different fields and explain social time, including organizational time, as heterogeneous and multi-layered phenomena. By highlighting the pluralistic and multi-dimensional nature of social time, this book discusses the broad range of ideas and insights related to time and temporality across various scientific disciplines, contexts, levels, and ontologies. The book consists of seven chapters covering the origin, role, and implications of standardized clock time, subjectively perceived time, endogenous and subjective temporality, socially constructed time, social time as a multi-layered context, different views to events, and the relationship between events and time. By drawing both from the classic writings and recent scholarship, this book underscores some of the important nuances in views on time and temporality.

Contents

1 Introduction — 1

2 Objective View of Time and Temporality: Time as a Tool for Organizing — 17

3 Subjective Time as Subjectively Perceived Temporal Dimensions of Objective Time — 67

4 Temporality—Endogenous and Subjective — 117

5 Socially Constructed Time and Social Time as a Context — 185

6 Events, Time, and Events-Based Time — 233

7 Some Challenges Related to Time and Temporality — 277

Index — 289

List of Figures

Fig. 2.1	Before time was invented	23
Fig. 3.1	Time-moving frame—Meeting is on Monday	81
Fig. 3.2	Ego-moving frame—Meeting is on Friday	82
Fig. 3.3	Ego-moving frame	82
Fig. 3.4	Time-moving frame	83
Fig. 4.1	Implicit and explicit temporalities	131
Fig. 4.2	The *possible shape* of our life as a combination of temporal aspects and temporal positions	135
Fig. 4.3	Possibilities, potentialities and becoming in irreversible time	163
Fig. 4.4	The model of ongoing temporality	166
Fig. 5.1	Temporal orientation of activities	200
Fig. 5.2	Concentric model of social time as a context	206
Fig. 5.3	A multi-layered concentric social time connected by events	208

List of Tables

Table 3.1	Comparison of assumptions of the ego-moving and time-moving frames	87
Table 3.2	A summary of Tang, Richter and Nadkarni's framework	89
Table 3.3	Deterministic versus hegemonic time	99
Table 4.1	Different types of pasts based on Oakeshott (1983, 1995)	160
Table 5.1	Temporal orientation of activities	199
Table 5.2	Layers of social time as context	204
Table 6.1	Comparison of the conceptualization of events and time in organization studies	235
Table 6.2	Temporal elements of structure/process based on Luhmann's reflexive selection process framework	241
Table 6.3	Possible selection criteria for events	241

1

Introduction

Having been asked once, "what is my research interest," and after replying that I am interested in time and temporality, I received the comment, "oh, you know, I don't worry about time and temporality. I just follow the approach from physics, that there is no such thing as time." I was surprised, not so much that time and temporality could be considered uninteresting and irrelevant, but that there is no time in physics. I was convinced that time is addressed in physics and occupies a pretty central position in theoretical physics. However, after checking some sources, it turned out that theoretical physics could manage with very little time and even without time at all. While most theories in theoretical physics are atemporal, there are still some traces of time, for example, in thermodynamics, quantum gravity, and relativity (Callender, 2017). Still, as both Callender (2017) and Rovelli (2011, 2017) confirm, physics manage nicely without time, and time tends to mess up and complicate things unnecessarily. Weinersmith explains the situation with time in physics through the prism of humour by stating, "Aristotle said a bunch of stuff that was wrong. Galileo and Newton fixed things up. Then Einstein broke everything again. Now, we've basically got it all worked out, except for small stuff, big stuff, hot stuff, cold stuff, fast stuff, heavy stuff, dark

© The Author(s), under exclusive license to Springer Nature Switzerland AG 2022
K. Pulk, *Time and Temporality in Organisations*,
https://doi.org/10.1007/978-3-030-90696-2_1

stuff, turbulence, and *the concept of time*" (2017: 1 emphasis added). This statement, although expressed through humour, carries a certain amount of truth—in theoretical physics, time is mainly ignored (Callender, 2017). Rovelli (2011) even urges us to forget time. However, Callender claims that "time is that set of directions in which our physical theory can tell the best stories" (2017: 23).

Based on Callender's statement that time provides the best stories in physics, I believe that time and temporality not only provide the best stories in social and organizational studies but also explain aspects overlooked by atemporal theories. There are several publications in sociology that treat the different social aspects of time. Some of those works are also cited in the following pages (e.g., Gurvitch, 1964/1990; Harvey, 1989; Levine, 2006; Mumford, 1970; Nowotny, 1996; Zerubavel, 1991, 2003). In other words, over the years, there has been interest in time in sociology. Issues concerning time are also covered in psychology, and again, there are some references to literature from psychology related to time and temporality. It cannot be argued that time and temporality are entirely ignored in organization and management theories.

Some early works have explicitly placed time at the centre of management and organization studies, for example, Taylor, with his time and motion studies in 1911. Sorokin and Merton (1937) suggested incorporating time and temporality more systematically into management studies to look beyond objective clock time (time and motion studies by Taylor) to socially created aspects of time. Roy (1959) took the call from Sorokin and Merton seriously and provided a profound analysis of subjective socially constructed time and its importance in everyday organizational life. However, a more systematic representation of time and temporality in organization studies has only emerged relatively recently. Until recently, time, if included in organization theories, is either conceptualized from the perspective of Newtonian physics or left undefined. It could be that time has been avoided because it tends to multiply all the problems in our theorizing (Luhmann, 1995: 41). Another reason could easily be that: "The question of what time, in essence, has repeatedly proved unanswerable, and is probably the wrong question" (Luhmann, 2018: 122).

1 Introduction   3

Nevertheless, more recently, issues related to time and temporality in organization studies have attracted more extensive scholarly attention with increased attention on the different features and different concepts of time. For example, a standing working group focusing on time at EGOS (European Group of Organization Studies) has been granted to run 2019–2023. There are also several special issues on time and temporality in journals such as *Strategic Organization*, *Organizational and Cultural Psychology*, and *Management Studies* (e.g., Reinecke et al., 2020; Shipp & Fried, 2014a, 2014b; Simão et al., 2015). In addition, the Centre for Organization and Time at Copenhagen Business School, directed by Professor Hernes, organizes regular seminars on the topic.

While broader scholarly interest in matters related to time and temporality is very much welcome and has the potential for further advancements in studies related to time and temporality in organization studies, it is essential to have clear definitions of the terms to enable fruitful debates and improvements in theorizing (Aeon & Aguinis, 2017). The fact that "there is no single, overarching theory of time" (Shipp & Fried, 2014a: 4) indicates that there are no unified concepts for time and temporality. Fried and Slowik point out that:

> Time is an enigmatic aspect of reality that researchers from a variety of disciplines are now beginning to understand, including those in the behavioral sciences. Although many important strides have been taken toward gaining a fuller understanding of time in the areas of psychology, sociology, or organizational behavior…, these advances are "esoteric" and far from becoming common knowledge. (2004: 405)

Importantly, this fuzziness in relation to time and temporality is not a characteristic unique to organization studies. We can find similar vagueness and contradictions in physics (e.g., Callender, 2017), psychology (e.g., Klempe, 2015), and even philosophy (Bardon, 2013). Therefore, to create a shared understanding and enable a dialogue that could further develop the field, it is essential to clarify how we use these concepts, why, and what are the consequences.

Starting to work on issues related to time and temporality without a clear definition of terms could easily end up with something reminiscent of Shigeo Fukuda's non-moving optical illusion titled "Underground piano" (also known as "Piano in the mirror"). In his artwork, Fukuda created a mirror image that correctly presents a piano if viewed from a specific angle. However, if we look directly at the object used to create the reflection, we see a strange composition made of different piano parts.[1] This analogy tends to work also for time and temporality. Viewed from a certain angle (which tends to have resulted from a superficial glance), it may seem that there is a unified understanding of time and temporality. However, as soon as we start to pay attention to the details, the perfect reflection transforms into a messy setup presenting different and often unconnected features of time and temporality.

Often clock time based on Newtonian physics is referred to as the real thing (Bardon, 2013) or the "real stuff" (Bluedorn, 2002: 27). However, a closer look at physics reveals that the Newtonian concept of time is only one among many. For example, Callender, from the perspective of theoretical physics, claims that physical time is fragmented, and "the concept time includes many important features" (2017: 122) "but the connections amongst the features of time are thin" (2017: 138). Being necessarily not over-optimistic, Callender admits that in physics, "there may not be an answer to the Fragmentation Problem" (2017: 136). At the same time, he points out the possibility that the fragmentation problem may have more than one correct answer.

The fragmentation problem is not unique to physics but also seems relevant in management and organization studies (Aeon & Aguinis, 2017). Therefore, although found or at least starting to find their way to research agendas and publications in organization studies, it is often claimed that time and temporality are concepts that remain vague and elusive. While reading publications that address time and temporality, we can easily recognize that these concepts are often left unclarified and undefined. Put differently, the definitions of time and temporality are often treated as taken-for-granted knowledge. Consequently, it could happen that when people are referring to time and temporality, they do

---

[1] Image of the "Underground Piano" by Shigeo Fukuda https://micro.cibermitanios.com.ar/post/86166329778/shigeo-fukuda-piano.

so as if time and temporality have unified agreed upon and clear-cut meanings.

However, the conceptualization of these terms may differ significantly, resulting in inevitable confusion (Klempe, 2015), which, unfortunately, is not helpful. On the one hand, time could be viewed as a general term covering various aspects of duration. It could be viewed as an objective, measurable dimension of the world, independent of the individual observer or perceiver. On the other hand, the interpretation of an objective, measurable time is culturally contextualized (Lewis & Weigert, 1981; Simão, 2015), that is to say, the meaning of time is socially constructed (Hoy, 2009; Levine, 2006; Zerubavel, 1987, 2003) and culturally embedded (Lewis & Weigert, 1981). However, socially constructed time may refer to the semiotic meaning ascribed to different temporal dimensions of objective time or event time or the shared experience of intersubjective time or societal time. Subjective time could refer to existential time and subjective perceptions of objective clock time. Similarly, temporality may refer to relations between the past, present, and future and the temporal dimension of objective time, like tempo, duration, frequency, and so on. Therefore, it is easy to become confused.

This mixture of often undefined concepts and terms has led to situations where new researchers trying to enter the field seriously ask whether we are dealing with event-based time or socially constructed time when discussing or analysing social events? On the other hand, the relative messiness around terms and concepts leads to justified questions, such as what is the difference between time and temporality or what exactly do we mean by temporality and how do we define that? Indeed, sometimes, time and temporality are used as synonyms, which do not necessarily help clarify the distinction between these two terms. But as Reinecke et al. (2020: 2, emphasis added) rightfully claim: "The way we conceptualise time and temporality is critical for process organization studies since it shapes how we view and relate to organizational phenomena." I dare to extend this claim further to include, in addition to process organization studies, also other organizational theories—how we conceptualize time matters in general. However, while it is important to conceptualize time and temporality, it is also important to be explicit about how these terms are conceptualized.

To help make our approach to time and temporality explicit, Hussenot et al. (2020) have proposed using either "the ontology of time" or "the ontology of temporality." The ontology of time assumes time as a linear and sequential external dimension and as a standardized measure, a tool for coordination and management. The ontology of temporality refers to ongoing temporality (Schultz & Hernes, 2013), the ongoing re-configuring and re-definition of the past, present, and future, and the endogenous temporality (Hernes et al., 2020). I found this classification to be highly helpful because it turned out that distinctions based on labels like objective time and subjective or socially constructed time are imprecise and insufficient for tackling the ontological differences between various types of time and temporality as presented in the literature.

As none of the times and none of the aspects of time could be claimed to be superior or inferior to others, it is important to be aware of what we choose to pay attention to and what we choose to ignore and the possible consequences of our choices. Therefore, in our theorizing, we must stay attentive to the different aspects of time and temporality and how we choose to conceptualize them because "these initial decisions about time tend to have serious ramifications later" (Callender, 2017: 99). While Callender (2017) refers to the ramifications for theorizing, Simão et al. (2015) stresses that our conceptualization of time also has existential implications. Therefore, our conceptualization of time affects our relationship with ourselves and others and the world. Adam (1990) insists that because time plays an important role both in people's lives and in their thinking, and with every choice comes related consequences, it is important to understand all of its aspects in their totality and their dynamic relations.

Therefore, it could be argued that how time is conceptualized has a far-reaching impact on how reality is seen and responded to by actors. Moreover, the question is not so much about "one or the other," that is, objective time versus subjective time or clock time versus social time. Instead, it is important to understand the relationships between different, simultaneously active and mutually non-excluding aspects of time. Luhmann (1980, quoted in Adam, 1990) argues that the question of time is a fundamental, if not a necessary, precondition to social theory. Consequently, the different aspects of time and the role of time in organizational theories cannot be less important because how organizational reality is imagined and responded to by actors is rooted in our view of time. That is, the conceptualization of time influences how reality is created and enacted.

In Chap. 2—The Objective View of Time and Temporality: Time as a Tool for Organizing—I discuss the most common role of time, which is organizing and coordinating social life, and the most common form of time addressed in organization studies, which is standardized clock time (Zerubavel, 1982). Standardized clock time refers to external and measurable time, time viewed as a background system external to human experience and events. Thus, Chap. 2 is rooted in the ontology of time. The concept of clock time refers to the atemporal time based on Newtonian theoretical physics, which views time as "absolute, true and mathematical" flowing "equably without relation to anything external" (Newton quoted in Whitehead, 1929/1978: 70). However, although clock time is seen as objective, continuous, linear, and quantifiable, existing independently of objects, actions, and events (e.g., Clark, 1985; Lee & Liebenau, 1999; Orlikowski & Yates, 2002), it turns out that standardized clock time is not entirely neutral and objective but a socially negotiated tool for coordination (Zerubavel, 1982). As socially negotiated, it is manipulated and entails elements of power. As a coordination tool, clock time has captured a lot of attention. For example, an entrainment theory is well-established in organizational studies.

Chapter 2 also covers the organizational, personal, and societal implications of monetized time. In organizations, time, viewed as a sacred resource, is linked directly to production planning, organizational efficiency, and effectiveness calculations (Bluedorn & Denhardt, 1988; Ciborra, 1999). For individuals, quantified and measurable time has led to almost constant time pressure and time famine. At the societal level, monetized time has resulted in continued acceleration, intensification, time compression, and short-termism. As the main tool for organizing everyday societal life and ideologies, we could argue that clock time has played a role in the climate crises (or just globally bad weather) we are witnessing.

The chapter argues that although clock time is a useful tool for social coordination, overemphasizing the importance of clock time leads to suboptimal outcomes for individuals, organizations, and societies. An objective clock time is not entirely objective, but a negotiated phenomenon, but as it is external to human experience, it does not necessarily sync with the person's subjective time of lived experience. However, when studying subjective time, it is important to distinguish between the subjective perception of the temporal dimensions of objective time (Chap. 3) and time as a lived experience (Chap. 4).

In Chap. 3—Subjective Time as Subjectively Perceived Temporal Dimensions of Objective Time—I focus on subjective time by discussing subjective time as subjectively perceived temporal aspects of objective time, including temporal dimensions like duration, frequency, or sequence (Zerubavel, 1987). Therefore, while moving from objective time to subjective time, we still stay in the ontology of time. Subjective time discussed in Chap. 3 is well covered in neuroscience and cognitive and experimental psychology and is often referred to as psychological time or inner time. While the focus is on subjective perceptions of time, time is treated as an external phenomenon—something all humans perceive. However, their perceptions may differ significantly and could be substantially biased. From the perspective of the organization, biased time perception could be costly. Due to the related high economic costs, biases in time perception and especially in duration estimation have attracted considerable attention. The term "planning fallacy" (Kahneman & Tversky, 1979) describes the systematic underestimation of the time required to complete a task.

Chapter 3 discusses the differences between the possible outcomes of ego-centric and time-centric approaches to time. As both approaches are built on the spatial metaphor, this highlights the main shortcoming related to the use of the spatial metaphor of time. However, both ego-centric and time-centric approaches include questions about such characteristics of subjective time as time orientation (past, present, or future), temporal depth (immediate or distant), and agency (an actor or time). All three aspects, time orientation, temporal depth, and agency, have important implications in organizations. The question about who has agency—the actor or time—is particularly fascinating. Ascribing agency to either an actor or time influences how reality is interpreted and enacted. The chapter discusses what happens when an actor is left with very limited or entirely without temporal agency, that is, the ability to do temporal work (Flaherty, 2002, 2003), and concludes that being forced to face objective and external time without temporal agency is mentally and emotionally overwhelming. Therefore, humans are not well equipped to deal with an "absolute, true and mathematical" time flowing "equably without relation to anything external" (Newton quoted in Whitehead, 1929/1978: 70).

Chapter 4—Temporality as Endogenous and Subjective—is rooted in the ontology of temporality. As temporality is a complex term, Chap. 4 is the longest in the book and could be more challenging to follow than other chapters. However, I nevertheless hope that those interested in temporality grounded in the ontology of temporality could find this chapter useful. Temporality is one of the central concerns in phenomenology, developmental and cultural psychology, and process studies. Instead of being conceptualized as an external category, time is described as an internal feature of humans, things, and events (Mead, 1932/2002). Time is viewed as a dimension of their being in the world. Inner or "own time" (Hernes, 2014: 49) refers to unique, personal, or organizational temporal structuring. In other words, inner time has "its own unique path of unfolding, supported by its own specific contingencies, the production of its unique past, and its own unique choices for future aspirations" (Hernes, 2014: 51).

Although the subjective temporality covered in this chapter is also endogenous, my intention in emphasizing them separately is to stress that endogenous temporality is not something granted to human beings only. In other words, my argument is that endogenous temporality is not limited to temporal idealism but applies to entities and events other than humans. As indicated by the quote from Hernes above, endogenous temporality refers to becoming, to the ongoing configuration of our past, present, and future experiences and expectations, and to the realization of our possibilities and actualization of potential. Subjective temporality refers to the lived experience of time, maintaining our perceived temporal continuity in the passing of time. On the one hand, viewing time as continuously and irreversibly passing gives time agency. It allows us to argue that time is productive, creative, and destructive. On the other hand, it enables the temporal agency of the subject to create its own time while carrying through time.

Endogenous and subjective temporality presupposes the openness of the past and future and the immanence of the past and future in the present. The immanence of the past and future in the present means that in addition to the agency of time (time as a productive force) and the temporal agency of the subject (ability and capability to do temporal work and manage our becoming), we can talk about a temporal structure to our agency (Emirbayer & Mische, 1998). Put differently, to view the past and future as constitutive elements of the present, our temporal focus could be directed predominantly either to towards the past, present, or future, affecting our decision- and sense-making and relationship to reality.

In Chap. 5—Socially Constructed Time and Social Time as a Context—Bluedorn and Denhardt (1988, p. 300) claim that "time is a fundamentally social construct," and therefore, the concept of clock time is too simplistic to explain organizational life. Bluedorn and Denhardt's claim is supported, for example, by McGrath and Rotchford (1983), Clark (1985), Das (1993), and Hassard (1989, 1996). These authors all suggest that social analysis requires a theory that considers the various subjective times (note the plurality here) despite the dominance of clock time. Those different subjective times tend to be more cyclical than linear (Hatch, 2002) and context specific (Clark, 1985; Hassard, 2002). Also, as standardized clock time is negotiated and rooted in rationality instead of nature (Zerubavel, 1982), it highlights the need to pay attention to the semiotic meaning of measured time.

Chapter 5 focuses on intersubjective time, the plurality of social times and their possible collisions, and intentional temporal work as temporal structuring in organizations. Chapter 5 pays special attention to the temporal orientation of activities, which is often overshadowed by an individual or social temporal orientation. It draws attention to the temporal orientation of organizational activities and outlines the role of the temporal orientation of activities in recognizing and grasping possibilities.

The second part of the chapter is devoted to analysing social time as a multi-layered context. It is based on the concentric model introduced in child development (Bronfenbrenner, 1979) and adjusted for cultural psychology by Tateo (2015). Moving from micro-time through meso-time and meso-time to macro-time, the chapter highlights, on the one hand, the temporal embeddedness of social time across its layers and, on the other hand, the ongoing mutual shaping and forming across all layers. Departing from the argumentation presented by Tateo (2015) and Marsico (2015) that negotiation between layers occurs at the borders of the layers, I argue that the separation of social time layers is arbitrary. There are no clear-cut borders between the layers but more like a blurred transition. Therefore, I argue that there is no ongoing negotiation taking place somewhere on the borders with the direction from either micro to macro or macro to micro. Instead, the transformation of all layers occurs in relation to events and through the internal connections within events and the mirroring that transcends through the layers.

Defining the ontological grounding for Chap. 5 is somehow challenging. On the one hand, it works on the basis of the socially shared semiotic meaning of objective time, which belongs to the ontology of time. On the other hand, all the social time layers as well as the socially shared semiotic meanings of objective time are evolving through time. Therefore, they are temporal. In other words, these are not static states but evolving phenomena in their becoming. This aspect of social time is rooted in the ontology of temporality.

Chapter 6—Events, Time, and Events-Based Time—is devoted to events, time, and their reciprocal relations. While it is agreed that events play a central role in recognizing time, how events, time, and their relationships are defined may differ significantly. Chapter 6 discusses four different approaches to events, time, and their theorized relationships. First, Luhmann's structure/process framework of events seems to combine the ontology of time and temporality by allowing us to analyse structure based on the ontology of time and process based on the ontology of temporality. In his framework, almost like weaving a fabric, Luhmann combines objective and measurable time as a structure with the temporality of processual events resulting in an elegant and plausible explanation of the becoming of organizational time.

The second approach argues that time is in events and events work as signifiers of time (Clark, 1985). This approach claims that the meaning of time stems from events. Although this approach claims that it works based on event time and not clock time, it follows a weak process view of time, and therefore, it is still grounded in the ontology of time, where events, as signifiers of time, have their clear meaning and significance.

The third approach is conceptualized as the sequential view of time. Contrary to the preceding approach, this view sees discrete events occurring in time or changes in states happening over time. Still, in both cases, the ontological assumptions follow the ontology of time. According to this approach, events are ordered sequentially in time, their meaning and significance and position in time are fixed. The fourth approach to time and events is presented as an events-based time. This approach is grounded deeply in the ontology of temporality. It views events as open and transcending in their becoming, while the becoming could always become otherwise. An events-based time is grounded in the view of "immanent temporal trajectory," according to which "distant events are immanent parts of actors' experience of time" (Hernes et al., 2021: 732). In this approach events are time; thus, there is no distinction between the two terms. Events-based time enables us to break free from the constraints of sequential time and conceptualize time not as a linear line but as a dynamic field of possibilities.

Chapter 7—Challenges Related to Dealing with Time and Temporality in Organization Studies—outlines some of the challenges we may face when studying issues related to time and temporality in organization studies. This chapter focuses on possible problems related to our deeply rooted spatial thinking and unquestioned use of spatial metaphors. This chapter discusses difficulties to think and theorize about time caused by our culturally rooted and socially taken-for-granted approach to time and our simultaneous living in and living time.

References

Adam, B. (1990). *Time and social theory*. Polity Press.
Aeon, B., & Aguinis, H. (2017). It's about time: New perspectives and insights on time management. *Academy of Management Perspectives, 31*(4), 309–330. https://doi.org/10.5465/amp.2016.0166
Bardon, A. (2013). *A brief history of the philosophy of time*. Oxford Scholarship Online. https://doi.org/10.1093/asprof:oso/9780199976454.001.0001

Bluedorn, A. C. (2002). *The human organization of time: Temporal realities and experience*. Stanford University Press.

Bluedorn, A. C., & Denhardt, R. B. (1988). Time and organizations. *Journal of Management, 14*(2), 299–320.

Bronfenbrenner, U. (1979). *The ecology of human development: Experiments by nature and design*. Harvard University Press.

Callender, C. (2017). *What makes time special?* Oxford University Press.

Ciborra, C. U. (1999). Notes on improvisation and time in organizations. *Accounting, Management and Information Technologies, 9*, 77–94.

Clark, P. (1985). A review of theories of time and structure for organizational sociology. In S. B. Bacharach & S. M. Mitchel (Eds.), *Research in the sociology of organizations. A research annual, volume 4* (pp. 35–79). JAI.

Das, T. K. (1993). Time in management and organization studies. *Time and Society, 2*, 267–274.

Emirbayer, M., & Mische, A. (1998). What is agency? *American Journal of Sociology, 103*(4), 962–1023.

Flaherty, M. G. (2002). Making time: Agency and the construction of temporal experience. *Symbolic Interaction, 25*(3), 379–388.

Flaherty, M. G. (2003). Time work: Customizing temporal experience. *Social Psychology Quarterly, 66*(1), 17–33.

Fried, Y., & Slowik, L. H. (2004). Enriching goal-setting theory with time: An integrated approach. *Academy of Management Review, 29*(3), 404–422.

Gurvitch, G. (1964/1990). Varieties of social time. In J. Hassard (Ed.), *The sociology of time* (pp. 67–76). Macmillan.

Harvey, D. (1989). *The condition of postmodernity: An enquiry into the origins of cultural change*. Blackwell.

Hassard, J. (1989). Toward a qualitative paradigm for working time. *International Social Science Journal, 119*, 93–104.

Hassard, J. (1996). Images of time in work and organizations. In S. R. Clegg, C. Hardy, & W. R. Nord (Eds.), *Handbook of Organization Studies* (pp. 581–598). Sage.

Hassard, J. (2002). Essay: Organizational time: Modern, symbolic and postmodern reflections. *Organization Studies, 23*(6), 885–892.

Hatch, M. (2002). Essay: Doing time in organization theory. *Organization Studies, 23*(6), 869–875.

Hernes, T. (2014). *A process theory of organization*. Oxford University Press.

Hernes, T., Feddersen, J., & Schultz, M. (2020). Material temporality: How materiality 'does' time in food organizing. *Organization Studies*. https://doi.org/10.1177/0170840620909974

Hernes, T., Hussenot, A., & Pulk, K. (2021). Time and temporality of change processes. Applying an event-based view to integrate episodic and continuous change. In M. S. Poole & A. Van de Ven (Eds.), *The Oxford handbook of organizational change and innovation* (2nd ed., pp. 731–750). Oxford University Press. https://doi.org/10.1093/oxfordhb/9780198845973.013.27

Hoy, D. C. (2009). *The time of our lives: A critical history of temporality*. MIT Press.

Hussenot, A., Hernes, T., & Bouty, I. (2020). Studying organization from the perspective of the ontology of temporality: Introducing the event-based approach. In J. Reinecke, R. Suddaby, A. Langley, & H. Tsoukas (Eds.), *About time: Temporality and history in organization studies* (pp. 50–68). Oxford University Press. https://doi.org/10.1093/oso/9780198870715.003.0005

Kahneman, D., & Tversky, A. (1979). Prospect theory: An analysis of decision under risk. *Econometrica, 47*, 263–291.

Klempe, S. H. (2015). Temporality and the necessity of culture in psychology. In L. M. Simão, D. S. Guimarães, & J. Valsiner (Eds.), *Temporality: Culture in the flow of human experience* (pp. 3–22). Information Age Publishing.

Lee, H., & Liebenau, J. (1999). Time in organizational studies: Towards a new research direction. *Organization Studies, 20*(6), 1035–1058.

Levine, R. (2006). *A geography of time: The temporal misadventures of a social psychologist, or how every culture keeps time just a little bit differently*. Oneworld.

Lewis, D. J., & Weigert, A. J. (1981). The structures and meaning of social time. *Social Forces, 60*(2), 432–462.

Luhmann, N. (1995). *Social systems* (J. Bednarz, Jr. with D. Baecker, trans.). Stanford University Press.

Luhmann, N. (2018). *Organization and decision* (R. Barrett, trans.). Cambridge University Press.

Marsico, G. (2015). Developing with time: Defining a temporal mereotopology. In L. M. Simão, D. S. Guimarães, & J. Valsiner (Eds.), *Temporality: Culture in the flow of human experience* (pp. 23–40). Information Age Publishing.

McGrath, J. E., & Rotchford, N. L. (1983). Time and behavior in organizations. *Research in Organizational Behavior, 5*, 57–101.

Mead, G. H. (1932/2002). *The philosophy of the present*. Prometheus.

Mumford, L. (1970). *The myth of the machine: The pentagon of power*. Harcourt, Brace, Jovanovich.

Nowotny, H. (1996). *Time: The modern and postmodern experience.* Polity Press.
Orlikowski, W. J., & Yates, J. (2002). It's about time: Temporal structuring in organizations. *Organization Science, 13*(6), 684–700.
Reinecke, J., Suddaby, R., Langely, A., & Tsoukas, H. (2020). Time, temporality, and history in process organization studies: An introduction. In J. Reinecke, R. Suddaby, A. Langley, & H. Tsoukas (Eds.), *About time: Temporality and history in organization studies* (pp. 1–14). Oxford University Press. https://doi.org/10.1093/oso/9780198870715.003.0001
Rovelli, C. (2011). Forget time. *Foundations of Physics, 41*, 1475. https://doi.org/10.1007/s10701-011-9561-4
Rovelli, C. (2017). *The order of time.* Allen Lane.
Roy, D. F. (1959). 'Banana time': Job satisfaction and informal interaction. *Human Organization, 18*, 158–168.
Schultz, M., & Hernes, T. (2013). A temporal perspective on organizational identity. *Organization Science, 24*(1), 1–21.
Shipp, A. J., & Fried, Y. (2014a). Time research in management: Using temporal ambassadors to translate ideas into reality. In A. J. Shipp & Y. Fried (Eds.), *Time and work, volume 1: How time impacts individuals* (pp. 1–10). Psychology Press.
Shipp, A. J., & Fried, Y. (Eds.). (2014b). *Time and work, volume 2: How time impacts groups, organizations and methodological choices.* Psychology Press.
Simão, L. M. (2015). Introduction: Time—not always the same. In L. M. Simão, D. S. Guimarães, & J. Valsiner (Eds.), *Temporality: Culture in the flow of human experience* (pp. xi–xiv). Information Age Publishing.
Simão, L. M., Guimarães, D. S., & Valsiner, J. (Eds.). (2015). *Temporality: Culture in the flow of human experience.* Information Age Publishing.
Sorokin, P. A., & Merton, R. K. (1937). Social time: A methodological and functional analysis. *American Journal of Sociology, 42*(5), 615–629.
Tateo, L. (2015). Temporality and generalization in psychology: Time as context. In L. M. Simão, D. S. Guimarães, & J. Valsiner (Eds.), *Temporality: Culture in the flow of human experience* (pp. 463–481). Information Age Publishing.
Taylor, F. W. (1911). *The principles of scientific management.* Harper & Brothers.
Weinersmith, Z. (2017). *Science: Abridged beyond the point of usefulness.* éditeur non identifié. https://books.google.ee/books?id=AyPLvQEACAAJ
Whitehead, A. N. (1929/1978). *Process and reality.* The Free Press.
Zerubavel, E. (1982). The standardization of time: A sociohistorical perspective. *American Journal of Sociology, 1*, 1–23.

Zerubavel, E. (1987). The language of time: Toward a semiotics of temporality. *The Sociological Quarterly, 28*(3), 343–356.
Zerubavel, E. (1991). *The fine line: Making distinctions in everyday life.* The Free Press.
Zerubavel, E. (2003). *Time maps: Collective memory and the social shape of the past.* University of Chicago Press.

2

Objective View of Time and Temporality: Time as a Tool for Organizing

It is hard to overestimate the essential role of time in societies as a tool for organizing and coordinating activities (Adam, 1990, 2004; Clark, 1985; McGrath & Rotchford, 1983). Organizing activities in any social group presupposes temporal coordination (Zerubavel, 1982: 4), and temporal coordination requires a shared temporal reference. Although parents with young children may disagree, coordinating activities at the family level could be relatively easy while still requiring some sort of temporal reference. Respectively, at the level of group, community, city, or nation, the complexity of coordination and the need for shared temporal reference increase (Zerubavel, 1982).

The shared temporal reference for coordinating activities has varied from community to community, closely linked with the activities and practices central to the community in question. For example, Adam (1990) describes temporal reference systems rooted in organic periodicities like cycles of the moon, tide, and seasons. Agricultural societies have been and still are organized according to seasonal rhythms (Reinecke & Ansari, 2015), as seasonal rhythms play a crucial role in organizing agricultural activities, much more than a clock or calendar. Both Adam (1990, 2004) and Zerubavel (1981, 1987) describe temporal reference systems based on religious beliefs and organized around religious holidays and highly pragmatic systems grounded in market days, and so on. The common features of all the mentioned time reckoning systems are that they are highly functional but only at the local level. The main aim of local time reckoning systems is not an objective measurement of time or precise timekeeping but coordinating activities and organizing everyday life in accordance with "a span of time that would seem to be necessary by the nature of those activities" (Neustadter, 1992: 383). Viewing time as a tool for social organizing is an instrumental view of time.

Malinowski (1990) claims that a shared time reckoning system is a practical necessity for every human group that needs to coordinate its activities, map chronological order of both the past and future events, and measure the duration of periods. Underlying these qualities of time, Malinowski refers to chronological clock time. Based on Newtonian physics, chronological clock time claimed to represent an objective, linear, measurable time independent of objects, actions, and events (e.g., Clark, 1985; Lee & Liebenau, 1999; Orlikowski & Yates, 2002; Watt, 1991). Newtonian time has the status of a noun, and it is treated as a real thing (Bardon, 2013). Viewing time as chronological clock time existing beyond human perceptions or experiences represents temporal realism (Bardon, 2013) and it is based on the ontology of time (Hussenot et al., 2020). Often clock time is referred to as "real, not just the right stuff, but the real stuff" (Bluedorn, 2002: 27 Emphasize in origin). Clock time is made real by precise and accurate measurability that serves as a reification of time (Neustadter, 1992). The objective measurement of time makes it into something concrete and divisible.

> We record the passage of time in seconds, minutes, hours, days, months, years, decades, centuries, and eras, as if everything has its place upon a single objective time scale. Even though time in physics is a difficult and contentious concept, we do not usually let that interfere with the commonsense of time around which we organize daily routines. (Harvey, 1989: 201)

Chronological time tracked by the endless ticking of the clock enables us to map the sequence of activities and agree on the chronological order of events as an objective social fact. Metering reality out in minutes, hours, days, weeks, months, and years means that chronological time has an objective, quantifiable chronometric nature (Watt, 1991), making it a suitable tool for measurement. Clock time enables us to objectively measure such temporal features of time as duration, tempo, interval, frequency, and periodicity (Zerubavel, 1987).

Industrial and contemporary post-industrial societies have chosen chronological clock time rooted in Newtonian physics as the dominant form of time, which has become a profoundly taken-for-granted aspect of social life (Adam, 1990, 2004). The concept of clock time refers to atemporal time. Clock time is atemporal in the sense that although clock time allows for tracking the temporal features of time mentioned above, it does not pay attention to the deeper temporal relations between the past, present, and future. Instead, it views time as "absolute, true, and mathematical" flowing "equably without relation to anything external" (Newton quoted in Whitehead, 1929/1978: 70). In the following pages, I discuss the rationality behind "choosing" chronological clock time as the dominant form of time and some of the consequences of that choice at the level of societies, organizations, and individuals.

2.1 An Objective View of Time: Standardized Clock Time

Zerubavel points out that "in the modern Western world, the prevalent *standard temporal reference framework* is the one based on the use of clock time, the Gregorian calendar, and the Christian Era" (Zerubavel, 1982: 3 emphasis in original). It is important to recognize that chronometric time depends on calendars, which typically revolve around the significant event (Baars, 2012). For example, the birth of Christ marks the beginning of the Christian era and the Gregorian calendar while also marking a zero point or beginning from where chronometric time can start to measure time (count years) in the Christian cultural context. Although Muslims or Jews follow their specific calendars, the underlying logic remains the same—without a calendar, chronometric time would not know when to start counting (Baars, 2012). With clocks and calendars, chronological time enables timekeeping (Hernes, 2014; Wiebe, 2010). It is worth highlighting that neither the global use of the Gregorian calendar nor the globally accepted standardized time is self-evident. Although the globally shared calendar is an essential social accomplishment, I will not dive into the details related to the implementation of the Georgian calendar.[1] In the following pages, I will discuss the emergence of clock time as a global standard and its role in contemporary society and organizations.

According to Berger and Luckmann, the prevailing temporal reference framework based on clock time is so deeply rooted that:

> Clock and calendar ensure that, indeed, I am *a man of my time*. Only within this temporal structure does everyday life retain for me its accent of reality. Thus, in cases where I may be *disoriented* for one reason or another ... I feel an almost instinctive urge to *reorient* myself within the temporal structure of everyday life. I look at my watch and try to recall what day it is. By these acts alone, I re-enter the reality of everyday life. (Berger & Luckmann, 1991: 42)

Although being so deeply rooted, clock time as we know it—a globally accepted standardized time—is a relatively new concept. In the article titled "The Standardisation of Time: A Sociohistorical Perspective," published in 1982 in the *American Journal of Sociology*, Zerubavel provides a fascinating historical overview of the development and implementation of the clock time.[2] According to Zerubavel (1982: 5), clock time started its gradual climb to its current throne only 240 years ago when in 1780, Geneva preferred to begin to use "mean time," a clock time as we know it today, instead of solar time. Before 1780 clock time was used, but it was a direct reflection of solar time (Ibid). Importantly, solar time is a local

---

[1] In the case of interest, we can find more information in Zerubavel, E. (1981) *Hidden Rhythms: Schedules and Calendars in Social Life*. Chicago: University of Chicago Press. Some details could also be found in Bluedorn, A.C. (2002) *The Human Organization of Time: Temporal realities and experience*. Stanford, CA: Stanford University Press, in pages 160–163.

[2] Detailed description about the implementation of standardized clock time in the United States could be found, for example, from Bartky, I. (2000) *Selling the True Time: Nineteenth-Century Timekeeping in America*. Stanford, CA: Stanford University Press. See also Hamerla, R. (2006) *An American Scientist on the Research Frontier: Edward Morely, Community, and Radical Ideas in Nineteenth-Century Science*. Dordrecht, the Netherlands: Springer.

time, varying across degrees of longitude. Following local times while coordinating activities in local communities worked without problem until the development of railway transportation and the instantaneous communication enabled by the invention of the telegraph and the telephone. Related to these developments, local communities faced a need for coordination at the super-local level with the precision of odd minutes. Before these developments, accuracy in time tracking was not an urgent need. Instead, activities were organized based on natural periodicities and accorded a reasonable span of time viewed as necessary for their completion (Neustadter, 1992). "It was not until the revolution in communication that the situation began to change in any significant way" (Zerubavel, 1982: 5). According to Zerubavel's review, the British Post Office gave "the initial push toward standardizing time reckoning on a super-local level," "when it started to run all its mail coaches throughout Great Britain in accordance with a uniform standard time" (Zerubavel, 1982: 6), which was Greenwich mean time (GMT).

Due to the small number of the British Post Office services, the importance of Greenwich mean time remained limited until the broader rise of railway services. With the spread of railway networks in the UK, starting from 1840, previously autonomous communities, each operating independently according to their local times, "gradually became interrelated parts of a single systemic whole" (Zerubavel, 1982: 7) glued together by a single uniformed standardized time and precise timetables. "Through the use of timetables, the railroads could coordinate passengers, cargo, and other trains to meet a specific train when it was at a station" (Okhuysen & Bechky, 2009: 465). The precise railway schedules based in uniform time were routinely published in the local newspapers. As there was a time discrepancy between the railway schedules based on GMT and local community time, people started to call the time used in the railroad timetables *railway time*. An interesting side-effect of the railway time is the institutionalization of timetables (Zerubavel, 1982).

Similar developments took place in the United States, flavoured with specific challenges stemming from the much larger size of the railroad network, broader physical coverage, and lack of a single centre like London was for the UK. As a result, each railway company in the United

States operated on all its own lines based on the local time at its headquarters. The consequences were messy and confusing:

> Thus, the New York Central, for example, used New York time throughout its entire system, while the Pennsylvania used Philadelphia time. While things were relatively orderly at the level of each particular railroad company, the situation was quite chaotic at the level of each particular community. At the train station in Buffalo, for example, there were three different clocks indicating three different times. While one of these showed Buffalo time, the second was set on New York time and was relevant only to passengers using the New York Central trains, whereas the third was set on Columbus time and was relevant to passengers using the Lake Shore and Michigan Southern trains. (Zerubavel, 1982: 8–9)

In its attempts to enhance its operational effectiveness and security, the United States railway network recognized the need for the standardization of time reckoning across the North American continent. To tackle this challenge, in 1876, the chief engineer of the Canadian Pacific Railway proposed the idea to divide the entire world into 24 time zones with a one-hour difference from one another (Zerubavel, 1982). The decisive breakthrough for clock time came just 136 years ago as a result of debates and negotiations in 1884 when at the International Meridian Conference, the Greenwich meridian as the prime was agreed as an international time reckoning system (Zerubavel, 1982). It is important to mention that although the concept of standardized time was agreed in 1884, this agreement did not mean that countries shifted to the new time reckoning system overnight. Instead, the agreement marked the start of the gradual global adaptation to standardized time. For example, France adopted GMT in 1911 and the Netherlands as late as 1937. Although few, there are still some countries and regions which do not follow the internationally agreed time zones. These places, according to the time zone atlas from 2010, are Newfoundland (an island in Canada), Venezuela, Iran, Afghanistan, India, Nepal, Myanmar, North-Australia, South-Australia, and Norfolk and Lord Howe islands.

According to historical overviews (e.g., Bartky, 2000; Hamerla, 2006; Zerubavel, 1982), the globally accepted standardized time reckoning

2 Objective View of Time and Temporality: Time as a Tool... 23

system, which replaced a multitude of local solar times and has become profoundly taken for granted, is not only a reflection of social activities but also a product of debates, negotiations, and lobbying. Necessarily not everybody was happy about switching from solar time to clock time. For example, the gentleman in Fig. 2.1. Indication of a semi-forced adaption to clock time in all spheres of social life comes from the complaint or statement published in the *Indianapolis Daily Sentinel* in November 1883, "The sun is no longer to boss the job. People must eat, sleep and work by railroad time. People will have to marry by railroad time. Ministers will be required to preach by railroad time. Banks will open and close by railroad time; notes will be paid or protested by railroad

Fig. 2.1 Before time was invented
(By permission of Leigh Rubin and Creators Syndicate, Inc.)

time" (quoted in Bartky, 2000: 14). Consequently, everybody was forced to organize his or her life in respect to all kinds of social aspects of life according to railroad time.

The decision of the International Meridian Conference in 1884 marked the shift from a time reckoning system anchored in nature to a socially based system anchored in rationality (Bartky, 2000: 19). The different time zones do not follow the meridian lines accurately but in addition to physical and geographical criteria are also drawn according to legal, political, social, and economic criteria. That is to say, clock time anchored in rationality serves particular legal, political, social, and economic interests (i.e., Harvey, 1989; Luhmann, 2018; Nowotny, 1996; Macnaghten & Urry, 1998), being "an expression of political, economic and social power" (Neustadter, 1992: 383). In addition, Harvey underscores "the relations between money, space, and time as interlocking sources of social power" and stresses that the common-sense rules about time are the continuous targets of "frustrated power struggles" (1989: 227). With the question of power comes a question of moral issues (van de Scott, 2020). Rationality could be viewed as a function of power, priorities, and values. Therefore, the adoption of standardized time as a dominant temporal reference for organizing everyday life raises questions such as in whose interest, why, how, when, and with what consequences it is applied (Dougherty et al., 2013).

Why write such a lengthy presentation about the history of clock time? I think it is important to understand the broader background of *objective*, standardized clock time, the causes and roots of its emergence, and the worldview related to it. Since it is not rooted in nature but in the principles of formal or instrumental rationality (Grey, 2017) emphasizing optimization and maximization, clock time represents a significant shift in the time reckoning system in the modern world. Formal or instrumental rationality is concerned with achieving a particular result most efficiently and effectively. As Bluedorn (2002: 105) points out: "Efficiency is usually good, but effectiveness is always better ... Efficiency is about how; effectiveness is about why." Still, the questions related to being efficient and effective from whose perspective and with what consequences remain open. Answers to these questions are concerned with substantive or value rationality (Grey, 2017) and focus on ends, not means.

Luhmann points out that it may be the case that "rationality is coupled with being discharged from responsibility," used as an excuse or "presentable explanation" (2018: 136) for our actions. Echoing Luhmann's concerns, Grey (2017) refers to the Holocaust as a grim example of formal rationality and technical efficiency. While an extreme case, the Holocaust illustrates the danger associated with detaching ends from means (Grey, 2017). Using formal or instrumental rationality as a presentable explanation can easily lead us astray because we lose sight of the values and ends. The ends can be viewed as a future, and for the future, the substantive or value rationality should also be considered. "Judgments about rationality have to include the future. But the future is and remains unknown" (Luhmann, 2018: 370). While the future remains unknown, whose future and how the distant future is taken account of also remain open and should be considered when justifying something as rational.

The act of replacing nature as the anchor for reckoning time with economic rationality has had its consequences. Lukács states that subsuming organizational practices to economic rationality transforms "the basic categories of man's immediate attitude to the world: it reduces space and time to a common denominator and degrades time to the dimension of space" (Lukàcs, 1973: 89). In the modern world, time is recognized from the perspective of effectiveness and efficiency accompanied by a focus on the short term (Hahn et al., 2015; Harvey, 1989; Marginson & McAulay, 2008). Nowotny (1996) shares both the concern about short-termism and Luhmann's concern about the possible consequences of ignoring our responsibilities stated above. Nowotny sees short-termism and being discharged from responsibility as closely related issues, claiming that "Short-term interactions negate time, and where time is neglected, responsibility also dwindles" (1996: 14). Sadly, a similar view is extended to reality. This means that the rationalist short-term approach to time combined with a declining sense of responsibility is also reflected in the rationalist short-term view of reality with a declining sense of responsibility. As our reality includes both our social and natural environment, Jaques' observation that "In the form of time is to be found the form of living" (Jaques, 1982/1990: 129) is reaffirmed.

Mikita (2013) claims that with the prevalence of economic rationality, mythological thinking is disappearing. He argues that mythological thinking is essential for long-term thinking and sustainability because mythological thinking enables humans to perceive time as a long-term duration and without mythological thinking humans are not able to learn to think longer than a few decades.

Indeed, according to Bluedorn (2002: 136), the Iroquois indigenous people of North America used extended time horizons to think ahead seven generations, which is well beyond the decision-maker or his/her direct offspring or contemporaries. Thinking ahead seven generations is in sharp contrast to the *economic short-termism* prevailing in modern organizations and societies (Hahn et al., 2015; Laverty, 1996). Being able to have such a long-term perspective on the future requires a supportive social imaginary. The *social imaginary* is a concept described as:

> The way ordinary people *imagine* their social surroundings ... carried in images, stories, legends ... it is shared by large groups of people, if not the whole society ... it is that common understanding which makes possible common practices, and a widely shared sense of legitimacy. It incorporates a sense of the normal expectations we have of each other, the kind of common understanding that enables us to carry out the collective practices that make up our social life. (Taylor, 2004: 23–24)

Social imaginaries belonging to deep cultural structures refer to the "phenomenological reality of images" (Augustine et al., 2019: 1936). Augustine et al. note that:

> Imaginaries encompass basic *cosmologies* of the world, as well as a moral basis for evaluating action. Cosmologies are belief systems regarding the foundational premises for making sense of the world, such as the origin, components, and mechanics of the social and material world. (2019: 1936, italics in the original)

Consequently, the social imaginary defines the prevailing social logic and sets, among other things, explicit constraints on policymaking (Reichel & Perey, 2018). Perey (2013) distinguishes between an "economic imaginary" and an "ecological imaginary," labelling the modern social imaginary as an "economic imaginary." In his view, the modern social imaginary that frames our decision-making is grounded in economics, which suffers from short-termism (Hahn et al., 2015; Laverty, 1996). In contrast to an economic imaginary characterized by short-termism, the ecological imaginary would enable a more balanced long-term orientation.

Compared to the contemporary mainstream worldview oriented on ever-increasing temporal acceleration (Harvey, 1989), economic growth, productivity (Lukàcs, 1973), and endless consumption (Nowotny, 1996; Reichel & Perey, 2018), the way the Iroquois imagined the future and how far into the future they imagined was based on a different temporal perspective and accompanying value system. I would like to note that it is probably not just a coincidence that the worldview of indigenous people was not rooted in economic rationality dictated by clock time but included mythological thinking about man and the earth and the universe and their mutual relationships. It is probably not just a coincidence that in the modern world, where the rationalistic approach to time puts its imprint on our value system, our thinking, and behaviour, there is not much place for mythological thinking. Compared to the usual timeframes in organizations, which tend to revolve around monthly budgets, quarterly profits, and annual financial performance (Laverty, 1996), accompanied by the CEO's five-year median tenure (Harvey, 1989; Marcec, 2018), we can say that Mikita (2013) is even too generous in proposing "a few decades" as the average length of our vision of the future.

2.2 Clock Time in Management and Organization Studies

It is not surprising that standardized clock time, which has become a deeply taken-for-granted aspect of social life (Adam, 1990, 2004) and the dominant form of time in industrial and contemporary post-industrial societies (Harvey, 1989; Neustadter, 1992; Zerubavel, 1982), has also become the most dominant and widespread conceptualization of time in modern organizations (i.e., Bluedorn & Denhardt, 1988; Clark, 1985; Crossan et al., 2005; Czarniawska, 2004; Hassard, 2001; Sorokin &

Merton, 1937). Although many organizational processes are described as having a cyclical nature (e.g., there are specific repeated patterns of activities), they are still plotted against a clock time seen as real (Bluedorn, 2002), objective (Watt, 1991), linear (Chia, 1999; Zerubavel, 1987), and measurable (Clark, 1985). While in everyday organizational life, the *realness* of clock time is more like a *common-sense* (Harvey, 1989) taken-for-granted background knowledge (Neustadter, 1992), clock time's measurability has attracted a lot of attention.

Studies taken from the chronological clock time view represent the realist perspective and focus on covering a broad spectrum of time management topics in organization and management research. For example, concepts like *just-in-time, time to market, lead time, response time, cycle time* (Ciborra, 1999: 86), *time and motion, time allocation, time budget, time management, forecasting*, and *time series analysis* (Lee & Liebenau, 1999: 1051) are well represented in management studies. All the mentioned *time studies* deal with some objective and quantifiable *real* aspects of time while aiming to improve efficiency and effectiveness, the overall economic performance of an organization, and the accumulation of wealth (Hassard, 2001).

The interest in time management spread from the railway and communication sectors to the organization and management studies at the end of the nineteenth century and beginning of the twentieth century. In the wave of industrialization, mechanical periodicity, dictated by the clock, gained importance in society in general and in factories in particular by replacing the organic nature-dictated periodicity (Neustadter, 1992) common in agricultural societies and the largely self-determined (ir)regularity and intensity of artisans (Hassard, 2001). With the rise of the Scientific Management promoted by Frederick Taylor, attention in organization and management studies was turned to the measurability and manageability of time. Choosing clock time as its departure point, Scientific Management, or "Taylorism" emphasized time as a resource. Taylorism ratified the measurability of time and turned it into a commodity we can sell or buy (Harvey, 1989; Hassard, 2001; Neustadter, 1992). Based on the measurability of time, Taylorism monetized time and led to time management in industrial organizations with the aim of allocating, budgeting, measuring, and spending time with scientific precision (Adam, 1990; Clark, 1985; Hassard, 2002). As a result of the commoditization of time, people were subordinated to the clock.

> Through the subordination of man to the machine the situation arises in which men are effaced by their labor; in which the pendulum of the clock has become as accurate a measure of the relative activity of two workers as it is of the speed of two locomotives … Time is everything, man is nothing; he is at the most the incarnation of time. Quality no longer matters. Quantity alone decides everything: hour by hour, day by day. (Marx quoted in Lukàcs, 1973: 89–90)

Even if not applied in its totality (Clark, 1985), Scientific Management is still a thriving concept within industry. It is easy to agree with Lukács that quality characterized by handmade craft is available in the category of luxury only, while mass production focuses on quantity. Still, I do not agree with Lukács' statement that quantity alone is what matters. Complementary to quantity comes speed, which seems to matter even more than or at least as much as quantity. Leaving aside the Asian sewing factories, probably the most infamous in its ultimate devotion to time and speed management is Amazon. Driven by data, Amazon relies on continuous data tracking, paying attention even to delays as small as 0.1 of a second. Amazon metrics indicate that a 0.1-second delay in a page loading leads to a 1% decrease in customer activity (Anders, 2012), which in turn may translate into fewer purchases. While most of the goals at Amazon are related to customer objectives, reports indicate that Amazon systematically monitors its employees (Bloodworth, 2019). All warehouse workers at Amazon are equipped with chips (Bloodworth, 2019), indicating how much time they spend on different activities.

Reports have revealed that the rigid and strict time management system in Amazon warehouses has led to inhuman working conditions where there is no time left to have lunch or go to the toilet (Bloodworth, 2019). While officially 30 minutes are allocated for a lunch break, this is insufficient to walk from the workstation to the employees' canteen due to the enormous size of the buildings[3] and tight security control system

---

[3] For example, according to Channel 4 News (2013), the size of one of Amazon's warehouses or *fulfilment centres* in the UK is nine standard-sized football stadiums.

(Bloodworth, 2019). Finding a bottle with urine between the shelves shows that employees at Amazon try hard to reduce so-called *idling*, as toilet breaks are counted as *idle time*, resulting in penalty points (Bloodworth, 2019). What has happened and most probably is still happening at Amazon (and probably many other workplaces) is exactly what several authors have pointed out—monetized time, as an element of social power, will be a target of social struggles (i.e., Harvey, 1989; Luhmann, 2018; Macnaghten & Urry, 1998; Nowotny, 1996).

> The battle over minutes and seconds, over the pace and intensity of work schedules, over the working life (and rights of retirement), over the working week and day (with rights to 'free time'), over the working year (and rights to paid vacations), has been, and continues to be, right royally fought. (Harvey, 1989: 231)

This predicted fight over time is vividly expressed by Amazon.[4] Amazon has literally created *a clock-tyrannized* environment, where "activities are not accorded a span of time that would seem to be necessary by the nature of those activities but are bound instead by mechanically imposed units of clock time" (Neustadter, 1992: 395). In this environment, grounded in mechanical periodicity dictated by clock time, organic nature-dictated periodicity is decisively and forcefully suppressed (Neustadter, 1992: 387, 392), including the periodic need for toilet breaks.

Despite the extremely negative examples of clock-based time management at Amazon, the essential role of mechanical clock time-based periodicity with the standardized temporal reference framework is undeniable in the current era of automatization and digitalization, where many activities and services are expected to run 24/7, either across organizations or national borders or even globally. What is also undeniable is the need to order different activities, sequence tasks, and synchronize processes within and across organizations to get anything done (McGrath & Kelly, 1986). The temporal coordination of interrelated tasks is linked to

---

[4] Interview with James Bloodworth discussing working conditions in Amazon warehouses on | SVT/TV 2/Skavlan—available at https://www.youtube.com/watch?v=7mm-jcSYQas.

organizational performance, efficiency, and effectiveness (Bluedorn, 2002; Claggett & Karahanna, 2018). In addition, temporal coordination is also closely linked to risk management and security. Going back to the railways, precise coordination is crucial to avoid collisions, and safety concerns formed an important part in lobbying for standardized time implementation (Hamerla, 2006; Okhuysen & Bechky, 2009). Tight and exact schedules are part of managing landing and take-off at airports. In some other cases, withholding information and under-coordinating activities could be fatal. For example, the case of *friendly fire* described by Snook (2000 cited in Weick, 2009: 18–20) where:

> In the no-fly zone of Iraq on 14 April 1994, twenty-six people riding in *two US Army helicopters died instantly when two US Air Force F-15 fighter planes* misidentified the helicopters as Russian Hind aircraft and shot them down (Snook 2000). That incident of 'friendly fire' occurred despite the fact that all four aircraft were under the air traffic control of a nineteen-person AWACs crew flying above them and they were the only four aircraft being tracked by the crew. (Weick, 2009: 18)

Snook, as an Army Lt. Colonel and a survivor of friendly fire (Weick, 2009), provides several theoretical explanations about what went wrong. Among other explanations, Snook highlights Thompson's (1967) theory of interdependence, stressing that "different types of interdependence necessitate different coordinating mechanisms: pooled interdependence requires standardisation, sequential interdependence requires plans, and reciprocal interdependence requires mutual adjustment" (Weick, 2009: 19). In this specific friendly fire case, "all three forms of interdependence were present," while the appropriate coordinating mechanism was missing (Snook, 2000:152–173 in Weick, 2009: 20). In addition to Thompson's interdependence theory, Snook introduces "practical drift theory." "Practical drift is the 'slow uncoupling of local practice from written procedure'" (Weick, 2009: 20). If all interdependent units have made their local practical drifts and loosened coordination of routines at the local level, while assuming that other units are still following the original set of rules, then when suddenly required to work closely with other units, the cooperation fails due to a lack of coordination.

2.3 Clock Time and Coordination Challenges

Clock time is an essential tool for regulating, sequencing, synchronizing, and entraining "various dimensions of temporality" (Zerubavel, 1987: 343), such as tempo, speed, duration, frequency, acceleration, deceleration, timing, and urgency in organizational activities (Ancona et al., 2001; Zerubavel, 1987). Coordination, defined as a "*temporally unfolding and contextualized process of input regulation and interaction articulation to realise a collective performance*" (Faraj & Xiao, 2006: 1157 emphasis added), is a central aim of organizations to integrate interdependent tasks into meaningful collective action (Okhuysen & Bechky, 2009). "At its core, coordination is about the integration of organizational work under conditions of task interdependence and uncertainty" (Faraj & Xiao, 2006: 1156). Coordination may be required for sequencing activities, planning what should come before (earlier) compared to something else, which should come after (later), ordering of tasks, and determining the timing of different tasks (Claggett & Karahanna, 2018) or timing the use of scarce resources (Okhuysen & Bechky, 2009). For coordinating activities and scheduling, scarce resources timetables serve as tools for mapping activities temporally (Ballard & Seibold, 2003). For example, all the booking systems work on the timetables for scheduling resources like seats on a train or flight, or rooms for accommodation, classrooms, conferences, operations, birthday parties, and so on. Timetables based on clock time are an essential tool for coordinating what resources (like seats or rooms) are reserved for whom, when, and for how long.

Although plotted against the linear concept of time, most organizational processes have a cyclical nature (Pérez-Nordtvedt et al., 2008), which means that they are carried out or executed in a periodic or quasi-periodic manner with a certain rhythm, that is, with a certain periodicity, tempo, and phases (Ancona & Chong, 1996; Pérez-Nordtvedt et al., 2008). Some coupling is required between the various cyclical processes for interaction to take place (Bell & Kozlowski, 2002; Clayton, 2012). Depending on the size of the organization and the complexity of its structure, environment, and existing interdependencies, multiple performance cycles must be coordinated to secure organizational effectiveness (Bluedorn, 2002; Ofori-Dankwa & Julian, 2001; Pérez-Nordtvedt et al., 2008). Routines are described as possible coordination mechanisms (Claggett & Karahanna, 2018; Okhuysen & Bechky, 2009). I claim that routines also require coordination, and even the subtasks of one routine may require coordination. Therefore, depending on the level (Ballard & Seibold, 2003; Ofori-Dankwa & Julian, 2001) at which organizational action should be analysed, it is possible to view routines as recurring practices, serving both as coordination mechanisms and as a target for coordination.

For example, in our recent study conducted in a ship design and construction company, we found that regular or routinized meetings served to coordinate routines from the different functions involved in ship construction (Hernes & Pulk, 2019). These meetings performed as coordination mechanisms with both structural and relational elements (Claggett & Karahanna, 2018). My personal working experience from the accounting in an international publicly listed timber company is that in order to secure timely external financial reporting, both month and quarter-end closing routines were scheduled with an accuracy of up to 30 or even 15 minutes. The whole month-end closing of accounts to external reporting was scheduled from three days before the actual month-end closing of general ledger accounts to the 12th day after the actual closing of the general ledger accounts. The whole month-end closing cycle lasted 15 days, involved 11 different types of actors across companies, national borders, and time zones, and was repeated from month to month.

The month-end closing routines served as a structured coordination mechanism (Claggett & Karahanna, 2018) for those 11 different types of actors and for the routinized tasks they were carrying out. For example, the various actors included business controllers responsible for local factories, country accounting services (chief accountants usually serving more than one legal entity), the global support service centre, and external outsourcing partners, group controllers, treasury, and so on. These different actors were responsible for carrying out different routinized recurring practices in the organization, for example, calculations of inventory and goods in transit, accounts payable and other accruals, consolidated value-added tax reports, reconciliation of bank accounts, and adjustments of the value of financial instruments, such as futures and options, in the general ledger.

The required input from these various actors was coordinated by a detailed timetable containing up to 300 lines representing different tasks (quarterly and year-end more than 1000 lines representing various subtasks), scheduled to up to 15 minutes accuracy and supplemented with the responsible actor and exact time for task completion. The special "online-tool," which was available on the company's intranet, complemented the closing schedule. This online-tool enabled actors to follow the progress of the month-end closing in real time. All parties involved needed to tick a box to confirm the completion of the specific task they were responsible for. Ticking the box allowed other actors to follow the progress of the routine and see when they can start to work on the task assigned to them. The task completion confirmation in the "tool" was equipped with a time stamp making it possible to check who has been deviating from the schedule and by how much, and who has therefore caused delays in the entire process, revealing the relationship between the temporal regularity and administrative control (Neustadter, 1992).

Therefore, routines not only are tools for coordination but also themselves require coordination. The higher the number of participants involved and the more significant the interdependence, the greater the coordination and the greater the precision required. Bluedorn (2002: 146) points out that "Schedules are rhythmic templates, and rhythms are one way times differ." In organizations, overall performance depends on the coordination of interdependencies of various functions performed by multiple actors acting in their specific rhythms based on their particular schedules. This leads us to entrainment theory.

2.3.1 Entrainment

Sequencing activities is only one possible form of coordination. Therefore, instead of sequencing, coordination may refer to the synchronization of different cycles (Bluedorn, 2002; Pérez-Nordtvedt et al., 2008) or some sort of entrainment between the cycles. Either synchronization or entrainment could be required between the organization's performance cycles and environment (e.g., Ancona & Chong, 1996; Ancona et al., 2001; Pérez-Nordtvedt et al., 2008), between organizations, or across organizational divisions (e.g., Eisenhardt & Brown, 1998; Sinha & Van de Ven, 2005), across functions in an organization (e.g., Kotlarsky et al., 2015; Ofori-Dankwa & Julian, 2001), between the activities of different working groups or teams (e.g., Bechky, 2003; Labianca et al., 2005), between the team members of inter-organizational management teams (e.g., Standifer & Bluedorn, 2006), between individuals in a working group (e.g., Kelly & Barsade, 2001; McGrath & Kelly, 1986), and also between the individual and the organization (Shipp & Richardson, 2021).

Entrainment is a broadly used term referring to the process of interaction between two or more independent cyclical processes described according to their individual rhythms, that is, according to a certain periodicity, tempo, or phase (Pérez-Nordtvedt et al., 2008; Ross & Balasubramaniam, 2014) through which these relatively independent rhythmical processes will establish and maintain consistent and relatively stable relationships. According to Ofori-Dankwa and Julian (2001), entrainment theory represents a highly complex theory in organization studies. Entrainment theory considers the multiple cycles with different temporal rhythms in different functional units that coexist simultaneously, which are, at the same time, becoming integrated and oscillate in harmony. Clayton points to the different forms of entrainment, claiming that "Entrainment between rhythmic processes may thus be one to one, one to many, or many to many, and be symmetrical and asymmetrical" (Clayton, 2012: 49). Entrainment is symmetrical when temporal patterns of interacting individuals or teams become mutually entrained to one another (McGrath & Kelly, 1986). Entrainment is asymmetrical when interacting cycles have different strengths (Pérez-Nordtvedt et al., 2008), and one cycle dominates over other(s) by dictating or entraining the rhythm and pace, while the dominated cycle lacks any influence towards the dominating cycle (Bluedorn, 2002). In the literature, the dominating cycle, which determines the rhythm, is called a "time giver" or "zeitgeber" (Bluedorn, 2002). The time giver is "the entraining force, the rhythm that captures another rhythm" (Bluedorn, 2002: 150). The time giver is external to the rhythm which is being entrained. Usually, managers have the power to decide the dominant cycle, but also, a cue from the external environment may act as a time giver (Ancona & Chong, 1996). In organizations, each functional department has its dominant cycles, leading to a vibrant and dynamic environment with the multiplicity of simultaneously coexisting dominant cycles (Ofori-Dankwa & Julian, 2001). Therefore, entrainment may also happen when one cycle is simultaneously being influenced by and influencing several others. McGrath and Kelly describe this vibrancy as a "dynamic equilibrium," stating that:

> The multiple independent cycles of activity of the members of a social system become coordinated with one another into a temporally patterned system of activity that is characterized by a *dynamic equilibrium* rather than by a fixed *homeostatic pattern*. (McGrath & Kelly, 1986: 90 *emphasis added by the author*)

In the context of human behaviour, entrainment refers to the adaptive (Ross & Balasubramaniam, 2014) or coping (Pérez-Nordtvedt et al., 2008) function. Entrainment could be voluntary or involuntary (Ross & Balasubramaniam, 2014), intentional (Ancona & Waller, 2007), or unintentional (Richardson et al., 2007). Research in experimental psychology has revealed that, as a rule, musicians are better at sensing and following temporal rhythms. Professional training has been pointed out as one possible explanation. However, it remains unclear whether musicians are better in their temporal judgements because musical training includes obtaining a mastery of the temporal components of music like rhythm, tempo, and intervals, that is, a "capacity to process temporal information" (Grondin, 2020: 124), or because of genetic factors. In other words, we cannot ignore the possibility that musicians become musicians, firsthand, because of their superior "ability to cope with the temporal demands" (Ibid), and training plays only a secondary role. Even if the latter is highly possible, training on temporal components and practicing temporal judgement still seems to affect our ability to make more accurate temporal estimations (Montare, 1988). Therefore, it seems to be possible to improve our "sensing of time" or "time sensitivity." Tang et al. (2020) have clustered time sensitivity as an individual-level state-like temporal construct (see also Table 3.2 in Chap. 3) described as being "malleable, fleeting, and externally induced" (Tang et al., 2020: 212). But it is also possible that some individuals in general have a greater synchrony preference, which is viewed as individual-level temporal disposition or trait-like and "stable, enduring, and internally caused" (Tang et al., 2020: 212).

If there is a possibility that some individuals have a greater preference for synchrony or entrain their action with others, there should be an equal possibility that others have lower or no preference for synchrony or entrainment. It is claimed that entrainment is natural to humans (i.e., McGrath & Kelly, 1986; Ross & Balasubramaniam, 2014), meaning that people generally tend to entrain their activities. Consequently, entrainment could happen unintentionally. Unintentional entrainment can occur when individuals interact socially by paying attention to their social interaction (Clayton, 2012). For unintentional entrainment to happen, the roles of physical proximity and relational coordination are highlighted (Claggett & Karahanna, 2018; Richardson et al., 2007). The current trend to reduce social proximity through digitalization and remote working solutions most probably reduce unintentional entrainment in organizations. Reduced social proximity may mean that coordination may require more conscious efforts compared to high social proximity environments.

Voluntarily or deliberate (Shipp & Richardson, 2021) entrainment may happen when organizations or individuals feel the pressure to align their internal rhythms to the rhythms of the cycles in the broader socioeconomic or organizational environment, and they entrain consciously (Shipp & Richardson, 2021). In other words, organizations or individuals make a conscious voluntary effort to entrain their rhythms to an external time giver. On the other hand, contrary to voluntary entrainment, there may emerge situations where people are forced to entrain. Indeed, Shipp and Richardson (2021) argue that individuals may either passively or actively resist entraining and follow their own timing and pace instead or only entrain to a certain degree. Most probably, everyone who has or had the privilege of being a parent of a teenager knows what involuntary entrainment means. Trying to get your teenager out of bed to catch his or her morning classes could require tremendous effort, and the poor child does not have much choice other than to entrain involuntarily or risk missing school. In organizational settings, involuntary entrainment may happen due to external pressure or top-down forced schedules. In the case of resistance or reluctance to entrain, individuals may choose to leave the organization (Shipp & Richardson, 2021). Pérez-Nordtvedt et al. (2008: 789) also point to *pseudo-entrainment* which they describe as coincidental synchronization happening for a limited period by chance and mimicking entrainment while lacking any real tempo and/or phase adjustment.

Although entrainment is often defined as the synchronization of the phase and tempo of different cyclical activities (Ancona & Chong, 1996), entrainment is not necessarily *all-or-nothing*. Instead, it may vary by degree and type (Shipp & Richardson, 2021). One possible outcome of entrainment is synchronization, which means that the periodicity, tempo, and phase of two or more processes will coincide precisely one-to-one. But as said, synchronization is only one possible outcome, and entrainment may lead to a variety of outcomes and behaviours (Bluedorn, 2002; Clayton, 2012), including resistance (Shipp & Richardson, 2021) as mentioned before. Phase entrainment refers to the relatively stable alignment of the timing (when) of two or more activities (Pérez-Nordtvedt et al., 2008). The cycles' rhythms may entrain in-phase, anti-phase, or in between in-phase and anti-phase (Clayton, 2012). If cycles are occurring exactly simultaneously, they are in-phase; if one cycle is occurring exactly midway through the other, they are anti-phase (Clayton, 2012). The rhythm of one cycle may lead or lag behind another or others (Bluedorn, 2002). The cycle may also occur as "out of phase" (Pérez-Nordtvedt et al., 2008: 787) when it is not aligned with other cycles. Tempo entrainment denotes establishing a relatively stable relationship between oscillations of cycles (Bluedorn, 2002).

Generally, entrainment is viewed as something positive and superior to disentrainment (Blagoev & Schreyögg, 2019). A person entrained in organizational rhythms is more productive than a person that is not entrained—an organization with cycles entrained to each other is more efficient than an organization with cycles that are not entrained. An organization entrained to environmental cycles is more effective compared to the one which is not entrained. Still, based on examples from jazz music, Clayton (2012) claims that there is no single ideal form for entrainment, but "the ideal relationship is inherently dynamic, and playing involves meaningful variations within the permissible range of looseness and out-of-phase-ness" (Clayton, 2012: 54). Based on the fact that the jazz metaphor is widely used in organization studies (i.e., Bastein & Hostager, 1992, 1998; Crossan et al., 2005; Hatch, 1997, 1998, 1999; Kamoche & Cunha, 2001; Kamoche et al., 2003), we should remain open to the idea of the advantages of disentrainment. For example, Blagoev and Schreyögg (2019: 1818) "challenge the orthodox view of entrainment as an ideal synchronous relation between organizations and their environments." Based on Luhmann's statement that we should *"give up the idea of full synchronisation with the environment"* (Luhmann, 1995: 43 emphasis in original), Blagoev and Schreyögg (2019: 1821) claim that "organizations necessarily temporally uncouple, at least from some external rhythms," because otherwise, "the distinction between organizational and societal temporality would necessarily collapse."

Therefore, it seems reasonable to avoid viewing entrainment as a kind of one-size-fits-all solution or taken-for-granted path to organizational effectiveness (Letiche & Hagermeijer, 2004). For example, Ofori-Dankwa and Julian (2001) have raised various questions worth pondering. Questions like when different cycles should be entrained and when it could be more beneficial that they not be entrained, when is entrainment necessary or desirable, and with which entities should an organization seek to entrain: customers, suppliers, or regulators? Could disentrained cycles have some advantages, and if so, what might these advantages be? Which factors lead to entrainment, and which stop or inhibit entrainment from occurring? Why can some individuals and organizations entrain with relative ease while others seem to struggle? (Ofori-Dankwa & Julian, 2001: 426–427). Analysing possible answers to these questions could be eye-opening for the organization, and perhaps even enabling it to enhance its competitive position. Alternatively, answering these questions may help to identify inefficient but "hardly reversible temporal lock-ins" (Blagoev & Schreyögg, 2019: 1818) and reveal how some of these have emerged.

While organizational entrainment treats time as circular and rhythmic (Pérez-Nordtvedt et al., 2008), the tempo and periodicity of cycles are usually controlled by clock time, at least when we are talking of cycles in an organization. However, the rhythms of cycles could also be regulated based on event time (Avnet & Sellier, 2011), requiring different management approaches (Crossan et al., 2005). While synchronization and coordination based on clock time is more predictable and focused on planning, synchronization and coordination based on event time demands more flexibility to deal with the higher levels of unpredictability associated with events (Pérez-Nordtvedt et al., 2008). The latter seems to be applied more often in the case of an external time giver (Pérez-Nordtvedt et al., 2008) (for event time, see Chap. 6).

Moreover, as a rule, different activity cycles are plotted against an irreversible flow of clock time. That is to say, the focus in organizations is never just on reoccurring activity cycles and the possible coordination problems between these cycles. Usually, organizational performance is planned and evaluated in linear time as an accomplishment over time achieved through sequential steps (Langley et al., 2013; Yoon & Barton, 2019). Consequently, time is fundamental in the ongoing reproduction of organizational practices (Rowell et al., 2017), demanding simultaneous managerial attention to both the cyclical and chronometric features of time, as well as linear and event time (Dougherty et al., 2013).

2.3.2 Some Considerations Related to Entrainment Theory

There are several aspects related to entrainment theory worth additional attention. First, contrary to the approaches prevailing in mainstream psychology, which use such metaphors as a filter, resource pool, spotlight, and tend to ignore the temporal biases of actors, Jones (2019) emphasizes the rhythmic nature of human attentional behaviour. Jones argues that our interaction with the world happens through events and depends on synchrony, which enables us to "engage with an event *as it happens* ... in the moment" (2019: 1, emphasis in original). That is to say, our interaction with the world, our synchronization with the events taking place in the world, is based on event time, not clock time, and happens within time instead of over time. According to Jones, our attention (ability to attend) is not a constant but the way we pay attention has its own temporal rhythm. Jones (2019) argues that human attention has a cyclical nature and that attending is a "dynamic activity that involves the interaction of an attender's internal rhythms with the external rhythms that make up an event in the world around us" (Jones, 2019: 1).

As a dynamic and continuous activity, attention exerts fluctuating energy in time. This means that managers could benefit from paying attention to the cyclical nature of human attention when trying intentionally to alter or entrain organizational rhythms at the individual, team, or functional level (Ancona & Waller, 2007). Unfortunately, as Jones stresses, we do not know much "about how people coordinate their attending *in time* with unfolding events" (Jones, 2019: 2, emphasis in original). She claims that "Attending can be viewed as an activity that relies on the in-the-moment activities of an attender to unfolding event relationships" (Jones, 2019: 2).[5]

Second, most of the research on temporal coordination and entrainment is conducted in an environment of a high level of temporal certainty. This means that coordination and entrainment are viewed as happening over time through a situated and incremental temporal structuring based on clock time. The assumption is that it takes time to achieve an entrainment between organizational processes and the external pacer or *zeitgeber*. In other words, it takes time to establish temporal fit (Pérez-Nordtvedt et al., 2008; Kunisch et al., 2017) typically validated against clock and calendar. In addition, entrainment theory relies on the assumption that the rhythm of the external pacer remains stable and recognizable over a long enough period to allow incremental entrainment to take place. However, Geiger et al. (2020) argue that these assumptions are invalid in settings of high temporal uncertainty, where "the timing of critical events cannot be known in advance and temporal misalignment creates substantial risks" (2020: 1). Geiger et al. (2020) claim that coordination and entrainment in organizations operating in settings of high temporal uncertainty depend on the ability to recognize and understand both clock time and unpredictable event time. Echoing Jones' claims

---

[5] Based on these notions and emphasizing both the role of time and attention in synchronization, Jones has developed a dynamic attention theory introduced in her recent book *Time Will Tell: A Theory of Dynamic Attending* published by Oxford University Press in 2019.

presented above, Geiger et al. (2020) highlight the need to decide on and apply an adequate rhythm of performed activities immediately (in the moment) without an external pacer, that is, without time to try and adjust and modify over time to achieve temporal fit. According to Geiger et al. (2020), the prerequisite for deciding and applying an adequate rhythm in the context of high temporal uncertainty is the ability to enact temporal autonomy rooted in previous training.

Third, although most of the studies on coordination and entrainment focus on ongoing issues and the current challenges faced by individuals or organizations, addressing these issues and facing these challenges may demand a much longer time orientation. For example, in light of the Sustainable Development Goals (SDGs) of the United Nations, Schultz and Hernes (2020) study the interconnected coordination challenges around food consumption and production. Tackling industry-wide and global organizational coordination problems, they exit from the traditional borders of theorizing in terms of the sequencing or entrainment of objectively measurable cycles or rhythms. Instead, Schultz and Hernes (2020) highlight the need to find ways to coordinate between food-sector organizations and consumers in the distant future. It is evident that to accomplish ambitious targets on that kind of scale, schedules and clock time alone fall short.

Indeed, there is a growing body of literature highlighting the role of shared temporal structures (e.g., Aeon & Aguinis, 2017; Claggett & Karahanna, 2018; Orlikowski & Yates, 2002; Reinecke & Ansari, 2015; Standifer & Bluedorn, 2006; Yakura, 2002) as a socially constructed shared understanding (Berger & Luckmann, 1991; Zerubavel, 1981) which both enable and constrain time coordination in organizations. Temporal structures include external temporal patterns, which are formalized and independently *observable* (Barley, 1988) consisting of *descriptive* (Schultz & Hernes, 2020) aspects of time like timing, timelines, schedules, duration, opening and closing times, frequency, bank holidays, and so on (Aeon & Aguinis, 2017). Often, we consider these temporal patterns as objective, that is, these aspects of time indicate commonly understandable measurable temporality matching a realist perspective of time (Bardon, 2013) and the ontology of time (Hussenot et al., 2020).

However, there is also a growing body of literature stressing that objectively perceived and readily observable temporal patterns represent just a surface-level element of temporal structures but that temporal patterns include less visible deeper elements (Barley, 1988; Rowell et al., 2017; Schultz & Hernes, 2020). Rowell et al. (2017: 309, 310) introduce these deeper level elements as *more implicit* temporal orientations and *largely implicit* temporal conceptions. According to them, the former stands for the shared understanding of "the properties of time in which temporal patterns are positioned" and the latter for "manners of valuing and attending time" (Rowell et al., 2017: 312). The specific socio-cultural system conditions both deep-level elements of temporal structures in terms of national culture, language, institutional arrangements (Adam, 1990; Bluedorn, 2002; Zerubavel, 2003) (for socially constructed time, see Chap. 5), departing from an objective view of time. With the idea of interdependent, mutually reinforcing, and conceptually distinct types of temporal structures, Rowell et al. (2017) support Bluedorn's (2002) claim that all time is socially constructed. That is to say, even when temporal patterns may occur based on an objective and real time, their establishment and maintenance are grounded in deep temporal elements, which in turn are influenced by surface-level temporal patterns (Rowell et al., 2017). I will come back to temporal structures as a social phenomenon and their role in guiding and constraining our behaviour in organizations in Chap. 5, where I discuss the socially constructed nature of deep temporal structures that work beneath and give meaning to the temporal patterns.

2.4 Some Consequences of Clock Time

Modern societies and organizations choosing to organize their activities according to clock time, which represents temporal realism, have chosen their view of reality and adequate behaviour to cope with that reality. By structuring modern social life, clock time alters the consciousness of people and societies. It is important to notice that by choosing their way of coping with reality, people also create reality in which every choice they make comes with specific related consequences. So, what does the reality created by clock time look like? What are the consequences related to the chrono-centric worldview?

The clock enables us to measure time precisely, and time is perceived as something that can be saved or used according to our preferences. This has several consequences. For example, having an instrumental approach to time, people budget their time daily; they plan, use, and allocate it. People use time as a resource or commodity by spending, saving, selling, and even wasting it (Hall, 1983). As a commodity, quantified labour time has become an integral component of production (Adam, 1990, 2004; Clark, 1985; Hassard, 2001; Lee & Liebenau, 1999). Time as a resource presupposes active management and planning (Crossan et al., 2005) and imposes the problem of allocation (Orlikowski & Yates, 2002). Clock time, viewed as a resource, is "measured by person-time units or man-hours" (Lee & Liebenau, 1999: 1043; see also Hassard, 2001). As a measurable and quantified resource, clock time is directly linked to production planning, organizational efficiency, and effectiveness calculations (Bluedorn & Denhardt, 1988; Ciborra, 1999). In the words of Hassard (2001: 134), "As technological determinism dominates modernist perceptions of time, so correct arithmetical equations are seen as the solutions to time problems—there are finite limits and optimal solutions to temporal structuring." According to Ciborra (1999: 86), "In modern management, time is looked at as a fundamental business performance variable, even more important than money." Within organizations, time is estimated, measured, and used as a tool for measurement, coordination, regulation, and control (Clark, 1985; Hassard, 2002; McGrath & Rotchford, 1983; Purser & Petranker, 2005).

Monetization has resulted in viewing time as a scarce resource (Adam, 2004), and speed (as the case of Amazon illustrates) has become an important competitive advantage (Hernes et al., 2013). Harvey (1989) argues that the concept of *turnover time of capital* made up of production time with the time of circulation is extremely important for profit generation. "The faster the capital launched into circulation can be recuperated, the greater the profit will be" (Harvey, 1989: 229). Therefore, *time to market* is an important aspect of competitiveness requiring speed and acceleration, which in turn leads to the shortening of production or product life cycles, waste (Harvey, 1989; Hassard, 2001; Nowotny,

1996), and *forgetting* (Czarniawska, 2013). While there is no doubt that excess waste is a social and environmental burden, organizational *forgetting* can have either positive (Martin de Holan & Phillips, 2004; Tsang & Zahra, 2008) or negative consequences (Coraiola & Derry, 2019; Mena et al., 2016). On the one hand, organizational forgetting might be seen as desirable as an enabler of unlearning (Nystrom & Starbuck, 1984) and, as such, a precondition for learning (Bettis & Prahalad, 1995). Being unable to forget anything overburdens individuals with unnecessary details. On the other hand, *forgetting* caused by time pressure may mean that fewer resources in the form of past experiences are available (Argote, 2013). Therefore, organizational forgetting is viewed as leading to a loss of knowledge, competencies, and capabilities. Organizational forgetting is also associated with corporate irresponsibility consequences (Coraiola & Derry, 2019; Mena et al., 2016).

Viewing time as an irreversible sacred resource has created the perception of acute time pressure and urgency. Maruping, Venkatesh, Thatcher and Patel (2015: 1315) define perceived time pressure as "a scarcity of time available to complete a task or set of tasks relative to the demands of the task(s) at hand." The chronic shortage of time is marked using phrases like time deficit (Bianchi et al., 2005), time famine (Robinson & Godbey, 1999), and time crunch (Zuzanek, 2004). Based on previous research, Maruping et al. (2015) note that perceived time pressure could have both positive and negative outcomes. Robinson and Godbey (1999: 37) share this viewpoint claiming that "there is also a social element to time pressures that is highly desirable for humans". Robinson and Godbey (1999) emphasize the role of time pressure in establishing and maintaining our temporal routines, which in turn, by intentional action, help to structure time. Referring back to the Great Depression, they claim that those who managed to establish "new routines with new time pressure around which the rest of life could unfold" (Robinson & Godbey, 1999: 38) generally coped better with unemployment. Their point is that without any time pressure it is easy to lose oneself in the sequence of empty forgettable days.

The concept of time pressure is linked directly to the concept of time deepening. Time deepening is based on the assumption that under pressure, people are able to expand the number of things they do. Robinson and Godbey (1999: 30) point out that time deepening has emerged as a strategy to deal with the continuous acceleration of social pace (see also Harvey, 1989; Nowotny, 1996). As a strategy to "squeeze out more from the same amount of time," time deepening includes multitasking (Bluedorn, 2002: 107–108). At the same time, polychronicity (see Bluedorn, 2002, Chap. 3) as a preference to being simultaneously engaged in two or more tasks without attempting to get more things done or do them faster is a different concept. Robinson and Godbey (1999) list several strategies to achieve time deepening; for example, instead of choosing and concentrating on one activity, people attempt to accomplish more activities in the same timeframe or even at once (multitasking), or substituting time-consuming leisure activities with quicker ones, or trying to be very precise and fast in their activities. Although the assumption is that time pressure leads to time deepening (Robinson & Godbey, 1999), there is no reason to ignore the possibility that time deepening adds to perceived time pressure. Consequently, it seems to be a kind of a "chicken-and-the-egg" problem.

However, perceived time pressure experienced in different life spheres in conjunction with urgency, defined as "a concern for time and a feeling of being chronically hurried" (Maruping et al., 2015: 1315), tends to have a negative impact both on team or organizational performance (Maule & Svenson, 1993) and on individual employee wellbeing (Roxburgh, 2004). Organizational performance may suffer due to chronic time pressure because of the negative impact on the quality of organizational decision-making and behaviour (Maule & Svenson, 1993). "A feeling of being chronically hurried" (Maruping et al., 2015: 1315) is associated with negative stress-related health problems (Lehto, 1998; Zuzanek, 2004). As a rule, the adverse effects on organizational performance and employee health have wider societal consequences, contributing to chronic time pressure as one of the most significant challenges in contemporary organizations and societies (Kleiner, 2014; Rosa, 2003; Szollos, 2009).

Neustadter (1992: 390) states that "Western conceptions of time are seen to be pathological." People have become servants of the clock, which sets the tempo of everyday life. There is never enough time, and faster is always better. Indeed, Eisenhardt and Brown (1998) found that decision-making speed in top management teams is positively correlated with organizational effectiveness in high-velocity environments. However, others have found that the feeling of being rushed in decision-making may create regret even if the outcome of the decision is positive (Connolly & Zeelenberg, 2002; Inbar et al., 2011). Bluedorn, claiming that "speed kills" (2002: 108), takes it many steps further from regret and dissatisfaction with our decision-making process caused by speed (Inbar et al., 2011). Namely, Bluedorn (2002) literally refers to strong positive relationships between the pace of life, perceived time pressure, stress, and coronary heart disease rates (Zuzanek, 2004). Speed or an overly fast pace is associated with burnout and many stress-related mental health issues, such as anxiety and depression (Rosa, 2003; Roxburgh, 2004; Wajcman, 2016). It seems that even children in kindergarten and elementary school need *minutes of silence* as an essential valve that helps them relax and calm down in generally hectic and rushing surroundings.

Still, the tempo of everyday life has accelerated even more with digitalization (Wajcman, 2016). In many areas of life, together with digitalization and the broader use of advanced computer technologies, clock time is replaced by "instantaneous time" (Macnaghten & Urry, 1998). Macnaghten and Urry provide a list of instantaneous time indicators (see also Harvey, 1989: 286), which have become standard across developed industrial countries during recent years. While related to different spheres of life, common features of these indicators are short-termism in both work-related and personal relations, instant availability of new goods, technologies and services, and increased waste. I will not present here the entire list but, for example, concerning work-related relationships, Macnaghten and Urry (1998:150) underline:

> a heightened 'temporariness' of products, jobs, careers, natures, values and personal relationships;
>   the growth of short-term labour contracts, what has been called the just-in-time workforce, and how this generates new forms of insecurity.

With the rise of on-demand platforms based on digital technology, we have witnessed exactly that—a gig economy with a temporary on-call gig worker. Although *gigs* could be appreciated by older teenagers and young adults as a convenient way to earn some income, being a gig-worker generally tends to mean lower social security and no concern for employee wellbeing (Bloodworth, 2019). Some other indicators on the list provided by Macnaghten and Urry (1998) seem familiar, including those at the heart of today's concerns about the environment and sustainability and debates about consumerism and its hard to bear consequences for the environment:

> technological and organizational changes which break down distinctions between night and day, working week and weekend, home and work, leisure and work;
> the growth of 24-hour trading so that investors and dealers never have to wait for the buying and selling of securities and foreign exchange;
> the proliferation of new products, flexible forms of technology and huge amounts of waste;
> the growing volatility and ephemerality in fashions, products, labour processes, ideas and images;
> the increasing disposability of products, places and images in a *throwaway society*;
> extraordinary increases in the availability of products so that we do not have to wait to travel anywhere in order to consume some new style or fashion. (Macnaghten & Urry, 1998: 150)

And last but not least:

> an increasing sense that the *pace of life* has become too fast in contradiction with other aspects of human experience. (Macnaghten & Urry, 1998: 150)

Therefore, instantaneous time has two main consequences. First, based on bits and advanced computer technologies, instantaneous time is speeding everything up by allowing us to make decisions in nanoseconds, meaning that "Contemporary social and organizational practices are based on time-frames that lie beyond conscious human experience. Time is organized at speeds beyond the feasible realm of human consciousness" (Hassard, 2001: 138).

Yet another outcome of speed is *intensification* (Bakken et al., 2013), also called *time-space compression* (Harvey, 1989; Hassard, 2002). Instantaneous time *dissolves the future* (Macnaghten & Urry, 1998: 150)

2 Objective View of Time and Temporality: Time as a Tool... 49

in the extended present leaving us without a perspective for something else or something different. Or as Fuchs points out, without any "indeterminate anticipation of what is yet to come" (Fuchs, 2013: 77). Harvey describes the result of time-space compression on our view of the world in the following words:

> Space appears to shrink to a *global village* of telecommunications and a *spaceship earth* of economic and ecological interdependencies—to use just two familiar and everyday images—and as time horizons shorten to the point where the present is all there is (the world of the schizophrenic), so we have to learn how to cope with an overwhelming sense of *compression* of our spatial and temporal worlds. (1989: 240 emphasis in original)

Fraser (1996 in Nowotny, 1996), in his foreword to Nowotny's *Time: The Modern and Postmodern Experience* expresses similar concerns by arguing that the technological and societal changes are so rapid that "to make their integration into the recent past and onrushing future [is] impossible. The environment created by individuals and societies thus outruns the adaptive capacities of their creators and leads to a loss of temporal horizons, or … extended present" (Fraser in Nowotny, 1996: 5).

In addition to leading to a pathological time, for example, both Harvey (1989) and Fuchs (2013) make reference to schizophrenic time. Intensification or time-space compression has, through shortened time horizons, led to *chronocentrism* (Fowles, 1974: 66). Fowles (1974: 67) claims that "Chronocentrism … is an intellectual error." Chronocentrism praises the importance of the present over the past and future. It undermines the importance of the future and over-estimates the importance of the present. The following quotes cited by Fowles (1974) are examples of endorsing temporal locale and highlighting its significance, that is, chronocentrism:

> By changing our relationship to the resources that surround us, by *violently* expanding the scope of change, and, most crucially, *by accelerating its pace*, we have *broken irretrievably with the past*. We have cut ourselves off from the old ways of thinking, of feeling, of adapting. *We have set the stage for a*

completely new society, and we are now racing toward it. (Alvin Toffler, 1970: 19 cited in Fowles, 1974: 66 *emphasis added*)

The way to proceed is clear, and the necessary steps, although they are new ones for human society, are well within human capabilities. Man possesses, for *a small moment in his history*, the most powerful combination of knowledge, tools, and resources the world has ever known. He has all that is physically *necessary to create a totally new form of human society—one that would be built to last for generations*. (Dennis Meadows, 1972: 183 cited in Fowles, 1974: 67 emphasis added)

Breaking away from the past, violently changing and expanding our relationships with our environment, expressing almost arrogant confidence that at present we know exactly how the future looks and what is best for that future, and denying or ignoring any hidden potential or emerging possibility are symptoms of chronocentrism. Chronocentrism, in its extreme form, may lead to the point where there is only the present without the future (Hassard, 2002). An over-emphasized present may lead to a temporal monotony, to existential atemporality, the annihilation of possibilities, and denial of potential (Neustadter, 1992). A temporal monotony, the present only without any future perspective, creates a perceived static view of an environment, which, in turn, contributes to boredom (Watt, 1991). Boredom, defined as "a distorted sense of time in which time seems to stand still" (Greenson, 1953: 7 in Watt, 1991: 323) is associated with negative feelings like depression, stress, hopelessness, loneliness, and distractibility (Watt, 1991). I will return to boredom caused by a distorted sense of time in more detail in the next chapter. At the moment, I would like to stress the paradox of time that in the case of chronocentrism, under the dominance of the present, life could be perceived as static and atemporal despite its fast pace—a kind of spinning wheel phenomenon or like a mad hatter's tea party in Alice's Adventures in Wonderland (Carrol, 1865/2008). The mad hatter's tea party was never-ending or starting a six o'clock tea party. It was never-ending or starting because the clock was always six, which was the *proper time* (Nowotny, 1996) for tea. As it was always *teatime*, there was no time to do the dishes or refresh the table but just move around the table to have

2 Objective View of Time and Temporality: Time as a Tool... 51

at least a *new* seat (Carrol, 1865/2008). There was no option of escaping the tyranny of time—*teatime* was all that existed.

The perception of the present without the future could lead to unsustainable practices. It gives the impression that both coming events and the environment have abundant, exploitable standing reserves (Bakken et al., 2013). As a pushback to thoughts expressed by Toffler and Meadows cited above, Mumford points to the shortcomings related to a chronocentric view of time, stating that:

> In fact, no generation before our own has ever been so fatuous as to imagine it possible to live exclusively within its own narrow time-band, guided only by information recently discovered; nor has it ever before this accepted as final and absolute the demands of the present generation alone, without relating these demands to past experiences and future projects and ideal possibilities. (Mumford, 1970: 282)

Although today, 40 years after Mumford's grim predictions, we are forced to face the climate crisis, questioning both the sustainability of humankind's future and the broader ecosystem of our planet as a result of the chronocentric worldview. We are so far from a human society that will *last generations* that schoolchildren worldwide are protesting with school strikes for the climate led by Greta Thunberg. And they have a legitimate point—there is very little left for the coming generations. As Nowotny states:

> The future of our children is no longer predominantly interpreted in individual terms—as the desire for social advancement and well-being—but as a question of collective survival. It is the time of the next generation which is being argued about now. (1996: 52)

Another movement in society working against the ever-increasing speed and acceleration is the Slow Movement, a term coined by Carl Honoré (2004) in his international best-seller *In Praise of Slow*. In his book, Honoré emphasizes that the current endeavour to accomplish everything as fast as possible has become a globally accepted societal standard, almost like a *cult of speed*. As a contra force to the *cult of speed*, which includes fast food, fast fashion, and social media, the Slow Movement praises attentiveness to local communities and fairness, sustainability, and values the simple life with real human contact. Contrary to the idea that faster is always better, slow movement emphasis quality and appropriate speed over quantity and unquestioned fastness.

Concerns about our ability to maintain our humanity in the chronocentric fast-paced world we live in, characterized by continuous measurement and calculation, are expressed by Romer (2010 referred in Bakken et al., 2013). Romer (2010: 198 quoted in Bakken et al., 2013: 19) suggests that "it is almost as if the precision with which we can measure time is an indicator of our existential lostness." That is to say, our internal psychological time and existential-phenomenological time, which I will discuss in the next chapters, may not necessarily sync with chronometric and chronological clock time. Although these different times may not sync, this does not mean that we should ignore them. On the contrary, following Adam's (1990) call, we should try to understand all the different times with their specific features and reciprocal influence.

2.5 Limitations of Clock Time

Contemporary postmodern developed societies are organized based on clock time. It turns out that the clock time we are so familiar with is neither objective nor absolute, even if it is sometimes described that way (i.e., Lee & Liebenau, 1999: 1038). Zerubavel claims that "[clock time] is not an absolute time. It's something we share, but it's not objective, because objective would be the natural or the logical, and—in the case of time—the physical" (Sabetta & Zerubavel, 2019: 60). James (1922 referred to in Sorokin & Merton, 1937: 616) is no less critical, viewing "the concept of *objective* time as a useful fiction." Clock time is neither natural nor physical time, and thus, it is neither objective nor absolute. Instead, it is a human creation (Bluedorn, 2002), a socially agreed time (Sorokin & Merton, 1937), which does great work in solving coordination problems stemming from interdependencies and intersubjectivity (Berger & Luckmann, 1991) of social action.

According to Neustadter (1992: 380), "The clock made possible a temporal environment that is spatial, quantitative, fast-paced, efficient and predictable." The predictability of a temporal environment is an important feature referring to regularity. According to Mumford (1963: 269), "The first characteristic of modern machine civilisation is its temporal regularity." An ability to predict the temporal regularity of social life enables us to control it, at least to some extent, while once again opening questions related to power—who controls whom, what, when, and why. Therefore, clock time may not necessarily be so neutral and external to human affairs as it is often described. Instead, it may be serving the interests of some social groups better than others (Harvey, 1989; Nowotny, 1996), and it may be both a target and a tool for manipulation (Luhmann, 2018; Zerubavel, 2003).

Although linear time or clock time is still the most dominant and widespread conceptualization of time in modern organizations (Bluedorn & Denhardt, 1988; Clark, 1985; Crossan et al., 2005; Sorokin & Merton, 1937), and despite its importance in organizational life, it has several limitations. These limitations have caught the attention of many authors (e.g., Bluedorn & Denhardt, 1988; Clark, 1985; Das, 1993; Hassard, 2002; McGrath & Rotchford, 1983). For example, Hassard (2002: 585) claims that "working time is a much richer phenomenon than is portrayed in mainstream industrial sociology. Dominant perspectives, such as functionalism and structuralism, mostly fail to capture the complexity of industrial temporality." Das (1993) echoes similar thoughts by pointing out that the concept of clock time, which ignores the human actor, falls short of understanding organizational phenomena in their complexity. The mentioned complexity of industrial temporality, which mainstream clock time-based perspectives fail to capture, includes a plurality of times. This plurality of times emerges from a relative, subjectively perceived, and experienced time (Clark, 1985; Tesluk & Jacobs, 1998). A plurality of relative, subjective times informs and gives meaning to our action in contrast to singular, objective, and measurable clock time (Bluedorn & Denhardt, 1988; Nowotny, 1996). See Chaps. 4 and 5 for a more detailed elaboration.

Standardized clock time as a negotiated and socially agreed concept overrules many local time reckoning systems, whereas the latter would reflect the rhythm of social activities at the local level much better. Consequently, we should not be surprised to find alternative systems for time reference, which in particular circumstances may make more sense and work much better than standardized clock time (see Reinecke & Ansari, 2015). When these local alternatives arise, we should not be surprised by possible clashes between the time reckoning systems based on local times and standardized time (Rifkin, 1987). I will come back to the plurality of time reckoning systems and social times in Chap. 5. Although we can find arguments against clock time and in favour of cyclical nature-based time (i.e., Adam, 1990; Nowotny, 1996), Boorstin claims that clock time liberated mankind "from the cyclical monotony of nature" (1983: 1).

However, while we can agree that something lasts so long or moves or responds as fast or accelerates or slows down on the basis of objective terms, the semantic meaning of the speed, duration, tempo, and so on is not objective but context-specific depending on the nature of the specific activity and its background (Zerubavel, 1987, 1991, 2003). Therefore, even if we use clock time as an objective measurement tool in many situations, we rely on the subjective qualitative interpretation of objectively measured time. For example, we can agree that objectively something takes 45 minutes. Still, we can ask, what does this mean? Is this optimal, too long or too short? The answer depends. Most probably, 45 minutes is too long if you are suffering a heart attack and waiting for a response to the emergency call. At the same time, 45 minutes between flights at Frankfurt Airport could be just optimal if catching a flight inside the Schengen area, but too short if catching a flight to the United States. Indeed, according to Sorokin and Merton (1937: 619), objective clock or calendar time "becomes significant only when it is transformed into social time," when its meaning is defined by social activities. Clock time is an emergent social tool for organizing "otherwise chaotic, individually varying, activities" (Sorokin & Merton, 1937: 628).

While there is nothing wrong with clock time per se, narrowing our conceptualization of time to measurable clock time has, for a long time, been seen as an overly limited approach (i.e., Adam, 1990, 2004; Baars,

2012; Clark, 1985; Hassard, 2002; Neustadter, 1992; Nowotny, 1996). Therefore, we should not neglect all other aspects of time and focus only objectively on it as an external and objective measure (Adam, 1990, 2004; Clark, 1985). Narrowing our realities to an overly rationalistic worldview directed by chronometric time may not serve our best interests (Baars, 2012). According to Neustadter (1992: 396), "Time, as measured, can become the enemy of time as lived." But not only, because *time, as measured*, can also become the enemy of creativity and innovation (Dougherty et al., 2013; Dougherty & Dunne, 2011; Hjorth et al., 2018; Styhre & Sundgren, 2011), and thus jeopardize organizational or even societal renewal and continuity.

Still, we cannot forget the main merits of clock time. As a globally accepted standardized time, it allows internationally shared temporal reference and time reckoning systems and has enabled institutionalized concepts such as appointments and timetables (Zerubavel, 1981, 1982). It is hard to imagine the modern world without these *inventions*. One of the indications that clock time is being "woven into the fabric of existence to the extent that it determines and coordinates all social life" (Neustadter, 1992: 395) is perhaps the fact that allegedly, we are no longer being forced to "marry" or "eat" according to "railroad time" (Bartky, 2000: 14). Yes, people can debate whether it is reasonable to switch between summer and wintertime, but hardly anybody challenges the shared reference system grounded in clock time. Recent reflections on the temporal lostness caused by COVID-19-related lockdown and isolation show that we need some kind of temporal structuring and coordination. Without a temporal structure provided by clock time and an accompanying *timeline*, we may easily find ourselves *disoriented* (Berger & Luckmann, 1991: 42), floating helplessly without a clear direction.

2.6 Conclusion

Standardized clock time is a socially agreed tool for organizing at the super-local level. Clock time enables us to coordinate activities at various levels, locate events in time, and agree on the chronological order of events. With the help of calendars, clock time enables us to pattern various realms of social life into more or less coherent systems. In organizations, clock time is a central tool for planning and costing activities and coordinating, synchronizing, and entraining various functions and activities. Clock time allows us to measure and calculate time as a resource. However, narrowing our conceptualizing only to an objective clock time alters our perception of reality. It constrains our attention and imagination, which in turn may jeopardize our creativity, ability to innovate, and see possibilities. Clock time, rooted in economic rationality, represents temporal realism rooted in the ontology of time and tends to lead us to a mechanical world view alienated from organic periodicities and mythological thinking. It has clear limitations in explaining physical, social, or psychological phenomena, processes, or experiences that may not follow clock time's linear logic.

References

Adam, B. (1990). *Time and social theory*. Polity Press.
Adam, B. (2004). *Time*. Polity.
Aeon, B., & Aguinis, H. (2017). It's about time: New perspectives and insights on time management. *Academy of Management Perspectives, 31*(4), 309–330. https://doi.org/10.5465/amp.2016.0166
Ancona, D. G., & Chong, C. L. (1996). Entrainment: Pace, cycle, and rhythm in organizational behavior. In B. M. Staw & L. L. Cummings (Eds.), *Research in organizational behavior* (Vol. 18, pp. 251–284). Elsevier.
Ancona, D. G., Okhuysen, G. A., & Perlow, L. A. (2001). Taking time to integrate temporal research. *Academy of Management Review, 26*(4), 512–529.
Ancona, D. G., & Waller, M. J. (2007). The dance of entrainment: Temporally navigating across multiple pacers. *Research in the Sociology of Work, 17*, 115–146.
Anders, G. (2012). Jeff Bezos gets it. *Forbes*, April 25. Retrieved February 20, 2020, from https://www.forbes.com/global/2012/0507/global-2000-12-amazon-jeff-bezos-gets-it.html?sh=55ed6a155fad
Argote, L. (2013). *Organizational learning: Creating, retaining and transferring knowledge*. Springer Science Business Media.

Augustine, G., Soderstrom, S., Milner, D., & Weber, K. (2019). Constructing a distant future: Imaginaries in geoengineering. *Academy of Management Journal, 62*(6), 1930–1960.
Avnet, T., & Sellier, A. (2011). Clock time vs. event time: Temporal culture or self-regulation? *Journal of Experimental Social Psychology, 47*, 665–667.
Baars, J. (2012). Critical turns of aging, narrative and time. *International Journal of Ageing and Later Life, 7*(2), 143–165.
Bakken, T., Holt, R., & Zundel, M. (2013). Time and play in management practice: An investigation through the philosophies of McTaggart and Heidegger. *Scandinavian Journal of Management, 29*, 13–22.
Ballard, D. J., & Seibold, D. R. (2003). Communication and organizing in time: A meso-level model of organizational temporality. *Management Communication Quarterly, 16*, 380–415.
Bardon, A. (2013). *A brief history of the philosophy of time*. Oxford Scholarship Online. https://doi.org/10.1093/asprof:oso/9780199976454.001.0001
Barley, S. R. (1988). On technology, time, and social order: Technically induced change in the temporal organization of radiological work. In F. A. Dubinskas (Ed.), *Making time: Ethnographies of high technology organizations* (pp. 123–169). Temple University Press.
Bartky, I. (2000). *Selling the true time: Nineteenth-century timekeeping in America*. Stanford University Press.
Bastein, D. T., & Hostager, T. J. (1992). Cooperation as communicative accomplishment: A symbolic interaction analysis of an improvised jazz concert. *Communication Studies, 43*(2), 92–104.
Bastein, D. T., & Hostager, T. J. (1998). Jazz as a process of organizational innovation. *Communication Research, 15*, 582–602.
Bechky, B. A. (2003). Object lessons: Workplace artifacts as representations of occupational jurisdiction. *American Journal of Sociology, 109*, 720–752.
Bell, B. S., & Kozlowski, S. W. J. (2002). A typology of virtual teams. *Group and Organization Management, 27*, 14–49.
Berger, P., & Luckmann, T. (1991). *The social construction of reality: A treatise in the sociology of knowledge*. Penguin Books.
Bettis, R., & Prahalad, C. K. (1995). The dominant logic: Retrospective and extension. *Strategic Management Journal, 16*(1), 5–14.
Bianchi, S. M., Casper, L. M., & King, B. R. (2005). *Work, family, health, and well-being*. Lawrence Erlbaum.

Blagoev, B., & Schreyögg, G. (2019). Why do extreme work hours persist? Temporal uncoupling as a new way of seeing. *Academy of Management Journal, 62*(6), 1818–1847.

Bloodworth, J. (2019). *Hired: Six months undercover in low-wage Britain*. Atlantic Book.

Bluedorn, A. C. (2002). *The human organization of time*. Stanford University Press.

Bluedorn, A. C., & Denhardt, R. B. (1988). Time and organizations. *Journal of Management, 14*(2), 299–320.

Boorstin, D. (1983). *The discoverers*. Random House.

Carrol, L. (1865/2008). *Alice's adventures in Wonderland*. Ebook produced by A. DiBianca & D. Widger. The Millennium Fulcrum Edition 3.0.

Channel 4 News. (2013). *Ex-Amazon workers talk of 'horrendous' conditions*. Retrieved September 23, 2020, from https://www.youtube.com/watch?v=gYUJjpIxkCU

Chia, R. (1999). A 'rhizomic' model of organizational change and trans- formation: Perspective from a metaphysics of change. *British Journal of Management, 10*, 209–227.

Ciborra, C. U. (1999). Notes on improvisation and time in organizations. *Accounting, Management and Information Technologies, 9*, 77–94.

Claggett, J. L., & Karahanna, E. (2018). Unpacking the structure of coordination mechanisms and the role of relational coordination in an era of digitally mediated work processes. *Academy of Management Review, 43*(4), 704–722.

Clark, P. (1985). A review of theories of time and structure for organizational sociology. In S. B. Bacharach & S. M. Mitchell (Eds.), *Research in the sociology of organizations. A research annual* (Vol. 4, pp. 35–79). JAI.

Clayton, M. (2012). What is entrainment? Definition and applications in musical research. *Empirical Musicology Review, 7*(1–2), 49–56.

Connolly, T., & Zeelenberg, M. (2002). Regret in decision making. *Current Directions in Psychological Science, 11*, 212–216.

Coraiola, D. M., & Derry, R. (2019). Remembering to forget: The historical irresponsibility of US big tobacco. *Journal of Business Ethics*.

Crossan, M., Cunha, M. P., Vera, D., & Cuhna, J. (2005). Time and organizational improvisation. *Academy of Management Review, 30*(1), 129–145.

Czarniawska, B. (2004). On time, space and action nets. *Organization, 11*(6), 773–791. https://doi.org/10.1177/1350508404047251

Czarniawska, B. (2013). Is speed good? *Scandinavian Journal of Management, 29*, 7–12.

2 Objective View of Time and Temporality: Time as a Tool... 59

Das, T. K. (1993). Time in management and organization studies. *Time & Society, 2*, 267–274.

Dougherty, D., Bertels, H., Chung, K., Dunne, D. D., & Kraemer, J. (2013). Whose time is it? Understanding clock-time pacing and event-time pacing in complex innovations. *Management and Organization Review, 9*(2), 223–263.

Dougherty, D., & Dunne, D. D. (2011). Organizing ecologies of complex innovation. *Organization Studies, 22*(5), 1214–1223.

Eisenhardt, K. M., & Brown, S. L. (1998). Time pacing: Competing in markets that won't stand still. *Harvard Business Review, 76*(2), 59–69.

Faraj, S., & Xiao, Y. (2006). Coordination in fast-response organization. *Management Science, 52*, 1155–1189.

Fowles, J. (1974). Future essay: On chronocentrism. *Futures, 6*, 65–68.

Fuchs, T. (2013). Temporality and psychopathology. *Phenomenology and the Cognitive Sciences, 12*(1), 75–104. https://doi.org/10.1007/s11097-010-9189-4

Geiger, D., Danner-Schröder, A., & Kremser, W. (2020). Getting ahead of time—Performing temporal boundaries to coordinate routines under temporal uncertainty. *Administrative Science Quarterly, 66*, 1–45. https://doi.org/10.1177/0001839220941010

Grey, C. (2017). *A very short, fairly interesting and reasonably cheap book about studying organizations* (4th ed.). SAGE.

Grondin, S. (2020). *The perception of time: Your questions answered*. Routledge.

Hahn, T., Pinkse, J., Preuss, L., & Figge, F. (2015). Tensions in corporate sustainability: Towards an integrative framework. *Journal of Business Ethics, 127*, 297–316.

Hall, E. (1983). *The dance of life*. Anchor Books/ Doubleday.

Hamerla, R. (2006). *An American scientist on the research frontier: Edward Morely, community, and radical ideas in nineteenth -century science*. Springer.

Harvey, D. (1989). *The condition of postmodernity: An enquiry into the origins of cultural change*. Blackwell.

Hassard, H. (2001). Commodification, construction and compression: A review of time metaphors in organizational analysis. *International Journal of Management Reviews, 3*(2), 131–141.

Hassard, J. (2002). Essay: Organizational time: Modern, symbolic and post-modern reflections. *Organization Studies, 23*(6), 885–892.

Hatch, M. J. (1997). Commentary: Jazzing up the theory of organizational improvisation. *Advances in Strategic Management, 14*, 181–192.

Hatch, M. J. (1998). Jazz as a metaphor for organizing in the 21st century. *Organization Science, 9*, 556–557.
Hatch, M. J. (1999). Exploring the empty spaces of organizing: How improvisational jazz redescribes organizational structure. *Organization Studies, 20*, 75–101.
Hernes, T. (2014). *A process theory of organization.* Oxford University Press.
Hernes, T., & Pulk, K. (2019). A temporal view of the interplay between continuous and episodic change. In *Academy of management proceedings.* Boston.
Hernes, T., Simpson, B., & Söderlund, J. (2013). Managing and temporality. *Scandinavian Journal of Management, 29*, 1–6.
Hjorth, D., Strati, A., Drakopoulou, D., & Weik, E. (2018). Organizational creativity, play and entrepreneurship: Introduction and framing. *Organization Studies, 39*(2–3), 155–168.
Honoré, C. (2004). *In praise of Slow: How a worldwide movement is challenging the cult of speed.* Orion Books.
Hussenot, A., Hernes, T., & Bouty, I. (2020). Studying organization from the perspective of the ontology of temporality: Introducing the events-based approach. In J. Reinecke, R. Suddaby, A. Langley, & H. Tsoukas (Eds.), *About time: Temporality and history in organization studies* (pp. 50–68). Oxford University Press. https://doi.org/10.1093/oso/9780198870715.003.0005
Inbar, Y., Botti, S., & Hanko, K. (2011). Decision speed and choice regret: When haste feels like waste. *Journal of Experimental Social Psychology, 47*, 533–540. https://doi.org/10.1016/j.jesp.2011.01.011
Jaques, E. (1982/1990). The enigma of time. In J. Hassard (Ed.), *The sociology of time* (pp. 21–34). Macmillan.
Jones, M. R. (2019). *Time will tell: A theory of dynamic attending.* Oxford University Press.
Kamoche, K., & Cunha, M. P. (2001). Minimal structures: From jazz improvisation to product innovation. *Organization Studies, 22*, 733–764.
Kamoche, K., Cunha, M. P., & Cunha, J. V. (2003). Towards a theory of organizational improvisation: Looking beyond the jazz metaphor. *Journal of Management Studies, 40*(8), 2023–2051.
Kelly, J. R., & Barsade, S. G. (2001). Mood and emotions in small groups and work teams. *Organizational Behavior and Human Decision Processes, 86*, 99–130.
Kleiner, S. (2014). Subjective time pressure: General or domain specific? *Social Science Research, 47*(1), 108–120.

Kotlarsky, J., van den Hooff, B., & Houtman, L. (2015). Are we on the same page? Knowledge boundaries and transactive memory system development in cross-functional teams. *Communication Research, 42*, 319–344.

Kunisch, S., Bartunek, J. M., Mueller, J., & Huy, Q. N. (2017). Time in strategic change research. *Academy of Management Annals, 11*(2), 1005–1064.

Labianca, G., Moon, H., & Watt, I. (2005). When is an hour not 60 minutes? Deadlines, temporal schemata, and individual and task group performance. *Academy of Management Journal, 48*(4), 677–694.

Langley, A., Smallman, C., Tsoukas, H., & Van de Ven, A. H. (2013). Process studies of change in organization and management: Unveiling temporality, activity, and flow. *Academy of Management Journal, 56*, 1–13.

Laverty, K. J. (1996). Economic "short-termism": The debate, the unresolved issues, and the implications for management practice and research. *Academy of Management Review, 21*(3), 825–860.

Lee, H., & Liebenau, J. (1999). Time in organizational studies: Towards a new research direction. *Organization Studies, 20*(6), 1035–1058.

Lehto, A.-M. (1998). Time pressure as a stress factor. *Society and Leisure, 21*(2), 491–512.

Letiche, H., & Hagermeijer, R. E. (2004). Linkages and entrainment. *Journal of Organizational Change Management, 17*(4), 365–382.

Luhmann, N. (1995). *Social systems*. Stanford University Press.

Luhmann, N. (2018). *Organization and decision*. Cambridge University Press.

Lukàcs, G. (1973). *History and class consciousness: Studies in Marxist dialectics*. MIT Press.

Macnaghten, P., & Urry, J. (1998). *Contested natures*. SAGE Publications.

Malinowski, B. (1990). Time-reckoning in the Trobriands. In J. Hassard (Ed.), *The sociology of time* (pp. 203–218). Macmillan.

Marcec, D. (2018). CEO tenure rates. Retrieved September 12, 2020, from https://corpgov.law.harvard.edu/2018/02/12/ceo-tenure-rates/

Marginson, D., & McAulay, L. (2008). Exploring the debate on short-termism: A theoretical and empirical analysis. *Strategic Management Journal, 29*, 273–292.

Martin de Holan, P. M., & Phillips, N. (2004). Remembrance of things past? The dynamics of organizational forgetting. *Management Science, 50*, 1603–1613.

Maruping, L. M., Venkatesh, V., Thatcher, S. M. B., & Patel, P. C. (2015). Folding under pressure or rising to the occasion? Perceived time pressure and the moderating role of team temporal leadership. *Academy of Management Journal, 58*(5), 1313–1333.

Maule, J., & Svenson, O. (1993). Theoretical and empirical approaches to behavioral decision-making and their relation to time constraints. In O. Svenson & J. Maule (Eds.), *Time pressure and stress in human judgment and decision making* (pp. 3–25). Springer Science+Business Media.
McGrath, J. E., & Kelly, J. R. (1986). *Time and human interaction.* Guilford Press.
McGrath, J. E., & Rotchford, N. L. (1983). Time and behavior in organizations. *Research in Organizational Behavior, 5,* 57–101.
Mena, S., Rintamäki, J., Fleming, P., & Spicer, A. (2016). On the forgetting of corporate irresponsibility. *Academy of Management Review, 41*(4), 720–738.
Mikita, V. (2013). *Lingvistiline mets.* Välgi Metsad.
Montare, A. (1988). Further learning effects of knowledge of results upon time estimation. *Perceptual and Motor Skills, 66,* 579–588.
Mumford, L. (1963). *Technics and civilization.* Harcourt Brace & World.
Mumford, L. (1970). *The myth of the machine: The pentagon of power.* Harcourt, Brace, Jovanovich.
Neustadter, R. (1992). Beat the clock: The mid-20th-century protest against the reification of time. *Time & Society, 1*(3), 379–398.
Nowotny, H. (1996). *Time: The modern and postmodern experience.* Polity Press.
Nystrom, P. C., & Starbuck, W. H. (1984). To avoid organizational crises, unlearn. *Organizational Dynamics, 12*(4), 53–65.
Ofori-Dankwa, J., & Julian, S. D. (2001). Complexifying organizational theory: Illustrations using time research. *Academy of Management Review, 26*(3), 415–430.
Okhuysen, G. A., & Bechky, B. A. (2009). Coordination in organizations: An integrative perspective. *The Academy of Management Annals, 3*(1), 463–502. https://doi.org/10.1080/19416520903047533
Orlikowski, W. J., & Yates, J. (2002). It's about time: Temporal structuring in organizations. *Organization Science, 13*(6), 684–700.
Perey, R. (2013, August). *Metabolic organization: Reframing ecological sustainability.* Presented at the Academy of Management Annual Conference, Orlando, FL, 9–13 August.
Pérez-Nordtvedt, L., Payne, G. T., Short, J. C., & Kedia, B. L. (2008). An entrainment-based model of temporal organizational fit, misfit, and performance. *Organization Science, 19*(5), 785–801.
Purser, R. E., & Petranker, J. (2005). Unfreezing the future: Exploring the dynamic of time in organizational change. *The Journal of Applied Behavioral Science, 41*(2), 182–203.

Reichel, A., & Perey, R. (2018). Moving beyond growth in the Anthropocene. *The Anthropocene, 5*(3), 242–249.
Reinecke, J., & Ansari, S. (2015). When times collide: Temporal brokerage at the intersection of markets and developments. *Academy of Management Journal, 58*(2), 618–648.
Richardson, M. J., Marsh, K. L., Isenhower, R. W., Goodman, J. R. L., & Schmidt, R. C. (2007). Rocking together: Dynamics of intentional and unintentional interpersonal coordination. *Human Movement Science, 26*, 867–891.
Rifkin, J. (1987). *Time wars: The primary conflict in human history.* Holt.
Robinson, J. P., & Godbey, G. (1999). *Time for life: The surprising ways Americans use their time.* Pennsylvania State University Press.
Rosa, H. (2003). Social acceleration: Ethical and political consequences of a desynchronized high-speed society. *Constellations, 10*(1), 3–33.
Ross, J. M., & Balasubramaniam, R. (2014). Physical and neural entrainment to rhythm: human sensorimotor coordination across tasks and effector systems. *Frontiers in Human Neuroscience, 8*, 1–6. https://doi.org/10.3389/fnhum.2014.00576
Rowell, C., Gustafsson, R., & Clemente, M. (2017). How institutions matter 'in time': The temporal structures of practices and their effects on practice reproduction. *Research in the Sociology of Organizations, 48*, 303–327.
Roxburgh, S. (2004). There just aren't enough hours in the day: The mental health consequences of time pressure. *Journal of Health and Social Behavior, 45*(2), 115–131.
Sabetta, L., & Zerubavel, E. (2019). Times of sociology. Eviatar Zerubavel in conversation with Lorenzo Sabetta. *Sociologica, 13*(2), 55–74.
Schultz, M., & Hernes, T. (2020). Temporal interplay between strategy and identity: Punctuated, subsumed, and sustained modes. *Strategic Organization, 18*(1), 106–135. https://doi.org/10.1177/1476127019843834
Shipp, A. J., & Richardson, H. A. (2021). The impact of temporal schemata: Understanding when individuals entrain versus resist or create temporal structure. *Academy of Management Review, 46*(2), 299–319.
Sinha, K. K., & Van de Ven, A. H. (2005). Designing work within and between organizations. *Organization Science, 16*, 389–408.
Sorokin, P. A., & Merton, R. K. (1937). Social time: A methodological and functional analysis. *American Journal of Sociology, 42*(5), 615–629.

Standifer, R. L., & Bluedorn, A. C. (2006). Alliance management teams and entrainment: Sharing temporal mental models. *Human Relations, 59*, 903–927.

Styhre, A., & Sundgren, M. (2011). Management regimes in science-based innovation: Control and uncertainty during early phases of new drug development. *Technology Analysis & Strategic Management, 23*(5), 567–581.

Szollos, A. (2009). Toward a psychology of chronic time pressure: Conceptual and methodological review. *Time & Society, 18*(2–3), 332–350.

Tang, S., Richter, A. W., & Nadkarni, S. (2020). Subjective time in organizations: Conceptual clarification, integration, and implications for future research. *Journal of Organizational Behavior, 41*, 210–234.

Taylor, C. (2004). *Modern social imaginaries*. Duke University Press.

Tesluk, P. E., & Jacobs, R. R. (1998). Toward an integrated model of work experience. *Personnel Psychology, 51*, 321–355.

Thompson, J. D. (1967). *Organizations in action*. New York: McGaw-Hill.

Tsang, E. W. K., & Zahra, S. A. (2008). Organizational unlearning. *Human Relations, 61*(10), 1435–1462.

van de Scott, L.-J. K. (2020). Temporal front and back stages: Time work as resistance. In M. G. Flaherty, L. Meinert, & A. L. Dalsgård (Eds.), *Time work: Studies of temporal agency* (pp. 83–101). Berghahn Books.

Wajcman, J. (2016). *Pressed for time. The acceleration of life in digital capitalism*. The University of Chicago Press.

Watt, J. D. (1991). Effect of boredom proneness on time perception. *Psychological Reports, 69*, 323–327.

Weick, K. E. (2009). Theory and practice in real world. In C. Knudsen & H. Tsoukas (Eds.), *The Oxford handbook of organization theory*. Oxford University Press. https://doi.org/10.1093/oxfordhb/9780199275250.003.0017

Whitehead, A. N. (1929/1978). *Process and reality*. The Free Press.

Wiebe, E. (2010). Temporal sensemaking: Managers' use of time to frame organizational change. In T. Hernes & S. Maitlis (Eds.), *Process, sensemaking, & organizing* (pp. 213–241). Oxford University Press.

Yakura, E. K. (2002). Charting time: Timelines as temporal boundary objects. *Academy of Management Journal, 45*(5), 956–970.

Yoon, I. H., & Barton, A. (2019). Turnaround leaders' shifting gears in *chronos* and *kairos* time. *Journal of Educational Administration, 57*(6), 690–707.

Zerubavel, E. (1981). *Hidden rhythms, schedules and calendars in social life*. University of Chicago Press.

Zerubavel, E. (1982). The standardization of time: A sociohistorical perspective. *American Journal of Sociology, 1*, 1–23.

Zerubavel, E. (1987). The language of time: Toward a semiotics of temporality. *The Sociological Quarterly, 28*(3), 343–356.

Zerubavel, E. (1991). *The fine line: Making distinctions in everyday life*. The Free Press.

Zerubavel, E. (2003). *Time maps: Collective memory and the social shape of the past*. University of Chicago Press.

Zuzanek, J. (2004). Work, leisure, time-pressure and stress. In J. T. Haworth & A. J. Veal (Eds.), *Work and leisure* (pp. 123–144). Routledge.

3

Subjective Time as Subjectively Perceived Temporal Dimensions of Objective Time

This chapter is the first of two chapters concentrating on subjective time. More precisely, in this chapter, I focus on intrasubjective time (Shipp & Jansen, 2021), that is, how individuals perceive and interpret temporal dimensions of objective time. Therefore, as in the previous chapter, this chapter follows the ontology of time. Perceptions of time, such as perceived duration, simultaneity, frequency, sequence, and regularity, refer to temporal dimensions of objective time that are well covered in disciplines like neuroscience and cognitive and experimental psychology. The main focus in these fields is on intrasubjective time—how an individual perceives and interprets objective time and relates to time. Attempts to find links between objective physical reality and our perceptions and sensory experiences belong to the realm of psychophysics, which is even older than psychology (Grondin, 2020; Mead, 1932/2002). The origin of psychophysics dates back to 1860, when Gustav Fechner published his book *Elemente de Psychophysik* (Grondin, 2020; Wearden, 2016). Studies in psychophysics have established some principles, for example, Vierordt's law and Weber's law[1] covering the links between physical reality as avail-

---

[1] For a more detailed explanation, see, for example, Grondin (2020). *The perception of time: Your questions answered.* New York: Routledge, and Wearden, J. (2016) The Psychology of Time Perception. London: Palgrave Macmillan.

able to our sensory systems and psychological reality, including psychological or inner time (Grondin, 2001; Wearden, 2016). Still, as these principles tend not to adhere to strict and straightforward laws, this allows the relationship between the two realities to be logarithmic, linear, or exponential with a wide variety of value estimates forcing us to look for additional explanations and psychological meaning (Grondin, 2020).

Attempts to measure the time passed between an event's physical manifestation and our perception have resulted in different psychophysical and behavioural methods. In general, studies in experimental psychology have revealed that our subjective perception of objective time with its different temporal dimensions is precisely that—subjective (Callender, 2017). We can even perceive repeated asynchronous stimuli as synchronous (Cravo & Haddad, 2015), which may seriously jeopardize our efforts to achieve the entrainment discussed in the previous chapter.

There is agreement that how we perceive temporal dimensions of objective time depends on many aspects, for example, our specific context and life situation, space, what we pay attention to and how, predictability, task demands and description, our emotional state, our age and sex, stimulus intensity, cognitive load, sensory modality, our body, and mental conditions, whether we are judging dimensions of time from a retro- or prospective perspective, the amount of caffeine we have consumed or the lack of it and interestingly, whether we are musicians or not (Callender, 2017; Cravo & Haddad, 2015; Grondin, 2020; Wearden, 2016). In the following pages, I discuss the main issues concerning our perception and estimation of duration and how they systematically undermine the accuracy with which we plan in everyday life or in work-related settings. I look at ego- and time-moving temporal frames stemming from the spatial metaphor of time, the perceived direction of time movement and temporal focus and depth, and the difference between temporal focus and temporal orientation. I conclude the chapter by discussing temporal agency.

3.1 Estimating Duration

While perceived and estimated duration is an integral component in organizational performance evaluations, planning, and forecasting, it is highly questionable how much we can trust our perceptions in this area. Already back in 1890, James recognized that "in general, a time filled with varied and interesting experiences seems short in passing but long as we look back. On the other hand, a tract of time empty of experiences seems long in passing, but in retrospect short" (James, 1890: 624). Therefore, in general, when paying conscious attention to time, waiting for an effect, like waiting for something to start, end, or be announced, or for somebody to arrive, answer, or show up, time seems longer (Grondin, 2020; Pedri & Hesketh, 1993). For example, when we are waiting impatiently for something exciting or pleasant, time seems to move slowly, and the duration of waiting feels long (Grondin, 2020). Being forced into the waiting role refers to a passive role with low agentic power (Johnsen et al., 2019). As the saying goes, "time is long for the one who is waiting." Time also seems to pass slowly when we are feeling bored, and we tend to feel bored if the duration of time seems empty and uneventful (Costas & Kärreman, 2016; Johnsen, 2016; Levine, 2006). Boredom, caused by empty and uneventful time, is often associated with the feeling of meaninglessness (Game, 2007; Gemmill & Oakley, 1992), which in turn is associated with a negative impact both on employee performance and on organization life in general (Costas & Kärreman, 2016; Loukidou et al., 2009).

On the other hand, when we are having fun or feeling happy, the duration of the event feels shorter (Callender, 2017). While actively occupied with something or having intense positive feelings, our attention is shared between processing non-temporal activities and counting *subjective temporal units* (Francis-Smythe & Robertson, 1999: 336). As a result, fewer subjective temporal units will be counted, and consequently, the passage of time feels shorter (Francis-Smythe & Robertson, 1999: 336).

However, Watzlawik's (2015) fieldwork in a hospice illustrates the influence our specific life situation may have on the perception of time. Watzlawik interviewed the residents at the hospice, who were facing the inevitable end of their life. Her findings show that when people are forced into a situation of waiting for something frightening, something they would instead prefer to avoid but necessarily cannot (such as a premature and unavoidable death), time seems to pass faster (Watzlawik, 2015). This means that when something frightening and unavoidable is approaching us, something we cannot control, we perceive time to be passing faster. However, it is important to note that although sensing duration as being short may lead to underestimating time, it does not automatically mean that chronometric time is judged to be short. And vice versa, that the subjective perception of the slow passage of time does not necessarily translate into the perception of the slow passage of objective chronometric time (Hawkins et al., 1988).

Watt (1991) points out that there is indeed an empirical conflict related to the depressed affect and the perception of time. Reports show that depressed affect influences the subjective experience of time, making it pass more slowly (i.e., Johnsen et al., 2019). At the same time, it seems to have no impact on "measures of time perception in the objective chronometric measurement" (Watt, 1991: 323). His study supports this claim by showing that high and low boredom-prone individuals did not differ in their estimates of the passage of objective or chronometric time. However, high boredom proneness was "associated with the subjective perception of the slow passage of time" (Watt, 1991: 326) that did not occur in the case of individuals with low boredom proneness.

Wearden (2005) describes the study results carried out in Manchester called the *Armageddon* experiment. *Armageddon* is an exciting, more or less violence-free meteor-destroying action movie from 1988 with Bruce Willis in the leading role (I even happen to have seen this movie on the big screen). In the described experiment, one group watched the mentioned movie for nine minutes, while the other group sat for nine minutes in a dull waiting room. In line with James' statement presented earlier, the first group assessed the passage of time as faster and the second group as slower than the actual passage of chronometric time. Compared to the waiting room group, the *Armageddon* group felt the event's duration was shorter (i.e., our interest in a task contributes to the perception that a period of time was shorter) (Francis-Smythe & Robertson, 1999). However, after a short break, in the second phase of the experiment, the

Armageddon period was judged to have lasted longer than the waiting room period. According to Wearden (2005: 152), "a time period (Armageddon) seems to fly when participants were in it (passage of time judgment) but is judged as relatively long after it has finished (retrospective time judgment)."

These examples show that the relationship between the perceived duration of objective time and the subjectively felt passage of time does not hold one to one or the other but varies. Moreover, based on her professional experience in cognitive psychology, Jones (2019) expresses her doubts about the results of time perception and estimations studied in laboratory settings. By emphasizing the dynamic nature of human attention,[2] Jones claims that the "majority of approaches to attention minimise the role of timing in both the tasks employed and with the concepts proposed" (2019: 4, see also pages 11–12). I prefer not to plunge into this debate, but in my view, Jones (2019) makes some interesting points and valid criticisms. I will continue with the retrospective and prospective judgement of the felt duration of tasks. It appears that depending on whether the time estimation for the task is given retrospectively or prospectively, it makes an important psychological difference (Callender, 2017).

3.2 The Difficulty with Predicting the Duration of Time

Grondin (2020) underlines that explicit judgements about duration depend on whether we estimate time in a retrospective or prospective way. Our retrospective judgements about time are influenced by our expectations about the duration of events and activities (Francis-Smythe & Robertson, 1999). Expecting a shorter duration leads to a shorter perceived time, and vice versa, an anticipation that something is taking longer leads us to feel in that way in our retrospective judgements (Grondin, 2020). Furthermore, experiments show that, in general, when people were asked to estimate duration or intervals retrospectively, they tend to

---

[2] See Jones, M.R. (2019) Time Will Tell: A Theory of Dynamic Attending. Oxford University Press.

judge these as lasting longer. Compared to immediate retrospective estimation, there is a tendency to overestimate the duration when estimating after a delay (Grondin, 2020; see also Wearden, 2005). By contrast, when people know beforehand (prospectively) that they are expected to estimate the duration or intervals, they tend to estimate these as short.

Time estimation is directly linked to planning and predictions. The literature reveals that people tend systematically to underestimate the time required to accomplish future tasks and the duration of future activities and events (Buehler et al., 1997; Francis-Smythe & Robertson, 1999; Roy et al., 2005; Tversky & Kahneman, 1974). The underestimation of the time needed to complete future tasks is so systematic that Kahneman and Tversky (1979) coined the term *planning fallacy* to highlight that problem. Planning fallacy represents a tendency to underestimate the time required to complete tasks despite being aware of past failures to keep deadlines (Kahneman & Tversky, 1979). The planning fallacy refers to optimistically biased estimations (Kahneman & Tversky, 1979) that we can complete the task or project according to planned schedules, even when you know that most similar tasks or projects have taken longer than planned and finished late (Buehler et al., 1997). Often these overly optimistic predictions appear to be "contaminated" by the predictors' "hopes and desires" and "wishful thinking" (Buehler et al., 1997: 245, 239). The planning fallacy is a systematic prediction error based on the optimistic confidence that, no matter what, we can manage and complete tasks or projects on time.

Kahneman and Tversky (1979) suggest that people can use either singular or distributional information for making temporal predictions. Singular information refers to the narrow focus on completing the specific task at hand. In contrast, distributional information considers general background information about the realized duration of similar tasks or projects (Roy et al., 2005). Thus, distributional information contains the analysis of the past experiences on how much time similar tasks have been required for completion and considers this information when making decisions or estimates about the current task/project. On the other hand, singular information does not take into consideration past realized experiences but makes estimations based only on the task/project at hand.

Kahneman and Lovallo (1993) supplemented singular and distributional information with inside versus outside view. The inside view is based on the singular information or specific knowledge of the task or project. The outside view is based on the average duration of past projects. To avoid or mitigate the adverse consequences of the planning fallacy stemming from incorrectly used memory and over-optimism, Kahneman and Lovallo (1993) recommended relying on the outside view, with which we can benefit from by considering statistical probabilities. These recommendations, however, are not supported by Griffin and Buehler (1999). They found that the predictive validity of both frequency-based predictions and case-specific judgements of probability is low, being in both cases overly optimistic. Consequently, Griffin and Buehler's (1999) findings do not support such a relatively easy remedy for the planning fallacy as relying on the outside view as recommended by Kahneman and Lovallo (1993). This, in turn, means that there is no easy ways to overcome our tendency to underestimate the required time.

Incorrect (Kahneman & Tversky, 1979) or unavailable memories about the actual passage of time related to a range of activities seem to be a plausible reason for such planning flaws. However, people may ignore their memories because it is challenging to see how to use them. How to "integrate the memories of the past into our understanding of the present and our expectations for the future" (Buehler et al., 2002: 270) may not be self-evident. Buehler et al. see this as "a central human challenge that we all face in every domain of our social life" (Ibid.). Alternatively, the inability to use our memories may stem from the fact that it could be challenging to identify an appropriate set of reference experiences because tasks, situations, and events differ. At this point, I cannot resist quoting a British rugby commentator and a former player, who has stated that "Each game is unique, and this one is no different [than] any other" (cited in Buehler et al., 2002: 255). In addition, people may also be unwilling to use their memory and recall their experiences but rather deny these if these are tied to adverse personal outcomes (Buehler et al., 2002). In other words, people may try to forget or suppress their personal or professional failures or shortcomings to keep up a more positive image.

To add to the prevailing explanation that people tend to underestimate the time required to complete a task because they are either unable or unwilling to use memories, Roy et al. (2005) propose the *memory bias account*. The memory bias account assumes that the "tendency to underestimate future duration may be due to a tendency to underestimate past duration. Thus, people remember tasks as taking less time than they did and, therefore, underestimate how long similar tasks will take in the future" (Roy et al., 2005: 738).

Although this assumption may seemingly run contra to the studies discussed earlier in this chapter, which claimed that in their retrospective estimations, people tend to overestimate the passage of time (see Grondin, 2020; Wearden, 2005, 2016), we need to consider the specific time scale used in the different studies. It is important to note that most of the study results discussed earlier are based on durations of seconds. The exception is Wearden's, 2005 Armageddon experiment, which used nine- and ten-minute intervals. But making time estimations on a different scale like days, months, or years could follow different patterns (Francis-Smythe & Robertson, 1999). Furthermore, in Wearden's experiment, the participants were asked to estimate the passage of time while watching the movie or waiting in the dull waiting room. Put differently, compared to trying actively to accomplish something, finish a task, or reach a goal, they had a relatively passive role with a low demand level. As a result, they had greater capacity to process temporal cues (Pedri & Hesketh, 1993) and count more subjective temporal units (Francis-Smythe & Robertson, 1999). We can argue that studying time perception by completing predesigned tasks in laboratory settings could have very little in common with the timing in everyday life (Jones, 2019). As Sorokin and Merton (1937: 622) claim, the perceived duration of time depends "not only [on its] absolute length but also on the nature and intensity of [its] qualities." That is to say, the perception of time may be influenced by our involvement in activities and the demands of a task (Cravo & Haddad, 2015; Pedri & Hesketh, 1993) as well as a specific situation.

While on a smaller scale, the planning fallacy is a common problem in our everyday lives (Buehler et al., 2002; Roy et al., 2005; Sanna et al., 2005), the costs of its consequences tend to rise proportionately with the size and duration of the undertaking (Flyvberg et al., 2002; Schnaars, 1989). The bigger the project, the greater the interdependencies; the longer it takes to complete a task, the more significant the tendency to underestimate its duration (Roy et al., 2005). Although the planning fallacy is far from just a problem of megaprojects (Buehler et al., 2002; Sanna et al., 2005), its consequences could be disproportionately high in the case of megaprojects. Interestingly, it has been found that individuals who considered themselves good at planning and estimating time turned out to be poor in judging the passage of time and estimating the duration required to complete tasks (Francis-Smythe & Robertson, 1999). Somehow counterintuitively, underestimating duration is highly salient in situations where "tasks are familiar" and that familiarity is complemented with a long period and incentives for quick completion (Roy et al., 2005: 754). Put differently, underestimation is likely when contractual terms grant bonuses on early completion and the field's leading experts are assessing the time required to complete the project, which is usually the case in business, manufacturing, and construction.

Concerning megaprojects, a recent and vivid example of a planning fallacy is Berlin Brandenburg Airport (BBA). The airport was finally opened on 31 October 2020, almost ten years later than the original opening date and three times over budget (Boon, 2020; Euronews, 2020). Its construction began on 5 September 2006, after almost 15 years of planning, most probably by the field's leading experts. According to the original plan, it was expected to open in five years (in October 2011), and the initial budget was 2.8 billion euros. In 2010, the official notification about a double increase in budget and postponement of the opening by two years was announced. Following the first postponement, the opening was postponed nine more times for different reasons, and the project's final cost increased gradually to almost 7 billion euros (Euronews, 2020). The project has earned the nickname "money-eating machine" due to its continuous need for subsidies (Ibid.). BBA is far from a black swan or lonely outsider. Another infamous example is the Sydney Opera House, which was planned to be constructed in 6 years but instead took 16 years to build, and the final cost of construction exceeded the initial budget by more than 1400%, jumping from 7 million to more than 100 million Australian dollars (Hall, 1980; Buehler et al., 2002; Sanna et al., 2005). To name some other well-known projects that ran over both deadline and their budgets, we can add the Channel Tunnel between

France and England or the Big Dig in Boston (Buehler et al., 2002; Roy et al., 2005).

On the one hand, it remains unclear exactly why people underestimate the past duration of tasks, especially the duration of tasks that required a long time to accomplish. On the other hand, predictions shorter than actual durations can create problems, and often expensive ones, in terms of both everyday life as well as organizational life. As Buehler, Griffin and Ross (2002: 270) state, we do not need probability analyses, as "accuracy and bias can be measured by the calendar and the clock." Recalling from the previous chapter that chronological time translates more than less automatically into monetary value underlines the planning fallacy's economic aspect. Ironically, instead of increasing our time predictions, careful forward planning may decrease the accuracy of predictions (Buehler et al., 1997). Despite that, Buehler et al. (2002) stress the usefulness and necessity of plans in guiding behaviour. Although predictions are associated with the planning fallacy, they claim that "Even if projects are typically completed later than predicted, they may be completed earlier than if no detailed plans or predictions were made" (Buehler et al., 2002: 262).

Moreover, before rushing to abandon prediction because of the systematic underestimation, we should recall a specific time elasticity. On the one hand, Parkinson's law of time states that "work expands to fill the time available for its completion." On the other hand, probably most of us, if not all, have personally experienced Horstman's corollary to Parkinson's law stating that "Work contracts to fit in the time we give it." In other words, without time estimations, however biased, there is a well-recognized tendency to procrastinate and use all the time available for task completion or to mobilize oneself just before the deadline and then rush to complete the task in the given time frame. However, both of these approaches may lead to suboptimal results providing additional support to continue time-predicting practices.

In addition to an optimistic singular inside view and the unavailability of memory (Kahneman & Tversky, 1979), biased memories (Roy et al., 2005), the inclination to deny or explain away negative personal outcomes and the overuse of best-case scenarios (Buehler et al., 2002), the familiarity and length of a task, overconfidence in knowledge, overoptimism fuelled by monetary incentives, and wishful thinking (Buehler et al., 1997), our predictions of the time required to accomplish future tasks seem to be influenced by how we see the movement of time—either from the past to the future or vice versa, from the future to the past. In other words, do we see time from an ego-centric or time-centric perspective (Callender, 2017), and this is what we will tackle next.

3.3 The Spatial Metaphor of Time and the Direction of "Flow"

Metaphors are regarded as powerful tools for understanding and moulding our beliefs and behaviours (Morgan, 1997). In Western thought, from Anaximander and Aristoteles to Kant, it is common to use a spatial metaphor for presenting time (Bambach, 2011; Núñez et al., 2006; Hassard, 2001; Wahidin, 2006). Zerubavel claims that "spatial metaphors pervade much of our thinking" (Zerubavel, 1991: 16), and although space and time are two different phenomena with different fundamental characteristics (e.g., Callender, 2017; Klempe, 2015), people use the observable "physical realities of space and motion" (Crilly, 2017: 2070) as analogies through which they construct an understanding of time in their minds (Núñez et al., 2006; Wahidin, 2006).

> It is very usual to present Time under the metaphor of a spatial movement. But is it to be a movement from past to future, or from future to past? … If the events are taken as moving by a fixed point of presentness, the movement is from future to past, since the future events are those which have not yet passed the point, and the past are those which have. If presentness is taken as a moving point successively related to each of a series of events, the movement is from past to future. Thus, we say that events come out of the future, but we say that we ourselves move towards the future. (McTaggart, 1908: 470)

While using a spatial metaphor helps us comprehend abstract constructs, as time is, through the concrete experience of space (Núñez et al., 2006), a metaphor of spatial movement raises a question about the direction of the movement. Bluedorn (2002), while pointing to the limitations of Newtonian time as being reversible and *even lacking direction*, claims that the direction of the flow of time "*is a profoundly fundamental attribute of time*" Bluedorn (2002: 25, emphasis added). If we agree with that claim, at least for the time being, and assume that time flows or at least this is how it seems to us as human beings, the question of the direction of the (perceived) movement of time remains open. Does time move or flow from the past via the present to the future or from the future via the present to the past? Again, there is no unified agreement on this question. Merleau-Ponty, echoing McTaggart's question above, describes two possible but opposing directions of the flow of time.

> We say that time passes or flows. We talk about the course of time…If time is similar to a river, it flows from the past towards the present and the future. The present is a consequence of the past, and the future a consequence of the present. (Merleau-Ponty, 2002: 477)

The first option proposed by Merleau-Ponty corresponds to the human experience of an irreversible forward-moving time—the direction of the course of life unfolding from birth to death without the possibility to change this direction. But Merleau-Ponty also offers an alternative view and instead of viewing the past pushing the present and the present pushing the future, he suggests that the future is "a brooding presence moving to meet him, like a storm on the horizon" (Merleau-Ponty, 2002: 478).

This alternative view of the direction of time's movement proposed by Merleau-Ponty points to the future, which emerges in front of us like a storm on the horizon. Indeed, both directions of the movement of time are represented in the existing theorization concerning the nature of the universe and human experience. In cognitive linguistics, the spatial metaphor of time with the associated idea of the movement's direction is used to understand variations in approaches to the future. For example, Boroditsky (2000), Boroditsky and Ramscar (2002), and Núñez et al. (2006) have used a spatial metaphor to make a distinction between ego-moving and time-moving perspectives. These perspectives stand for "representational schemas with which we frame the world" (Callender, 2017: 252). Zerubavel (1991: 11) points out that "A frame is characterized not by its contents but rather by the distinctive way in which it transforms the contents' meaning." Consequently, framing has a direct and significant influence on how we make sense of reality, for our meaning and decision-making. As such, a spatial representation of time is not common only among theorists and academics, but typically corporate executives employ spatial language when talking about the future (Crilly, 2017). Expressions like "moving through something," "leaving something behind," "looking forward to something," "moving away from or toward something," "approaching something," and "something is approaching" are all spatial metaphors used to describe temporal evolvement or movement in or over time. Using a spatial metaphor for time helps structure perceptions of the future, including the distance of the future. In this context, the distance of the future usually indicates a chronologically distant future and not necessarily a qualitatively distant or different future (Augustine et al., 2019). Therefore, a spatial metaphor helps to create an expected timeline for the future, set milestones, and plan the duration of future activities.

There are arguments about the appropriateness of presenting time spatially (Klempe, 2015), and not everybody agrees that time *flows* (i.e., Callender, 2017; Luhmann, 2018). Still, the river metaphor presented by Heraclitus that "You cannot step twice into the same river" is widely cited. The flowing river metaphor is viable in stressing the underlying assumptions of process theories (i.e., Langley & Tsoukas, 2010) by emphasizing the unfolding nature of reality. At the same time, for example, Merleua-Ponty expresses his reservation about the spatial river metaphor and the associated flow, stressing that in his eyes, "this often-repeated metaphor is in reality extremely confusing" (2002: 477). He insists that "Time presupposes a view of time. It is, therefore, not like a river, not a flowing substance" (Merleau-Ponty, 2002: 477). Merleau-Ponty warns his readers about the possible fallacy stemming from applying the flowing river spatial metaphor to time.

I will skip these big questions about whether time flows or not, or what its flowing means if it flows, for they are far too ambitious for this book and remain for others to debate. While assuming that time moves and its movement has direction, it is important to underline that whichever approach is chosen, it seems to have consequences for our attitudes towards the future. Metaphorically speaking, putting an observer into the river to witness its course (Merleau-Ponty, 2002) means that an observer is in time while the time is external to the observer. Relocating an observer from the river onto the riverbank does not improve the situation much more than making it possible for the observer to keep his/her feet dry. Time remains as an external force or variable. Therefore, next, we will look at how our relationship with the future and our temporal agency is influenced by the *perceived direction* of the time *external* to us.

3.3.1 Ego-Centric and Time-Centric Views of Time

McTaggart's (1908) quote in Sect. 3.3 indicates that a metaphor of spatial movement raises two questions. One question is about the direction of the movement, and another is about who or what has agency, that is, who or what moves. Therefore, experiencing time could be expressed in two different ways—we can view either time or ourselves as moving. These two views represent two ways people connect with the future—either through activity or through waiting (Minkowski, 1970). In the first case, Minkowski refers to the creative and agentic power stating that "Through its activity, the living being carries itself forward, tends toward the future, creates it in front of itself" (1970: 83). In the second case, the agency is assigned to time, leaving the person to witness how the future becomes present. "In activity, we tend toward the future. In expectation, on the contrary, we live time in an inverse sense; we see the future come toward us and wait for that (expected) future to become present" (Minkowski, 1970: 87).

In cognitive metaphor theory (i.e., Núñez et al., 2006), the same idea is expressed with the ego-moving and time-moving frames. To find experimental evidence on how spatial and linguistic assumptions prepare the ground for applying one or the other perspective and with what consequences, psychologists have used a well-known experiment (e.g., Boroditsky, 2000; Boroditsky & Ramscar, 2002; Callender, 2017; Crilly, 2017; Núñez et al., 2006) asking participants:

> On which day will the next Wednesday's meeting take place if moved forward two days?

3 Subjective Time as Subjectively Perceived Temporal...

In the English-speaking environment,[3] answers to this question tend to be shared relatively evenly between Monday and Friday (Ramscar et al., 2010). Crilly explains that "Ambiguity arises because people conceptualise space and time in different ways, leading to divergent understandings of what *moving forward* means when used in relation to time" (2017: 2371). The ambiguity is related both to who or what is moving and the direction of movement. Figure 3.1 presents the answer interpreted based on the time-moving frame where time is viewed as the actor (Carver, 2006). When time is considered moving with its direction from the future to the present, then *moving forward* is interpreted as time is moving closer to the respondents, or the answer to the question is Monday.

Respondents who interpret the movement through an ego-moving frame answered "Friday." Viewed from the ego-moving frame, moving the meeting forward means to reschedule it to take place later than initially planned. From the perspective of forward moving ego or self, a *forward moving* meeting is placed two days ahead of the self (Crilly, 2017) as presented in Fig. 3.2. The difference between these two approaches in anticipating something to happen or take place is quite significant. In the described example, an entire working week.

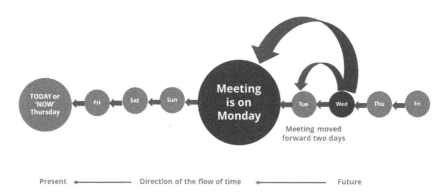

Fig. 3.1 Time-moving frame—Meeting is on Monday

---

[3] It is worth mentioning that there is some evidence that the results of using a spatial metaphor in cognitive linguistics depend on the language used. For example, Fuhrman et al. (2011) found significant differences in Mandarin speakers' and English speakers' answers to the question about the next Wednesday's meeting. Thus, other factors than just our perspectives on time could play a role in our frame choice.

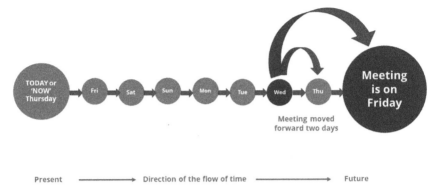

Fig. 3.2 Ego-moving frame—Meeting is on Friday

Fig. 3.3 Ego-moving frame
(Adapted from: Callender, C. (2017). *What makes time so special?* Oxford University Press, p. 254)

In both cases, the ego is attached to the series of *nows* but the temporal direction of these series is different (see Figs. 3.1 and 3.2 and Figs. 3.3 and 3.4). Therefore, depending on whether people perceive themselves moving or standing still and time moving instead, they interpret time—the respective distance or closeness of the same future event, and their agentic power—differently (Boroditsky & Ramscar, 2002). Notably, temporal framing and control beliefs are interrelated. Therefore, moving towards something or an ego-moving frame involves greater perceived agency and control than a time-moving frame. It is also important to note that whichever direction time is perceived to move, the underlying assumption is that time is sequential and something external to the ego or self.

3 Subjective Time as Subjectively Perceived Temporal... 83

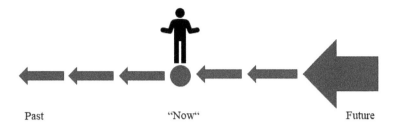

Fig. 3.4 Time-moving frame
(Adapted from: Callender, C. (2017). *What makes time so special?* Oxford University Press, p. 254)

In the ego-moving frame, we are moving towards the future event—"we are approaching" deadlines, exams, climate crises. Therefore, as presented in Fig. 3.3, the direction of the ego-moving frame's movement is from the past to the future. As "we are moving" actively towards the future, we sense that we have agency (Richmond et al., 2012); that is, we feel we are able to influence our context and control our performance and its outcomes (represented in Fig. 3.3 with the more prominent arrow). Usually, the ego-moving frame is used to express confidence in achieving our objectives (Crilly, 2017). In general, the agentic power is sensed to be stronger in the short run and decreasing in the long run due to the increasing uncertainty associated with a more distant future. Therefore, the ego-moving frame is "linked to prioritizing the present over the future" (Crilly, 2017: 2379). Concerning the future, the focus tends to be limited with an immediate short-term future.

As rooted in spatial metaphor, applying an agentic ego-moving frame to anticipated or imagined future events tends to lead to overestimating distances to future events or deadlines, seeing these as more distant than they may actually be (Kim et al., 2012). As a result of overestimated temporal distances, people applying the ego-moving frame tend to be late for appointments and complete unpleasant tasks at the last minute or even after deadlines (Crilly, 2017). Adding these tendencies to the other ego-moving frame characteristics, such as short-term focus and sensed high agency and control, it becomes tempting to tie the ego-moving frame to the planning fallacy. What makes it especially tempting is the effect of moving something forward from the perspective of an ego-moving frame, as Duffy and Feist (2014) point out, the future tasks are moved into the future simultaneously with the forwarding ego (see also Figs. 3.2 and 3.3). As such, in the ego-moving frame, future events, including the meeting of deadlines, tend to stay ahead of the ego (Núñez et al., 2006). Therefore, in the ego-moving frame, the deadline is like a visible line on the horizon. The horizon's visual line always seems to stay ahead and move together with the observer when the observer is sailing across the ocean. Hopefully, the deadline-horizon is ultimately reached.

In the time-moving frame, we see ourselves standing still and the future event moves towards us. Put differently, the future, in the form of a deadline, exam or climate crisis is *approaching us*, and the direction of movement is from the future to the past, as presented in Fig. 3.4. Applying the ocean and horizon example to the time-moving frame views a deadline or event like a coast approaching the observer across the ocean. The time-moving frame is associated with long-term future-oriented strategies (Nadkarni et al., 2016). It potentially amplifies future events and makes them appear more proximate and approaching faster (Turatto et al., 2007) than the ego-moving frame. For example, how the hospice guests, in Watzlawik's (2015) fieldwork discussed earlier in Chap. 2, expressed their temporal experience indicates an application of the time-moving frame. Because of the sensed proximity, procrastination is associated with the time-moving frame less often than with the ego-moving frame (Duffy et al., 2014). On the one hand, when we see something approaching as moving towards us or *happening* to us may create a sense of urgency that we should prepare for it, to get ourselves ready. On the other hand, the feeling of having no control over what is happening or what is about to happen could make the future loom larger and even create "a sense of fatalism" (Crilly, 2017: 2371).

My very personal experience of sensing time as moving towards me as an unavoidable destiny was when I was waiting for the day of my doctoral defence to arrive. I thought it would be liberating to know that my thesis has been accepted for the final defence. In my case, it wasn't like that at all. Instead, the day of the defence loomed over everything and over-shadowed all other matters. Relief came only after it was over. However, neither the expectation nor anticipation necessarily means passivity. On the contrary, it implies preparation, making choices and decisions about what and when to do and what activities to skip or postpone in light of the inevitable future moving towards us.

While the ego-moving frame is frequently used to voice our confidence about events over which we have control, the time-moving frame is used to describe uncertain events or events over which we lack influence and control. Still, the picture is not entirely black and white, and time-moving frames may not necessarily denote beliefs about a lack of confidence and low control (Richmond et al., 2012). A short-term perspective, associated with the ego-moving frame, tends to mean shorter planning horizons with short-range risk behaviour (high or low)—either seeking or averting risk in our short-term plans (Das & Teng, 2001). In contrast, the longer-term perspective, associated with the time-moving frame, refers to "long-range risk behaviour (high or low)" and "seeking or averting risk in longer planning horizons" (Das & Teng, 2001: 522). Crilly (2017) points out that time-moving frames could also be used to indicate uncertainty by executives who prioritize short-term objectives and signal capacity to influence the external environment. Trope and Liberman (2003) claim that perceiving future events as closer to the present (time-moving frame) leads to more detailed planning and preparation. Therefore, applying the time-moving frame may lead to careful planning for the event because it seems proximate, although the general time perspective is long term. Quite paradoxically, a person applying the ego-moving frame may, despite the associated short-term orientation, postpone more detailed planning as the future event is viewed as remaining ahead of the ego and, thus, more distant.

Both action modes associated with these two frames have their distinctive choices, which could be more or less beneficial depending on the circumstances. In organizational settings, the question is more about finding a balance between using these two frames in everyday and strategic organizational communication, decision-making and, of course, in action. For example, Slawinski and Bansal (2015) found that organizations that were able to *juxtapose* instead of *polarizing* the short- and long-term perspectives more likely recognized the complexity of issues concerning climate change and environmental sustainability and the need for comprehensive and coherent solutions. However, those organizations that were *polarizing* the short versus long term tended to apply the short-term approach. Table 3.1 presents the comparison of the main underlying assumptions of the two frames.

It is assumed that by following contextual cues, people can shift between the ego- and time-moving frames and "readily slide back and forth between the two ideas all the time" (Callender, 2017: 252). Following this assumption, individuals have a mixture of both frames and related action modes—long/short-term activity patterns and expectations—available to them. Furthermore, related to the assumption that sliding between the two frames is easy, it is assumed that people's relation to the future and present is dynamic and flexible.

Although it is disputed what exactly could be concluded from the use of one or another frame (Callender, 2017), acknowledging the existence of these two frames could help us understand differences in expressed agency, control beliefs, and perceived temporal proximity/distance. Our ability to slide between these two frames *nearly effortlessly* (Callender, 2017: 253) indicates the potential for intentional or unintentional nudging either towards an ego-moving or time-moving frame with the associated perception of control and perspectives towards the future. It is widely accepted that language plays an influential role in creating organizational reality. Therefore, shaping the dominant perspective or frame in organizations is within the reach of its managers. In other words, managers do not shape the way their subordinates think about time only through deadlines and schedules (Orlikowski & Yates, 2002) as discussed in the previous chapter but also through language and discourse (Ancona et al., 2001; Mohammed & Nadkarni, 2011).

Without doubt, confidence and self-reliance are essential for future-oriented action. Behind strategic decisions is the managers' belief that they can influence the course of events and achieve the promised results. Still, the ego-moving frame, with its short-term focus, offers little support in the fight against the general short-termism discussed in the previous chapter. Furthermore, with its tendency to overestimate the distance of the future, neither does it provide much support for addressing issues which, while requiring a longer-term perspective, need immediate attention, like sustainability and climate change. It is tempting to speculate about the relations between the general short-termism that characterizes the prevailing economic rationality and efficiency logic, the planning

Table 3.1 Comparison of assumptions of the ego-moving and time-moving frames

Type of cognitive frame	Temporal focus	Direction of movement	Who or what has agentic power? Who or what is moving?	The characteristics of the relationship between time and the individual	Distance/ closeness of the future	Certainty/ uncertainty	Possibility to switch between frames
Ego-moving frame	Short-term closed focus. The present is prioritized over the future	From the present to the future	The individual has agency; the individual is moving towards the future	The individual is actively pursuing his/her goals, influencing and controlling the environment and using time to achieve its objectives	Future is perceived as distant. There is a tendency to underestimate the distance of the future	Perceived high certainty, high self-reliance, and confidence	Yes, almost effortless sliding to time-moving frame
Time-moving frame	Long-term open-ended focus on the future	From the future to the present	Time has agency; time is moving—the future is approaching	The unavoidable future [time] holds agentic power. The individual can just prepare himself/herself but has no power to change the course of events or avoid the approaching future	Perceived proximity. There is a tendency to overestimate the proximity of the future	Perceived high uncertainty, low self-reliance	Yes, almost effortless sliding to ego-moving frame

fallacy caused by the unjustified optimism, overconfidence, and professional pride of experts, biased memories, and the ego-centric time perspective with its perceived high level of agency and short-term focus. It seems that between these listed aspects, there is a particular interconnectedness and mutual reinforcement.

3.4 Temporal Orientation, Focus, and Depth

Contrary to the effortless sliding between ego- and time-moving frames and the related future perspective and temporal agency, Ancona et al. (2001: 519) point out that "a temporal personality is unique for each actor" much "like a fingerprint." With the fingerprint metaphor, Ancona et al. (2001) refer to subjective time as a temporal trait (Tang et al., 2020), stressing the specific and unique way an actor relates to time and their disposition, attitude, and approach to time. Several scholars agree that our temporal personality is unique to us. Some agree that just like a fingerprint, our temporal personality, viewed as the equivalent of a subjective temporal orientation, has a trait-like nature (Chen & Nadkarni, 2017; Das & Teng, 2001), being "stable, enduring, and internally caused" (Tang et al., 2020: 212).

Others, while agreeing that our temporal personality is unique, view stable individual characteristics as insufficient to explain the behaviour of individuals (Crilly, 2017). Instead, they support the idea that how we relate to time—or our temporal orientation—is not determined by our temporal personality as a trait but depends on the situation (e.g., Ebert & Prelec, 2007). They state that our orientation towards time, as a state-like character, depends on the specific situation being "malleable, fleeting, and externally induced" (Tang et al., 2020: 212). However, it is worth mentioning that several scholars support the idea that the line between trait- versus state-like temporal constructs is arbitrary (Tang et al., 2020), and the distinction between the two could not necessarily be categorical but viewed as varying along a continuum (Shipp et al., 2009; Tasselli et al., 2018). That view could explain the contradiction that tends to arise in relation to the previously discussed ego- and time-moving frames when we try to follow the state-trait distinction too rigidly. Namely, temporal frames, according to the framework proposed by Tang et al., are classified as state-like temporal constructs (see also Table 3.2). At the same time, temporal focus and depth, also associated with frames, are classified as traits. The recent review article by Tang et al. (2020), where publications on time and temporality either at the individual or collective level published 1988–2018 in the field of organizational behaviour, strategy, entrepreneurship, and organizational theory are analysed, systemizes them into a two-by-two (state-trait and individual/collective) framework. Tang et al. (2020) provide a helpful framework for systematizing and clustering the different concepts. A summary of their classification is presented in Table 3.2.

Although, for example, Bluedorn and Denhardt (1988: 308) claim that "two of the fundamental differences among people are their overall temporal orientation and their differing abilities to project into and deal with the future," we will not find temporal orientation in Tang et al.'s (2020) framework. Missing the term temporal orientation is even more surprising considering that the short bio of two of the three authors list

Table 3.2 A summary of Tang, Richter and Nadkarni's framework

	Trait-like	State-like
Individual level	Temporal focus Temporal depth Time urgency Individual polychronicity Pacing style Consideration of future consequences Synchrony preference Time bifurcation	Time pressure Temporal frame Timelessness Time sensitivity Perceived control of time Time structure and purpose Future time perspective[a]
Collective level	Team time focus Temporal schemata Team time urgency Team polychronicity Temporal capacity Team temporal diversity Temporal transactive memory systems Organizational temporal culture	Collective time pressure Temporal shifts Time consciousness Temporal reflexivity Temporal coordination Shared temporal cognition

Source: Based on Tang et al., 2020: 213
[a]Could be defined as both a trait and a state

temporal orientation as one of their research interests (Tang et al., 2020: 233–234). However, in their framework, Tang et al. (2020) have clustered temporal orientation as a trait-like temporal construct under temporal focus to avoid what they themselves claim to be a "jingle-jangle problem fallacy" (Ibid.: 210–211, 224). I agree with them that the simultaneous and interchangeable use of the labels and concepts creates confusion. These terms are often left undefined when used in the literature, which makes it hard to follow when these terms refer to the same or different phenomena. In addition to examples presented by Tang et al., for example, Fuchs (2013) uses time orientation in headings and temporal orientation in the text as if these two concepts are synonyms.

Therefore, while referring to "the jingle fallacy," Tang et al. (2020: 224) prefer, instead of temporal orientation, the label temporal focus, described as representing "the extent to which individuals characteristically devote attention to the past, present, and future, and these three temporal foci are independent dimensions" (Tang et al., 2020: 224). Although it may seem contrary to Bluedorn and Denhardt's claim cited above, Bluedorn (2002) also suggests avoiding the temporal orientation label to describe *general* temporal direction or inclination. Following this, we could argue, for example, that Crilly's (2017) claim, that we can identify the directly unobservable temporal orientation through future-oriented behaviours, would be more precise when replacing temporal orientation with temporal focus. However, the concept of temporal orientation seems to be preferred when the interest is not *the general* temporal inclination but *the specific* temporal orientation (Orlikowski & Yates, 2002; Kim et al., 2019).

Bluedorn proposes that subjective temporality should be supplemented with another essential aspect: temporal depth. He defines temporal depth as "the temporal distances into the past and future that individuals and collectives typically consider when contemplating events that have happened, may have happened or may happen" (Bluedorn, 2002: 114). Although with this definition Bluedorn does not restrict temporal depth to the chronological distance to the past and future, nevertheless, temporal depth in the literature is defined as chronometric. The possibility of the distant to be qualitatively different is brought clearly out by Augustine et al. (2019). Focusing on the future, they claim that "the difference between the near and distant futures is not a matter of time horizon.

Instead, distance suggests that there are qualitatively different ways of representing and experiencing the future" (Augustine et al., 2019: 1933). They conceptualize the distant future as an abstract high-level construct, resulting from imagination and fantasy, which is ambiguous and full of unknown possibilities. As radically uncertain, the distant future tends to represent discontinuity from present and past experiences (Augustine et al., 2019: 1934). While Augustine et al. (2019) concentrate on the distant future, Hernes et al. (2020) extend the qualitative difference as the distance to the past. Using the term *epochal temporality*, they refer to the temporally distant as an imagined potential in either the past or future. They also relate distant to a discontinuity from the state of the provisionally stabilized present. The importance of "actualizing the potentiality of the distant past or future in the present" is in its power to enable "the development of potentially more radical solutions" (Hernes et al., 2020: 15), which in turn could support breakthroughs, radical shifts, or turnarounds in the course of action.

Notably, while Bluedorn (2002) defines temporal depth only as of the distance to the past or future, and Augustine et al. (2019) underscore the difference between the distant and near futures, Kim et al. (2019) found that some tea producers operated under the assumption of a *long-present*. The long-present perspectives were not associated with short-termism but with the view that the present has a duration. By introducing a long-present perspective, Kim et al. (2019) bring a breadth into the present, defined "not as an instant, but an extended duration, so that the present, past, and future are inseparable, connected by a set of processes that seemed only to end when the next year crops and income began" (Kim et al., 2019: 626), they are making a reference to Emirbayer and Mische's (1998) tripartite temporality discussed below. Also, while seeing *a long-present* extend, it is not viewed to have an infinite duration. Instead, it is still viewed to have an anticipated end, which makes it different from *the extended present* described below.

In addition to a state-trait continuum, according to Ancona et al., temporal personality is "the manner in which an actor understands and acts with respect to the temporal continuum" (2001: 519). This means that people act based on their understanding of time as a continuum across past, present, and future. Continuum refers to an imaginary line or row of nonempty points in the metric space. Once again, we are running into the challenges stemming from the spatial representation of time. In contrast to the continuum, Emirbayer and Mische, based on different scholars from pragmatism and phenomenology grounded in the ontology of temporality (Hussenot et al., 2020), have proposed a tripartite construction or "the chordal triad" (Emirbayer & Mische, 1998) of human agency. They stress the ongoing, unfolding nature of our subjective temporality (Emirbayer, 1997; Emirbayer & Mische, 1998). Emirbayer and Mische belong to the group of scholars who are not much interested in either a trait-like or a state-like nature of subjective time but in the processual and changing nature of our subjective temporal orientation and its agentic power (i.e., Langley, 1999; Langley & Tsoukas, 2010; Langley et al., 2013).

While acknowledging that one temporal orientation is dominant, Emirbayer and Mische (1998: 972) stress "a chordal triad of agency within which all three [temporal] dimensions resonate as separate but not always harmonious tones." Emirbayer and Mische (Ibid.) argue that "for each analytical aspect of agency one temporal orientation is the dominant tone, shaping the way in which actors relate to the other two dimensions of time." At the same time, "each primary orientation in the chordal triad encompasses as subtones the other two as well while also showing how this 'chordal composition' can change as actors respond to the diverse and shifting environments around them" (Ibid.). Therefore, temporal orientation combines all three directions, and while having a dominant but not a fixed orientation, it always contains all three. Put differently, we can be oriented towards the past, present, and future at any given moment, although depending on the unfolding situation, one or another dimension could dominate. While the dominant temporal orientation affects our relationship with the other two temporal dimensions, it also contains or consists of the other two (Emirbayer & Mische, 1998). At the same time, temporal orientation is far from being stable or fixed. Neither is it a one-dimensional temporal focus, but actors can recompose their tripartite temporal orientations in the unfolding emergent contexts.

Consequently, compared to temporal focus, temporal orientation is a different and more complex concept. I agree that temporal focus may be a more precise label to refer to *the general* temporal direction or inclination towards the past, present, *or* future. But it is important to underline that referring to focus directed to only one "independent dimension" instead of the combination of all three, temporal focus is a much narrower concept than temporal orientation. In addition, we should pay close attention to how temporal orientation is conceptualized—is it based on the ontology of time or on the ontology of temporality (Hussenot et al., 2020).

3.5 Wrestling with Time: Time Work and Temporal Agency

The distinctive temporal orientation of activities and events in organizations, which is simultaneously forming and being enabled and constrained by organizational temporal structures, is far from fixed. Temporal structures, "Like all social structures, … are ongoing human accomplishments, and thus provisional. They are always only *stabilized-for-now*" (Orlikowski & Yates, 2002: 687) because only stabilized-for-now temporal structures, and together with them the temporal orientation of activities, are subject to continuous change that could occur through social interaction and human agency either intentionally or unintentionally (Flaherty, 2011). In other words, humans have the ability to perform time work (Flaherty, 2002, 2003) and exercise temporal agency. However, Flaherty uses these terms as synonyms (e.g., Flaherty, 2002 and 2003 compared to 2011). I prefer to view time work as part of but not necessarily synonymous with temporal agency. According to Flaherty (2002, 2003, 2011), time work is an activity through which people are influencing their everyday experience of time. Including activities like making or allocating time for something, manipulating duration through velocity (either through acceleration or deceleration of time), modulating the frequency of specific activities and events (increasing, maintaining, reducing the number), regulating the sequence of events, activities, and interactions, deciding and choosing the timing for them (Flaherty, 2011), time work targets our perceptions and experiences of so-called objective, external time. An important note by Flaherty is that time work could be applied to modifying our own temporal experiences or others' temporal experiences (2011). But by modifying our own temporal experiences, we may unintentionally modify others' experiences (Flaherty, 2011).

In general, time work essentially concerns our relationships with time and our ability to do time work requires us to have temporal agency. However, I would argue that temporal agency is a more profound concept, including our ability and capability to influence, create, and recreate past, present, and future. In that sense, temporal agency is associated with phenomenological time (discussed in the next chapter). Still, the question of temporal agency is undeniably present in the case of the ego- and time-moving frames discussed in this chapter. In general, in the ego-moving frame, the individual is the one who has an agency, the confidence to achieve results, professional pride, and identity. The individual is the actor who does the movement, although the short-term focus usually guides this movement. And in the time-moving frame, the time has agency, and time is doing the moving. Respectively, the sensed uncertainty of a human actor is higher and confidence lower. Still, there is an anticipated future hiding different possibilities in both cases, and there is the possibility to switch, quite effortlessly, between these two frames. The ego-moving and time-moving frames are based on different assumptions (see Table 3.1) and applying dominantly either one or the other leads to different results (i.e., Crilly, 2017; Kim et al., 2019).

However, it is assumed that the individual can switch effortlessly between the two cognitive frames. The ability to make choices about activities and switch from one to the other frame means that the individual has temporal agency. He/she can select and re-select both his/her approach to the future and his activities in the present or short-term future to address the long-term future. Put differently, the individual has the ability and capability to "construct and reconstruct the temporal conditions that shape their lives" (Orlikowski & Yates, 2002: 686). But what if that is not the case? What if the person loses his temporal agency, his ability, and capability to "construct and reconstruct the temporal conditions that shape their lives" (Orlikowski & Yates, 2002: 686)? Why is it important to have temporal agency?

While trying to answer this question, we can add a twist with a couple of sub-questions. For example, when playing with the assumptions behind the ego- and time-moving frames, we can ask who or what has agency and what are the possible consequences. First, applying only one or the other frame without the option to slide between the two freely, the individual's temporal agency decreases significantly, meaning that the individual is stuck in one or the other frame, unable to have an alternative approach to create a relation to our future. We could hold an optimistic, self-confident, and, to some extent, a myopic view—a view based on the perception of controlling the environment and creating the course of events (Kim et al., 2019). The alternative approach is a less active or even relatively passive one—waiting, on the mercy of time, for something to happen, unable to actively shape the course of events. As we lose our ability to slide between the cognitive frames, we lose our ability to combine these different views and, respectively, to relate differently to time and to ourselves (Fuchs, 2013).

Second, if we assume that the individual is stuck in the time-moving frame, his/her agentic power could diminish to such a level that s/he feels unable to cause but only exists as an effect (Meisenhelder, 1985). If we follow the assumption that the individual cannot influence the course of events, then our relationship to time, to both the past and the present, but especially to the future, lacks any creative power making the future look fatalistic. This can easily happen if we are diagnosed with a terminal illness and need, often unexpectedly, to handle the fact that our time is limited (Watzlawik, 2015). If that happens, if we are suddenly forced to face our mortality, the future may collapse into the present. Situations like that do not only convey urgency about our use of time (Wahidin, 2006) or what can still or will happen but requires us to "accept what has happened" and "what is not going to happen" (Watzlawik, 2015: 219), neither of which is necessarily easy and self-evident.

Losing our perspective for the future could create a feeling that our past has become redundant as well. Sudden structural changes, both in society and in organizations, could also have such an effect. For example, in 1991, when Estonia regained its independence from Soviet occupation, the shift from the planned economy to a market economy triggered various parallel developments. Two of these were the privatization of formerly state-owned enterprises and, associated with that, the century's highest number of suicides among men, which reached a peak in 1994 with almost 500 cases. Most of these suicides were committed by middle-aged men who suddenly lost well-established careers and managerial positions in the privatized enterprises. In conjunction with their work-related positions, they lost their social status and identity, which destroyed both their future perspective and the meaning of their past, leaving them floating in limbo in an extended present. Losing our temporal perspective, either the past or future or both, challenges and even tears apart our relationship with reality. For comparison, the next peak in the number of suicides, reaching 220 cases, was reached in 2009 when the impact of the global financial crisis was reflected in the Estonian economy. While the economic and financial consequences of the global financial crisis were fairly devastating, its existential impact was much lower than the impact of the restructuring of the entire societal system.

Based on these examples, it could be concluded that experiencing financial loss, including personal bankruptcies, has significant consequences on our self-esteem and mental and physical well-being. However, these consequences are not directly comparable to the experienced existential crisis related to lost temporal continuity (see Chap. 4).

Concerning organizations, sudden structural changes, such as restructuring and mergers and acquisitions, could have a similar effect on the people involved. Especially so when downsizing is included, or an organization is swallowed during a hostile takeover (van Knippenberg et al., 2002), or in the case of an organization's death (i.e., Sutton, 1987) when a department or entire organization is facing closure. For example, when the Estonian branch of Danske Bank was closed and liquidated due to a money laundering scandal, it adversely affected many employees who had been working for the organization and who had done nothing illegal. A 54-year-old ex-employee of the Estonian branch described her personal experience as follows: "The organization you have worked in for twenty-seven years is liquidated. Suddenly, these twenty-seven years just disappear, and you lose everything that has been around you for half of your life." That kind of experience could be traumatizing.

3.5.1 Losing Our Temporal Agency

Studies show that lacking temporal agency and seeing our situation as futureless makes the present meaningless (Fuchs, 2013). Unable to shape temporal conditions that shape our time (Orlikowski & Yates, 2002) could force us to accept the dominance of "an independent, indeed inexorable" (Fuchs, 2013: 80), "abstract, absolute, unitary, linear, mechanical, and quantitative" (Orlikowski & Yates, 2002: 685) time flowing "equably without relation to anything external" (Newton quoted in Whitehead, 1929/1978: 70). We can imagine an external time imposed on the person. When an infinite time with agentic power that dictates everything leaves no room for pleasant surprises or any individual interventions, no creativity or spontaneity, no room for individuals to change or amend their relationship with it, it is too hard to bear. Characterized by continuous and monotonous passing, that kind of time represents a tyranny of time (see Table 3.3). As it turns out, our relationship with that kind of time could be tense. Dealing with that kind of time could be both mentally and emotionally challenging or even traumatizing (i.e., Fuchs, 2013; Johnsen et al., 2019; Meisenhelder, 1985; Wahidin, 2006). The ability to maintain a sense of agency with respect to time seems vital for our mental and emotional well-being.

Therefore, not only are high levels of time pressure and constant time famine, discussed in Chap. 2, exhausting but time overabundance with limited temporal agency could be as hard to manage.

For example, Johnsen et al. (2019) carried out their study based on interviews conducted in a high-security prison in Helsinki, Finland. They found that without the ability to dictate events in the present and "without a definite sense of attainable future" (Johnsen et al., 2019: 14), the inmates perceived time as an enemy to fight with "by *doing it*, by making it *their own*" (Johnsen et al., 2019: 14). On the one hand, the inmates struggled to fill their empty, meaningless days, to "make the present tolerable" (Johnsen et al., 2019: 15). On the other hand, they had a painful sensation that this empty, meaningless time that appeared to stand almost still was their life passing away irreversibly. For the inmates, the pressure of time seemed not as a shortage of time or time famine (Robinson &

Table 3.3 Deterministic versus hegemonic time

Type of cognitive frame	Temporal focus	Direction of movement	Who or what has agentic power? Who or what is moving?	The characteristics of the relationship between time and the individual	Distance/ closeness of the future	Certainty/ uncertainty	Possibility to switch between frames
Deterministic time	Short-term closed-ended present with no future	From the present to non-existence	Time is passing away—the present is fading away; the [ultimate] end [no future] is approaching	Time as a force terminating our existence holds agentic power. The only option for the individual is to accept the power of time and adapt	Perceived proximity of the future. The future is blended to the present, as the present is all that is left	Perceived high certainty, the fatalistic nature of time. Time is limited	No real possibility to change cognitive frames
Hegemonic time	Long-term closed-ended present	From the present to the past	Time as an external force dictates life while ceaselessly passing away	Time petrifies and subjugates the individual in his battle to preserve his temporal agency	The future is perceived as distant and hard to reach. The individual is left without a definite sense of attainable future	Deterministic time, continuing sameness creates the feeling of time standing still. Time is abundant	Limited possibility to create *pockets of time*

Godbey, 1999) discussed in Chap. 2, but as a "pressure of finitude" (Johnsen et al., 2019: 16). The inmates were acutely aware of the paradox of time—being simultaneously finitude and infinite.

The findings of Meisenhelder's (1985) studies on prison time conducted in the United States echo these results. Meisenhelder (1985) claims that time in prison is characterized by constant waiting. The sensed abundance of time, without any future perspective, translates into a burden. The continuous waiting fuels the sensed boredom, as does "the recurrent cycle of meaningless repetitious actions that make up prison routine" (Meisenhelder, 1985: 44). Tightly scheduled days with similar rhythms make time monotonous and slow. Consequently, the problem faced by inmates includes lacking possibilities to do time work. Tedious slow time becomes a burden instead of a resource. Lacking temporal agency, the prisoner is incapable of using time as a creative resource. Instead, waiting passively for time to pass is burdensome; time becomes a problem. "Extra time" or "adding time" is a punishment, not a reward.

The findings of Johnsen et al. and Meisenhelder are in line with Wahidin's (2006) findings, who carried out intensive fieldwork in prison establishments in England and Wales. Inmates describe the terrifying effects of essentially empty prison days that resemble so closely one another that time seemingly stands still, and the "objective" duration of time loses its meaning as all days mingle together in a timeless soup of time. As one of the inmates expressed it, "It is as if the nineteen years could have *all* been fitted in one year" (Wahidin, 2006, emphasis in the original). With that, it is not meant that time *flies* so quickly that 19 years feels like one. Rather, the time is so empty, uneventful, and tedious that we can easily pack everything that has happened or could happen in 19 years into just one. At the same time, the prisoner is acutely aware that s/he is "losing" a much more significant stake in their life than a year. In the words of Paulette (one of the interviewees in Wahidin's study):

> The boredom and isolation, I think, because every day is the same. It is just dreadful. Every single day is the same. It drives you mad! I don't know how to come out and you're sane. Because every single day is just actually the same as the day before. Your meals are at the same time. Everything. Oh, it's horrible. I'm telling you—it really is. (Wahidin, 2006)

The findings of the studies investigating prison time highlight that for humans, "abstract, absolute, unitary, linear, mechanical, and quantitative" (Orlikowski & Yates, 2002: 685) time is fundamentally unbearable. These studies indicate that individuals are poorly equipped to face external and absolute time. In their battles against the domination of time, the inmates used various coping strategies to claim some autonomy over time. Attempts to claim temporal autonomy included typical examples of time work like controlling and dictating what happens and when covering activities like "insult games, smoke breaks, trips to the canteen, 'rapping,' and even the more violent acts of fighting and rioting" (Meisenhelder, 1985: 48). The inmates also tried to *create time* (Meisenhelder, 1985) by either loading "everything into one day" (Wahidin, 2006) or making their own rhythm by going to sleep and waking up earlier compared to others, to get ahead of the daily schedule and have some quiet or their own time (Wahidin, 2006). Another technique to manage the abundance of time is *marking time* (Meisenhelder, 1985: 49) like time for reading or time for training. As Meisenhelder points out, marking time around pleasant activities can be used "to carve out meaningful moments ordered sequentially from raw, empty prison time" (Meisenhelder, 1985: 50). Therefore, to make chronometric time meaningful and bearable for themselves, humans need events as time markers (Jones, 2019) and temporal agency that allows them to relate these events and to both shape the temporality of these events and their lives.

Of course, we can argue that prisons represent a particular type of oppressive institution, where the absence of events, dull, empty, and meaningless days, and the loss of temporal agency are intentionally designed features of the punishment. As such, the experience of time in prison has little relevance in different organizational settings. It turns out that this assumption does not hold, and the implications of monotony, boredom, and social isolation have a much broader impact in different types of organizations across various settings. Calkins (1970) presents a typology of styles of time usage she identified in a rehabilitation institution, the ideology of which was to "be a home for each patient for the duration of his stay" (Calkins, 1970: 489). As Calkins assumes, because of this ideology, professional preferences related to time usage were not imposed on the patients, and the individual patient was probably granted "much greater latitude in how to choose to use his time while there than in similar medical settings" (Calkins, 1970: 489). Although the patients were not forced to follow a particular way to use their time, they still had relatively limited choices. Therefore, similar to the inmates in the prison studies, the centre's patients experienced an abundance of time with relatively limited temporal agency to deal with that time, to relate to it.

Calkins (1970) identified six styles of time usage—passing, waiting, doing, making, filling, and killing, each associated with a particular way of orienting towards and relating to time, a time management strategy, an awareness of time, and perceived temporal agency. Each style of time usage is also associated with a particular behaviour that is either contributing to or challenging the smooth running of organizational processes. Calkins proposes that similar styles of time usage and related behaviours could be found in diverse social settings "where people are also apt to have abundant time with relatively few alternatives for using it" (Calkins, 1970: 501). She refers to institutions like the army, educational programmes, and retirement communities. Although she does not highlight prisons, we can recognize the similarities between the time usage styles described by Calkins and the time management strategies described in the prison studies cited earlier. I would argue that the restricted time work or suppressed temporal agency could be an issue in business and manufacturing organizations as well. While the meaning and appropriateness of different time usage styles could be interpreted differently in different social settings, understanding the styles and associated behaviours could still be helpful.

Different time use styles and their features enable us to see the connections between our orientation towards time, perceived temporal agency and control, engagement in social interaction, anticipated future or the sensed lack of it, time awareness and time management strategies, and behaviour. Maybe excepting *making time*, in their pure form, Calkins' typology styles are more common in a social or organizational setting, where there is a perceived abundance of time with limited choices to use it and less often in other types of environments. Still, some features of these styles, as mechanisms for coping with boredom caused by the extended present (where there is a perception of the cutoff past, meaningless in the given situation and no real drive for the future), could be relevant in broader organizational settings. Moreover, although maybe not too widely covered (Johnsen et al., 2019), issues related to boredom are not strange in organizational studies (i.e., Costas & Kärreman, 2016; Fisher, 1993; Game, 2007; Gemmill & Oakley, 1992; Johnsen, 2016; Loukidou et al., 2009). Therefore, being aware of the coping mechanisms related to different time usage styles could help us understand and prevent undesirable or even deviant behaviours caused by meaninglessness and boredom in various organizational settings. Studies indicate that boredom in organizations could be costly in terms of errors, low performance and creativity, low employee job satisfaction, demotivation, and even depression (Fisher, 1993; Loukidou et al., 2009). Moreover, all the mentioned factors tend to have a spill-over effect outside the organization's borders into society.

3.5.2 Temporal Agency and Our Relations to the Future and Present

Notably, the factors contributing to organizational or work-related boredom are mostly the same as discovered in Calkins's (1970) study in a rehabilitation centre or the prison studies referred to earlier. However, surprisingly, monotonous or highly routinized work tasks are not necessarily the main reason for work-related boredom (Fisher, 1993; Gemmill & Oakley, 1992; Loukidou et al., 2009). Instead, several other aspects seem to play more significant roles, such as a lack of temporal autonomy to influence the present, for example, by deciding when to perform which tasks (Diefendorff et al., 2006), and the future and uncertain, missing or largely ambiguous relationship between the current work tasks and the future or, on the contrary, lacking expectations because of an assured and highly predictable future (Loukidou et al., 2009). Therefore, fast-speed intensive tasks could lead to boredom if not complemented with temporal agency and a meaningful future. Isolation could be viewed as both social isolation and the isolation of our future or from our creative power. This means that the temporal agony described in the prison studies could be much more common in organizations dominated by a chronometric view of time and societies characterized by chronocentrism (see the previous chapter) than we would think.

As Loukidou et al. (2009: 393) indicate, quoting Marks and Darden (1999), we tend to have either a problem of boredom or, in a worse case, a problem of depression when "*the present does not reach out to embrace the future*, meaning that, for the bored person, the current condition seems eternal." Without the future or without protention as the "indeterminate anticipation of what is yet to come" (Fuchs, 2013: 77), there is no goal to achieve something, to reach out for something. Recalling the described consequences of intensification or time-space compression discussed in the previous chapter, we can see some parallels—there is no escape from the extended present. "Time has stopped; there is no time … The past and future have collapsed into the present, and I can't tell them apart" (Melges, 1982: 177). Surprisingly, the monotonous and abundant prison time psychological experience has some similarities with the psychological experience of monotonous fast-paced instantaneous time and reminds us, once again, of the never-ending or never-starting mad hatter's tea party in Carrolls' *Alice's Adventures in Wonderland* (Carrol, 1865/2008). In both cases, the individual is stuck in the present lacking or having only limited temporal agency and future perspective.

Therefore, the extended present is a different concept to the long present described by Kim et al. (2019). While a long present, characterized by having a particular duration filled with various connected events, has a temporal depth (Kim et al., 2019), an extended present is described as an uneventful infinity being without becoming. Therefore, our past and/or future experiences directly influence our "current affective reactions," as indicated by Shipp and Jansen (2021). At the same time, our present experiences also affect both our past and future experiences, as the present is our locus of action (Mead, 1932/2002).

Respectively, in the case of both time compression and time overabundance, time ceases to be a resource we can use, spend, or save. Instead, time becomes "an object to be managed in an undifferentiated landscape which has to be marked out" (Wahidin, 2006). One of the most famous studies on time marking in organizations to have dealt with organizational or work-related monotony is Roy's (1959) "Banana Time," dating back more than 60 years. Roy was using participant observation to investigate job satisfaction and social interaction in the small group of factory machine operatives performing "very simple operations over an extra-long workday, six days a week" (Roy, 1959: 158). Roy found himself "fighting the clock" (Ibid.: 160) while "dealing with a formidable 'beast of monotony'" (Roy, 1959: 158). Spending his long workdays in the small room, forced to stand while having largely restricted leg movements, hands operating a clicking machine by repeating a simple routine with a low emotional tone and non-existent intellectual stimulus. Although Roy joined the small working group voluntarily to carry out his research, the way he describes his relation to and feelings towards time echoes the relations to and feelings towards time expressed by inmates in the studies described earlier (i.e., Johnsen et al., 2019; Meisenhelder, 1985; Wahidin, 2006).

Although Roy (1959: 160) states that "Before the end of the first day, Monotony was joined by his twin brother, Fatigue," the situation became tolerable when Roy noticed the time marking performed by the workgroup and when he started to participate in time work. Like inmates marking time around pleasant activities to give it some meaning and break its monotonous hegemony (Meisenhelder, 1985), so did the men in the small workgroup. They exercised their temporal agency by dividing the long working day by marking a series of *times* assigned to consume a snack or drink. Roy lists "coffee time, peach time, banana time, fish time, coke time, … lunchtime" (Roy, 1959: 162) and some verbally not recognized times like "window time, pickup time" (Ibid.) and quitting times for two colleagues. Therefore, finding the possibility to exercise some temporal agency, even if limited, could help to deal with the monotonous slowly passing time. However, considering that boredom could result from both an abundance and a shortage of time, marking and even more importantly, allocating time would also work in high time pressure circumstances allowing employees to create pockets of their own time, whether this time is coffee time or yoga time or chat time or smoke time or nap time or quiet time or time consciously allocated to share with our loved ones. While marking time would help deal with time perceived, felt, or conceptualized as a powerful external force, it presupposes some temporal agency.

Having temporal agency is a prerequisite for being able to enact temporal autonomy, which in turn could be helpful in *getting ahead of time* (Geiger et al., 2020: 1). Wahidin (2006) describes how the inmate tried to create some *own time* and get ahead of the daily schedule by going to bed and waking up much earlier than others. The recent study by Geiger et al. (2020) of Hamburg firefighters indicates that enacting temporal autonomy to get ahead of time is a strategy that is useful in entirely different organizational and temporal contexts than prisons. Although we can recognize the agentic power of time in both cases, the nature of the agency of time and the temporal situation in these studies were utterly different. While the inmate in Wahidin's (2006) research was struggling to deal with an abundance of inescapable time and its fixed, predictable, and monotonous rhythm, the firefighters were facing urgency caused by the shortage of time; they were racing with time while trying to deal with temporal contingencies (Geiger et al., 2020: 1). Again, we can argue that both prisoners and firefighters could be viewed as exceptional cases representing, to some extent, extreme circumstances. As such, the implications for more traditional or ordinary organizations are questionable. However, I would argue that to some extent, extreme cases help to highlight the importance of temporal agency, its essential role in dealing with time as an external force and make the struggles or even battles with it more visible than otherwise in so-called normal circumstances.

Having temporal agency, that is, having the creative power to shape our present, which is meaningfully connected to our past and future, and being able to influence our future, which is also meaningful and attainable, is vital to our mental, emotional, and physical well-being. Temporal agency enables us to prepare for the future. While it is easy to agree that preparing for the future in the sense of being ready for the future is important (Shipp & Jansen, 2021), it is not the only important aspect of preparing for the future. Exercising our temporal agency by preparing for the future in the present makes our perception of the present meaningful. It gives purpose to our action and makes maintaining temporal continuity possible without which we do not manage so well (Fuchs, 2013). However, it seems to be relatively easy to lose ourselves in the extended present that could be caused either by extensive time pressure or time compression as discussed in the previous chapter or, respectively, by a lack of time pressure.

In 2020, due to the worldwide COVID-19 pandemic, most of us have probably experienced the effects of the extended present in one or the other way. On the one hand, healthcare workers across countries have agonized under the time pressure caused by the unexpected overburden of work in high infection risk environments without any knowledge of when it will end. On the other hand, most others have agonized in mandatory or voluntary self-isolations, partial or complete lockdowns, constraint mobility, and social distancing. The emotional and physical well-being and mental health of people worldwide have been severely affected by health hazards, unexpected job and income losses, losses of loved ones, and separation from loved ones. For many people, the burning question is how to manage financially when the income sources have disappeared, and no one knows when the situation will ease. The sudden disruptions in our habitual social life caused by the pandemic have put us in limbo. To a greater or lesser extent, everybody has experienced boredom and isolation and has had to struggle to find a new daily rhythm to manage and keep up a meaningful existence in the passing time with limited or at least sharply decreased choices for using our time. As Fraisse argues:

> Temporal pressure is constricted, but it is also the framework within which our personality is organized. When it is absent, we are disoriented. There is nothing to bind the sequence of activities: we are alone. Human equilibrium is too precarious to do without fixed positions in space and regular cues in time. (1964: 141)

To a greater or lesser extent, we are all imprisoned by COVID-19. Unable to do much about the whole situation, everybody has been waiting for the COVID-19 pandemic to finally end. We are quite like prisoners whose "Every action is affected by the ubiquitous sense of having to wait for world time to pass so that one can finally return to the *outside*" (Meisenhelder, 1985: 44).

Without temporal agency, we cannot create or mark time; we will be unable to relate to time, to make it our own. Instead, time just passes by independent from us while robbing from us some of "our own time."

According to Meisenhelder, "The primary emotional effect associated with the universality of waiting seems to be that of boredom" (Ibid.). Boredom, while being different than depression, may lead to depression (Watt, 1991). The fact is that depression, together with other stress-related mental issues, like anxiety, has increased significantly during the pandemic across countries (i.e., Bueno-Notivol et al., 2020; Elflein, 2020a; Hyland et al., 2020; Salari et al., 2020; Ustun, 2021). Although waiting is probably not the only cause, it is still one of the main causes, as we all wait for the end of the pandemic and related constraints. Statistics show that substance and alcohol consumption has increased (i.e., Dumas et al., 2020; Elflein, 2020b; Pollard et al., 2020), allowing us to draw parallels with activities associated with *time filling* and *time killing* in Calkins' typology (Calkins, 1970). At the same time, Ustun (2021) found that compared to others, the depression scores were lower for those individuals who had maintained their ability to mark time either through their interactions with family members, making time for themselves, or keeping themselves busy with home education or work.

Therefore, to answer the question raised above, why is it important to have temporal agency, I would say that it is to make time bearable. As human beings, we need temporal agency to give meaning to our present through striving for a meaningful future. To make our present and future meaningful, we need events to mark time (i.e., Calkins, 1970; Jones, 2019; Meisenhelder, 1985; Roy, 1959) to create time and help us relate to time.

Without temporal agency, we are forced to face time as an external force continuously passing away and our life perishing with it. That type of relationship to time tends to be pathological (i.e., Fuchs, 2013). We need temporal agency, that is, our ability and capability to "construct and reconstruct the temporal conditions that shape [our] lives" (Orlikowski & Yates, 2002: 686); it facilitates "carving out of temporal existence (present, past, and future) from the passing of time" (Hernes, 2014: ix). Importantly, this no longer refers to subjectively perceived temporal dimensions of objective time but to another kind of subjective temporality that will be discussed in the next chapter.

3.6 Conclusion

So far, no universal law has been discovered that enables an easy and trustworthy translation from physical time to psychological or inner time. Instead, studies show that there are numerous ways and various reasons for how and why our perception of objective time is in one or the other biased or distorted. Studies in psychology show that we are doing relatively poorly in perceiving, estimating, and planning objective time objectively. Although individuals usually do not question the *passing* nature of time, their experiences of how quickly or slowly time passes or the length of a particular duration differ tremendously across individuals and specific situations. Our past experiences systematically fail to serve as a basis for estimating the duration of future tasks because our memories are either unavailable or biased or even willingly suppressed, leading to the planning fallacy. Our relationship with the future, viewed through either the ego-moving or the time-moving frame, influences our forward-looking estimates both about duration and temporal proximity. However, besides the future, our temporal focus or orientation could also be directed towards the past or present and have a different temporal depth.

Situations where our temporal agency is limited could be hard to bear. Studies show that time work to manipulate perceived duration and actual frequency, sequence, and timing is a part of our everyday coping mechanism. We do even worse when we are left without the ability and capability to exercise our temporal agency as a creative power to shape, create, and recreate our past, present, and future realities. When we are left with limited temporal agency, our ability and capability to construct and reconstruct the temporal conditions shaping our lives are constrained. Left with very limited or no temporal agency jeopardizes our mental and emotional well-being, indicating that time as objective, detached, and external is too much for us as humans to handle. Forced to face an objective time without any temporal agency is emotionally overwhelming. It could become an intolerable existential burden.

To sum up, our subjective perception of temporal dimensions of objective time or our cognitive time frames do not equal our subjective time and subjective temporality. Although that is not to say that these aspects are unimportant, they are important in shaping our relationship to time, as the reviewed literature has shown. Still, they are not sufficient to explain our relationship to time. Our subjective temporality has a more profound, more existential nature, discussed in the next chapter.

References

Ancona, D. G., Okhuysen, G. A., & Perlow, L. A. (2001). Taking time to integrate temporal research. *Academy of Management Review, 26*(4), 512–529.

Augustine, G., Soderstrom, S., Milner, D., & Weber, K. (2019). Constructing a distant future: Imaginaries in geoengineering. *Academy of Management Journal, 62*(6), 1930–1960.

Bambach, C. (2011). The time of the self and the time of the other. *History and Society, 50*, 254–269.

Bluedorn, A. C. (2002). *The human organization of time.* Stanford University Press.

Bluedorn, A. C., & Denhardt, R. B. (1988). Time and organizations. *Journal of Management, 14*(2), 299–320.

Boon, T. (2020). Breaking: Berlin's Brandenburg Airport opens almost 10 years late. *Simple Flying*, October 31. Retrieved November 3, 2020, from https://simpleflying.com/berlin-brandenburg-airport-open/

Boroditsky, L. (2000). Metaphoric structuring: Understanding time through spatial metaphors. *Cognition, 75*, 1–28.

Boroditsky, L., & Ramscar, M. (2002). The roles of body and mind in abstract thought. *Psychological Science, 13*, 185–189.

Buehler, R., Griffin, D., & MacDonald, H. (1997). The role of motivated reasoning in optimistic time predictions. *Personality and Social Psychology Bulletin, 23*(3), 238–247.

Buehler, R., Griffin, D., & Ross, M. (2002). Inside the planning fallacy: The causes and consequences of optimistic time predictions. In T. Gilovich, D. Griffin, & D. Kahneman (Eds.), *Heuristics and biases: The psychology of intuitive judgement* (pp. 250–270). Cambridge University Press.

Bueno-Notivol, J., Gracia-García, P., Olaya, B., Lasheras, I., López-Antón, R., & Santabárbara, J. (2020). Prevalence of depression during the COVID-19 outbreak: A meta-analysis of community-based studies. *International Journal of Clinical and Health Psychology, 21*(1). https://doi.org/10.1016/j.ijchp.2020.07.007

Calkins, K. (1970). Time: Perspectives, marking and styles of usage. *Social Problems, 17*(4), 487–501.

Callender, C. (2017). *What makes time special?* Oxford University Press.

Carrol, L. (1865/2008). *Alice's adventures in Wonderland.* Ebook produced by A. DiBianca & D. Widger. The Millennium Fulcrum Edition 3.0.

Carver, C. S. (2006). Approach, avoidance, and the self-regulation of affect and action. *Motivation and Emotion, 30*, 105–110.

Chen, J., & Nadkarni, S. (2017). It's about time! CEOs' temporal dispositions, temporal leadership, and corporate entrepreneurship. *Administrative Science Quarterly, 62*(1), 31–66.

Costas, J., & Kärreman, D. (2016). The bored self in knowledge work. *Human Relations, 69*(1), 61–83.

Cravo, A., & Haddad, H. (2015). When is now: Measuring how we perceive instants in time. In L. M. Simão, D. S. Guimarães, & J. Valsiner (Eds.), *Temporality: Culture in the flow of human experience* (pp. 115–126). Information Age Publishing.

Crilly, D. (2017). Time and space in strategy discourse: Implications for intertemporal choice. *Strategic Management Journal, 38*(12), 2370–2389.

Das, T. K., & Teng, B. S. (2001). Strategic risk behaviour and its temporalities: Between risk propensity and decision context. *Journal of Management Studies, 38*(4), 515–534.

Diefendorff, J. M., Richard, E. M., & Gosserand, R. H. (2006). Examination of situational and attitudinal moderators of the hesitation and performance relation. *Personnel Psychology, 59*, 365–393.

Duffy, S. E., & Feist, M. I. (2014). Individual differences in the interpretation of ambiguous statements about time. *Cognitive Linguistics, 25*(1), 29–54.

Duffy, S. E., Feist, M. I., & McCarthy, S. (2014). Moving through time: The role of personality in three real life contexts. *Cognitive Science, 38*(8), 1662–1674.

Dumas, T. M., Ellis, W., & Litt, D. M. (2020). What does adolescent substance use look like during the COVID-19 pandemic? Examining changes in frequency, social contexts, and pandemic-related predictors. *Journal of Adolescent Health, 67*, 354–361. https://doi.org/10.1016/j.jadohealth.2020.06.018

Ebert, J. E., & Prelec, D. (2007). The fragility of time: Time-insensitivity and valuation of the near and far future. *Management Science, 53*(9), 1423–1438.

Elflein, J. (2020a). Depression level increases during the COVID-19 pandemic worldwide June 2020, by age. *Statista*, November 5. Retrieved November 25, 2020, from https://www.statista.com/statistics/1184765/depression-level-increases-in-adults-due-to-covid-by-age-worldwide/#statisticContainer

Elflein, J. (2020b). U.S. mental health and substance abuse problems during COVID-19 June 2020, by age. *Statista*, September 4. Retrieved November 25, 2020, from https://www.statista.com/statistics/1168482/mental-health-substance-abuse-suicide-ideation-covid-age/

Emirbayer, M. (1997). Manifesto for a relational sociology. *American Journal of Sociology, 103*(2), 281–317.

Emirbayer, M., & Mische, A. (1998). What is agency? *American Journal of Sociology, 103*(4), 962–1023.
Euronews. (2020). Berlin airport opens 10 years late and three times over budget. Retrieved March 15, 2021, from https://www.euronews.com/2020/10/31/berlin-airport-opens-10-years-late-and-three-times-over-budget
Fisher, C. D. (1993). Boredom at work: A neglected concept. *Human Relations, 46*, 395–417.
Flaherty, M. G. (2002). Making time: Agency and the construction of temporal experience. *Symbolic Interaction, 25*(3), 379–388.
Flaherty, M. G. (2003). Time work: Customizing temporal experience. *Social Psychology Quarterly, 66*(1), 17–33.
Flaherty, M. G. (2011). *The textures of time: Agency and temporal experience.* Temple University Press.
Flyvberg, B., Holme, M. S., & Soren, B. (2002). Underestimating costs in public works projects: Error or lie? *Journal of the American Planning Association, 68*, 279–295.
Fraisse, P. (1964). *The psychology of time.* Eyre and Spottiswoode.
Francis-Smythe, J. A., & Robertson, I. T. (1999). On the relationship between time management and time estimation. *British Journal of Psychology, 90*, 333–347.
Fuchs, T. (2013). Temporality and psychopathology. *Phenomenology and the Cognitive Sciences, 12*(1), 75–104. https://doi.org/10.1007/s11097-010-9189-4
Fuhrman, O., McCormick, K., Chen, E., Jiang, H., Shu, D., Mao, S., & Boroditsky, L. (2011). How linguistic and cultural forces shape conceptions of time: English and Mandarin time in 3D. *Cognitive Science, 35*(7), 1305–1328.
Game, A. M. (2007). Workplace boredom coping: Health, safety, and HR implications. *Personnel Review, 36*, 701–721.
Geiger, D., Danner-Schröder, A., & Kremser, W. (2020). Getting ahead of time—Performing temporal boundaries to coordinate routines under temporal uncertainty. *Administrative Science Quarterly, 66*, 220–264. https://doi.org/10.1177/0001839220941010
Gemmill, G., & Oakley, J. (1992). The meaning of boredom in organizational life. *Group & Organization Management, 17*, 358–369.
Griffin, D., & Buehler, R. (1999). Frequency, probability, and prediction: Easy solutions to cognitive illusions? *Cognitive Psychology, 38*, 48–78.
Grondin, S. (2001). From physical time to the first and second moments of psychological time. *Psychological Bulletin, 127*, 22–44.
Grondin, S. (2020). *The perception of time: Your questions answered.* Routledge.

Hall, P. (1980). *Great planning disasters*. Weidenfeld & Nicolson.
Hassard, H. (2001). Commodification, construction and compression: A review of time metaphors in organizational analysis. *International Journal of Management Reviews, 3*(2), 131–141.
Hawkins, L., Frenclh, C., Crawford, B. D., & Enzlem, E. (1988). Depressed affect and time perception. *Journal of Abnormal Psychology, 97*, 275–280.
Hernes, T. (2014). *A process theory of organization*. Oxford University Press.
Hernes, T., Feddersen, J., & Schultz, M. (2020). Material temporality: How materiality 'does' time in food organizing. *Organization Studies.* https://doi.org/10.1177/0170840620909974
Hussenot, A., Hernes, T., & Bouty, I. (2020). Studying organization from the perspective of the ontology of temporality: Introducing the events-based approach. In J. Reinecke, R. Suddaby, A. Langley, & H. Tsoukas (Eds.), *About time: Temporality and history in organization studies* (pp. 50–68). Oxford University Press. https://doi.org/10.1093/oso/9780198870715.003.0005
Hyland, P., Shevlin, M., McBride, O., Murphy, J., Karatzias, T., Bentall, R. P., Martinez, A. P., & Valliéres, F. (2020). Anxiety and depression in the Republic of Ireland during the COVID-19 pandemic. *PsyArXiv.* https://doi.org/10.31234/osf.io/8yqxr
James, W. (1890). *The principles of psychology*. Macmillan.
Johnsen, R. (2016). Boredom and organization studies. *Organization Studies, 37*(10), 1403–1415.
Johnsen, R., Berg Johansen, C., & Toyoki, S. (2019). Serving time: Organization and the affective dimension of time. *Organization, 26*(1), 3–19. https://doi.org/10.1177/1350508418763997
Jones, M. R. (2019). *Time will tell: A theory of dynamic attending*. Oxford University Press.
Kahneman, D., & Lovallo, D. (1993). Timid choices and bold forecasts: A cognitive perspective on risk taking. *Management Science, 39*, 17–31.
Kahneman, D., & Tversky, A. (1979). Prospect theory: An analysis of decision under risk. *Econometrica, 47*, 263–291.
Kim, A., Bansal, P., & Haugh, H. (2019). No time like the present: How a present time perspective can foster sustainable development. *Academy of Management Journal, 62*(2), 607–634.
Kim, B. K., Zauberman, G., & Bettman, J. (2012). Space, time, and intertemporal preferences. *Journal of Consumer Research, 39*, 867–880.

Klempe, S. H. (2015). Temporality and the necessity of culture in psychology. In L. M. Simão, D. S. Guimarães, & J. Valsiner (Eds.), *Temporality: Culture in the flow of human experience* (pp. 3–22). Information Age Publishing.

Knippenberg, D., Knippenberg, B., Monden, L., & de Lima, F. (2002). Organizational identification after a merger: A social identity perspective. *British Journal of Social Psychology, 41*, 233–252.

Langley, A. (1999). Strategies for theorizing from process data. *Academy of Management Review, 24*, 691–710.

Langley, A., Smallman, C., Tsoukas, H., & Van de Ven, A. H. (2013). Process studies of change in organization and management: Unveiling temporality, activity, and flow. *Academy of Management Journal, 56*, 1–13.

Langley, A., & Tsoukas, H. (2010). Introducing "Perspectives on process organization studies". In T. Hernes & S. Maitlis (Eds.), *Process, sensemaking, & organizing* (pp. 1–26). Oxford University Press.

Levine, R. (2006). *A geography of time: The temporal misadventures of a social psychologist, or how every culture keeps time just a little bit differently*. Oneworld.

Loukidou, L., Loan-Clarke, J., & Daniels, K. (2009). Boredom in the workplace: More than monotonous tasks. *International Journal of Management Reviews, 11*, 381–405.

Luhmann, N. (2018). *Organization and decision*. Cambridge University Press.

McTaggart, J. (1908). The unreality of time. *Mind, 17*, 457–474.

Mead, G. H. (1932/2002). *The philosophy of the present*. Prometheus.

Meisenhelder, T. (1985). An essay on time and the phenomenology of imprisonment. *Deviant Behavior, 6*(1), 39–56.

Melges, F. T. (1982). *Time and the inner future*. John Wiley.

Merleau-Ponty, M. (2002). *Phenomenology of perception*. Routledge Classics.

Minkowski, E. (1970). *Lived time: Phenomenological and psychopathological studies*. Northwest University Press.

Mohammed, S., & Nadkarni, S. (2011). Temporal diversity and team performance: The moderating role of team temporal leadership. *Academy of Management Journal, 54*(3), 489–508.

Morgan, G. (1997). *Images of organization* (2nd ed.). SAGE Publications.

Nadkarni, S., Chen, T., & Chen, J. (2016). The clock is ticking! Executive temporal depth, industry velocity, and competitive aggressiveness. *Strategic Management Journal, 37*, 1132–1153.

Núñez, R. E., Motz, B. A., & Teuscher, U. (2006). Time after time: The psychological reality of the ego- and time-reference-point distinction in metaphorical construals of time. *Metaphor and Symbol, 21*(3), 133–146.

Orlikowski, W. J., & Yates, J. (2002). It's about time: Temporal structuring in organizations. *Organization Science, 13*(6), 684–700.

Pedri, S., & Hesketh, B. (1993). Time perception: Effects of tasks speed and delay. *Perceptual and Motor Skills, 76,* 599–608.

Pollard, M. S., Tucker, J. S., & Green, H. D. (2020). Changes in adult alcohol use and consequences during the COVID-19 pandemic in the US. *JAMA Network Open, 3*(9), e2022942. https://doi.org/10.1001/jamanetwork open.2020.22942

Ramscar, M., Matlock, T., & Dye, M. (2010). Running down the clock: The role of expectation in our understanding of time and motion. *Language & Cognitive Processes, 25*(5), 589–615.

Richmond, J., Wilson, J. C., & Zinken, J. (2012). A feeling for the future: How does agency in time metaphors relate to feelings? *European Journal of Social Psychology, 42*(7), 813–823.

Robinson, J. P., & Godbey, G. (1999). *Time for life: The surprising ways Americans use their time.* Pennsylvania State University Press.

Roy, D. F. (1959). 'Banana time': Job satisfaction and informal interaction. *Human Organization, 18,* 158–168.

Roy, M. M., Christenfeld, N. J. S., & McKenzie, C. R. M. (2005). Underestimating the duration of future events: Memory incorrectly used or memory bias? *Psychological Bulletin, 131*(5), 738–756.

Salari, N., Hosseinian-Far, A., Jalali, R., Vaisi-Raygani, A., Rasoulpoor, S., Mohammadi, M., Rasoulpoor, S., & Khaledi-Paveh, B. (2020). Prevalence of stress, anxiety, depression among the general population during the COVID-19 pandemic: A systematic review and meta-analysis. *Globalization and Health, 16*(57). https://doi.org/10.1186/s12992-020-00589-w

Sanna, L. J., Parks, C. D., Chang, E. C., & Carter, S. E. (2005). The hourglass is half full or half empty: Temporal framing and the group planning fallacy. *Group Dynamics: Theory, Research, and Practice, 9*(3), 173–188.

Schnaars, S. P. (1989). *Megamistakes: Forecasting and the myth of rapid technological change.* Free Press.

Shipp, A. J., Edwards, J. R., & Lambert, L. S. (2009). Conceptualization and measurement of temporal focus: The subjective experience of the past, present, and future. *Organizational Behavior and Human Decision Processes, 110*(1), 1–22.

Shipp, A. J., & Jansen, K. J. (2021). The "other" time: A review of the subjective experience of time in organizations. *Academy of Management Annals, 15*(1), 299–334. https://doi.org/10.5465/annals.2018.0142

Slawinski, N., & Bansal, P. (2015). Short on time: Intertemporal tensions in business sustainability. *Organization Science, 26*, 531–549.
Sorokin, P. A., & Merton, R. K. (1937). Social time: A methodological and functional analysis. *The American Journal of Sociology, 42*(5), 615–629.
Sutton, R. I. (1987). The process of organizational death: Disbanding and reconnecting. *Administrative Science Quarterly, 32*, 542–569.
Tang, S., Richter, A. W., & Nadkarni, S. (2020). Subjective time in organizations: Conceptual clarification, integration, and implications for future research. *Journal of Organizational Behavior, 41*, 210–234.
Tasselli, S., Kilduff, M., & Landis, B. (2018). Personality change: Implications for organizational behavior. *Academy of Management Annals, 12*(2), 467–493.
Trope, Y., & Liberman, N. (2003). Temporal construal. *Psychological Review, 110*, 403–421.
Turatto, M., Vescovi, M., & Valsecchi, M. (2007). Attention makes moving objects be perceived to move faster. *Vision Research, 47*(2), 166–178.
Tversky, A., & Kahneman, D. (1974). Judgment under uncertainty: Heuristics and biases. *Science, 185*, 1124–1131. https://doi.org/10.1126/science.185.4157.1124
Ustun, G. (2021). Determining depression and related factors in a society affected by COVID-19 pandemic. *International Journal of Social Psychiatry, 67*(1), 54–63. https://doi.org/10.1177/0020764020938807
Wahidin, A. (2006). Time and the prison experience. *Sociological Research Online, 11*(1), 127–138.
Watt, J. D. (1991). Effect of boredom proneness on time perception. *Psychological Reports, 69*, 323–327.
Watzlawik, M. (2015). Temporality, lifetime, and the afterdeath: Case studies from hospice patients. In L. M. Simão, D. S. Guimarães, & J. Valsiner (Eds.), *Temporality: Culture in the flow of human experience* (pp. 215–229). Information Age Publishing.
Wearden, J. H. (2005). The wrong tree: Time perception and time experience in the elderly. In J. Duncan, L. Phillips, & P. McLeod (Eds.), *Measuring the mind: Speed, control, and age* (pp. 137–158). Oxford University Press.
Wearden, J. H. (2016). *The psychology of time perception*. Palgrave Macmillan.
Whitehead, A. N. (1929/1978). *Process and reality*. The Free Press.
Zerubavel, E. (1991). *The fine line: Making distinctions in everyday life*. The Free Press.

4

Temporality—Endogenous and Subjective

In general, it is agreed that temporality is one of the most complex constructs in Western philosophy to grasp and explain (e.g., Chaudhary, 2015; Simão, 2015). Considering the concept's claimed complexity, it is no wonder that this is the longest chapter in this book. Indeed, there are many related and interrelated issues which require at least some attention. Temporality has caught the attention of philosophers and scholars from various fields. For example, temporality as endogenous and subjective has been one of the central interests and objects of theorization for phenomenologically oriented philosophers like Husserl, Heidegger, and Merleau-Ponty. However, it has also attracted process-inspired philosophers like Bergson, Mead, Whitehead, and pragmatists like James, Mead, and Pierce. But temporality is also addressed in developmental and cultural psychology (e.g., Roe, 2008; Valsiner, 2011), ageing studies (e.g., Baars, 2012), psychiatry (e.g., Fuchs, 2013), and organization studies (e.g., Hernes, 2014a; Schultz & Hernes, 2013). Common to these works across different fields is their grounding on the ontology of temporality (Hussenot et al., 2020).

Klempe (2015) argues that while in the premodern era subjectivity was mainly ignored, today there is a tendency to overlook the distinction between subjective and objective. However, ignoring either endogenous or subjective temporality or the difference between subjective and objective temporality could lead to misreading reality, misunderstanding people and misinterpreting events, situations and circumstances, ultimately leading to faulty conclusions and decisions. Therefore, this chapter is devoted to temporality as endogenous and subjective. Endogenous temporality is viewed as a broader concept, denoting the internal quality of an "entity's or substance's movement through time" (Hernes et al., 2020: 354). Consequently, endogenous temporality applies both to human subjects and to non-human objects, as well as to ideas and value systems. Subjective temporality is viewed as the experience of time as lived by humans. It also covers a selection of topics directly linked to subjective temporality as a lived experience, the basic structure of subjective temporality, temporal idealism, becoming in passing time, issues concerning pasts, futures, and the present, and the temporal structure of agency.

This chapter introduces the more *"esoteric"*[1] (Fried & Slowik, 2004: 405) view of subjective time and temporality as theorized by Husserl, Heidegger, and Merleau-Ponty. It could be true that the more esoteric aspect of subjective time has not become common knowledge (Fried & Slowik, 2004)—at least not yet, and at least not in organization studies. It could partly be that Bluedorn's (2002) *The Human Organization of Time: Temporal Realities and Experience*, which is widely referred to in both management and organization studies that focus on time and temporality, could be blamed for that. In his book, Bluedorn treats time as an external phenomenon and skips the phenomenological approach to time as an internal and subjective lived experience altogether. For example, in his review of Bluedorn's book, Vail (2003) yearns exactly for this certain amount of esotericism when criticizing that:

> While Bluedorn's analysis is internally consistent and impeccably referenced, it is directed quite clearly and explicitly on the outcomes of social action. Focus on outcomes is important in many cases and obviously makes up the vast majority of sociological output. However, constructionist work

---

[1] According to Cambridge Dictionary, esoteric means something that is "very unusual and understood or liked by only a small number of people, especially those with special knowledge" https://dictionary.cambridge.org/dictionary/english/esoteric

is most illuminating and satisfying when it progresses beyond the outcome to "catch the process" (Blumer, 1969) through which people achieve their outcomes. As is usually the case with constructionist explanations that focus on outcomes rather than process, I found many of his conclusions a bit underwhelming. (Vail, 2003: 768–769)

However, another reason why esoteric advances in time studies have failed to become common knowledge could be that "the action of common sense" (Merleau-Ponty, 2002: 490) tends to thematize or objectify time. Consequently, the focus of research on time and temporality tends to follow the ontology of time and remain at the objective, external and measurable level, as indicated in the previous chapters. In addition, the problem pointed out by Merleau-Ponty is how to make explicit time a subjective temporal dimension of our being which is not objective in the empirical sense (Merleau-Ponty, 2002: 482–483, 490). That is, subjective phenomenological time is not directly observable or measurable; there are no clear and visible causal relationships to track across or between tenses or even a straightforward positioning of experience or events in a linear temporal line. Therefore, the assumptions of the ontology of time do not allow us to study existential time.

In his review of Bluedorn's book, Vail expresses how he expected to see a more comprehensible analysis going beyond the outcomes of time and temporality. Vail's review reveals his yearning for analysis that opens up how temporal realities are created, how temporal experiences emerge, how temporal experiences and temporal realities mutually co-constitute one another, how humans organize time, and how time organizes humans, and maybe also, how humans and time mutually cocreate each other. In short, he wants to see the process. Indeed, time and temporality are central in process theories (Reinecke et al., 2020), as any process, by its nature, is temporal. Yet, when talking about time in the lived experience or subjective temporality, we are talking about something that is even "not a real process" (Merleau-Ponty, 2002: 478).

Considering the increasing number of publications focusing on time and temporality in organization studies and management, we can expect that besides external time and exogenous temporality, internal time and endogenous temporality will attract enough attention to become common knowledge. This chapter's focus moves from subjective perceptions of temporal dimensions of objective time to subjective temporality as "a measure endogenous to the entity's or substance's movement through time" (Hernes et al., 2020: 354). Therefore, this chapter's focus shifts from an exogenous temporality of external time to the endogenous quality that "belongs exclusively to the entity" (Hernes et al., 2020: 354). Two underlying assumptions run through this chapter. First, endogenous temporality is a source of becoming, and second, becoming is enabled by irreversibly passing time, which is simultaneously emerging and perishing.

4.1 Subjective Temporality as a Lived Experience

The concept of subjective temporality as a lived experience is central in phenomenology. Merleau-Ponty opposes the view of treating the past and the future as perceptions and recollections of "psychic facts" (Merleau-Ponty, 2002: 481). He insists that human experience is viewed as inextricably interwoven with time. As the quote from Merleau-Ponty indicates, the subjective temporality of lived experience is very different from the temporality of perceived dimensions of the objective time that we discussed in the previous chapter. In Heidegger's words, "Temporality makes possible the understanding of being" (Heidegger, 1982: 302) as a subjective experience not objective phenomenon. Husserl is very straightforward in stating, "one cannot discover the least trace of Objective time through phenomenological analysis," as the experienced now "is not a point of Objective time" (Husserl, 1964: 24) but belongs to a different sphere. Limiting our view of subjective time to a perception of temporal dimensions of objective, external, and measurable clock time and to our ability to predict the future and remember the past does not allow us to understand our own temporality, that is, our sensed continuity in the passing of time and our personal temporal connection to the world. However, it is hard to observe the experience of time in time, and according to Klempe (2015), subjective temporality has not necessarily been figured on the top of the research agendas, and thus has failed to become "common knowledge" (Fried & Slowik, 2004: 405).

Subjective temporality does not equal some kind of "inner time" as internalized objective time or intrasubjective temporality, described as "mental time travel" (Eacott & Easton, 2012; Shipp & Jansen, 2021). The idea of an intrasubjective temporality as mental time travel relies, once again, on a spatial metaphor. Following a spatial metaphor, the past is separated from the future, and "both episodic memory for past experiences and thinking about future personal events form a continuum" (Eacott & Easton, 2012: 167). The time-travelling metaphor gives the impression that we can *move* across the past, present, and future, as these are fixed, static, and unquestionable *places* (Bardon, 2013). Bergson contests this spatial and sequential ordering in favour of the multidimensional organization of temporal elements:

> If our conscious point A does not yet possess the idea of space—and this is the hypothesis which we have agreed to adopt—the succession of states through which it passes cannot assume for it the form of a line; but its sensations *will add themselves dynamically to one another* (Bergson, 1910: 103–104 emphasis added).

Consequently, the availability of past experience in subjective temporality differs from the psychological explanation of conscious past memories and future projections (Merleau-Ponty, 2002: 479). Instead, subjective temporality relies on the realization of intuitive intentions that "cling on to memories preserved *in the unconscious*" (Merleau-Ponty, 2002: 479). Additionally, both Heidegger and Merleau-Ponty stress that the temporality of lived experience is not intrasubjective (see, for example, Shipp & Jansen, 2021), but it rather belongs to a more existential *originary* or *primordial* temporality (Heidegger, 1927/1962; 1979; Merleau-Ponty, 2002).

Originary or primordial temporality is a non-sequential manifold in its wholeness. This unity cannot be divided into different and separated temporal dimensions of past, present, and future like objectively existing static units. Originary or primordial temporality could be viewed as always a unified whole that enables the emergence of different temporal dimensions and understandings of possibility. As Wong (2001) explains, "for Heidegger, originary temporality is the condition for the possibility of Dasein's understanding. Originary temporality is the necessary condition common to all Dasein[2] that allows for anything to make sense, or for any worldly comportment to be possible." According to Heidegger, "we shall have to ask how what confronts us *in the unity* of expecting [future], retaining [past], and enpresenting [present] can be validly asserted to be original time" (Heidegger, 1982: 260 *emphasis added*). On this point, Heidegger's views are compatible with Bergson, who states that:

> Nor need it forget its former states: it is enough that, in recalling these states, it does not set them alongside its actual state as one point alongside another, but forms both the past and the present states into an organic whole. (Bergson, 1910: 100)

The notion in existential phenomenology is that subjectivity constitutes lived time, and temporality is a dimension of subjectivity within which people manifest themselves by creating their relations to the world. Blattner, building on Heidegger, states, "Dasein, conceived in its extreme possibility of being, is time itself, not in time" (Blattner, 1999: 230). Merleau-Ponty follows this line of argumentation by claiming, "We must understand time as the subject and the subject as time" (Merleau-Ponty, 2002: 490). Therefore, "Subjectivity is not in time, because it takes up or lives time, and merges with the cohesion of a life" (Merleau-Ponty, 2002: 491). As not belonging to the world's objective dimension, subjective temporality emerges from the deeply intertwined relationships between the person's immediate experience, the world, and time, Merleau-Ponty concludes:

> Time is, therefore, not a real process, not an actual succession that I am content to record. It arises from my relation to things. Within things themselves, the future and the past are in a kind of eternal state of pre-existence and survival. (Merleau-Ponty, 2002: 478)

---

[2] With the term Dasein, Heidegger denotes human existence.

In these relations, time is viewed as irreversible (Bergson, 1910; Valsiner, 2011) and perishing (Hernes, 2014a; Mead, 1932/2002; Whitehead, 1929/1978). The irreversibility of time means that we cannot return to the same position we occupied earlier, even a moment before; we cannot be undone what is once done. Although now and then, but not always, it could be possible to correct what is done (Luhmann, 2018), it is never possible to undo something already done or repeat the exact experience. Perishability implies time neither stays still nor it ever returns; instead, it keeps moving on, and in passing by, it is gone forever; it vanishes. The intertwined relationships between the person's immediate experience, the world, and passing and perishing time mean, "we are always already living *in* time, and in some sense, we are always already *living* time. And although (unlike stones or trees) we can be aware of this, we cannot step out of time to observe it purely" (Baars, 2012: 144 *emphasis in original*).

Thus, the main challenge in analysing someone's (including our own) lived experience stems from the fact that tracking its chronological appearance or measuring it chronometrically does not say anything about its significance and the meaning ascribed to it. The meaning of lived experience emerges from simultaneously living in a time (in the passing flow of perishing time) and actively living time (*creating* time by combining different pasts and futures). The latter is emphasized by Theunissen (1991 cited in Fuchs, 2013: 81). However, we are unable to observe simultaneously happening processes because due to their simultaneity they remain unobservable (Luhmann, 2018). As they remain unobservable, we cannot influence them causally. Both observing something and producing effects requires time (Luhmann, 2018: 125). In other words, we cannot control what is taking place simultaneously, either "informationally or causally, either through knowledge or through action" (Luhmann, 2018: 128). Consequently, it is not so surprising that understanding subjective temporality as lived experience is challenging because of our inability to control these parallel processes of living in the time and actively living time or temporalizing ourselves. But what does it mean to "actively live time" or temporalize oneself?

4.1.1 Living Time and Ongoing Temporality

As underlined by Merleau-Ponty, time is neither our perceptions nor memories as *psychic facts* nor a sequential process we struggle to grasp; instead, we are actively living time. *Actively living time* means creating our temporal reality by (re)combining different pasts and futures in the continuously passing time. Therefore, our subjective temporality, that is, our lived experience of time, could be viewed as an ongoing configuration of three temporal dimensions (past, present, and future) influencing the way we connect to the outside world, make sense of that and create our own reality (Heidegger, 1927/ 1962; Hernes, 2014a; Merleau-Ponty, 2002). While creating our reality in the present through the different combinations of the pasts and futures, we are continuously reinterpreting their meaning, relevance, probabilities, and proximities. In other words, on an ongoing basis, we create our pasts and futures in the elapsing present (Luhmann, 2018; Schultz & Hernes, 2013).

While the idea of an ongoing temporality and importance of connecting past and future may sound abstract and theoretical, it has implications in empirically oriented studies in cognitive and social psychology (i.e., Abram et al., 2014) and development studies, including ageing (i.e., Baars, 2012), cultural psychology and cultural semiotics (Valsiner 2007, Valsiner, 2011), and organization studies (i.e., Hatch & Schultz, 2017; Schultz & Hernes, 2013). For example, in alignment with the logic of an ongoing temporality perspective, writers in cognitive and social psychology, such as Abram et al., state that the present being is perceived as "a continuity of the past and as a prelude to the future" (Abram et al., 2014: 76). From the perspective of psychology, Holman and Silver (1998) highlight how the overall span (or temporal depth, to use the term introduced by Bluedorn (2002) see previous chapter) may be either extended or narrowed. Meaning, our temporal span could range from distant past to distant future or from immediate past to immediate future, and thus, have a different influence on our experiences, our interpretation of situations, decision making, and behaviour. As a rule, a richer reservoir of past experiences (extended span) enables greater flexibility in constructing hypothetical future scenarios and see different possibilities (Abram et al., 2014; Luhmann, 2018).

In that sense, our ability to remember past experiences and to imagine and plan future ones is essential in our daily lives. Perceived temporal continuity, defined by Holman and Silver (1998: 1146) as "the overall span of cognitive involvement across the past, present, and future life domains," is closely related to a person's sense of self-identity (Abram et al., 2014) and perceived self-continuity (Hershfield, 2011). The inability to keep up the ongoing connections between the past, present and future is associated with various severe mental disorders or diseases like autism spectrum disorder (Lind & Williams, 2012), schizophrenia, depression (Fuchs, 2013), dementia, temporal disorientation, Alzheimer's disease (Blattner, 2020; Ryan et al., 2015) and even such pathologies as states of mania (Levine, 2006; Martin et al., 2018). Numerous empirical studies in cognitive psychology, clinical phenomenology, and psychiatry (i.e., Fuchs, 2013; Martin et al., 2018) validate the practical relevance of the seemingly highly theoretical nature of ongoing subjective temporality and its dynamics across past, present and future.

As in general, we tend to take for granted connections across the past, present and future, the inability to remember our recent past, that is, the inability to create new memories, known as anterograde amnesia, has inspired numerous movies. For example, in the romantic comedy *50 First Dates* by Segal et al. (2004), Lucy Whitmore (played by Drew Barrymore) lost her memory in a car accident, which made it hard for Henry Roth (played by Adam Sandler) to win her heart. Lucy could not remember anything from yesterday, including her encounter with Henry and her feelings towards him. A grimmer movie version of anterograde amnesia is featured in the movie *Memento* (Nolan et al., 2002). Leonard Shelby (played by Guy Pearce), the protagonist, can remember his life and keep his long-term memories intact until the day he and his wife fell victims to an attack. The attack led to his wife's rape and murder and Leonard's inability to form new memories. Therefore, since that event, Leonard has been suffering from anterograde amnesia, but compared to Lucy's 24-hour-memory, Leonard experiences short-term memory loss every fifteen minutes. Consequently, there is no ongoing temporal continuity, and Leonard experiences reality as a single stand-alone frame. He equips himself with complex Polaroid photographs and a tattoo system to build up his temporal reference system and for storing information that he is unable to remember. These movies highlight the importance of ongoing temporality of living experience and a critical role memory plays in experiencing time and constructing our personal identities (Callender, 2017; Klein & Nichols, 2012).

While the storyline in the movie is based on fictional script, there are real-life examples of people suffering with that condition. However, ongoing temporality does not belong to psychology only. For example, based on the concept of the *ongoing present* (Mead, 1932/ 2002), which stresses that we are constantly in the ongoing present, Schultz and Hernes (2013) introduced the term *ongoing temporality* in organization studies. Using the term *ongoing*, they highlight what is happening at the very moment (Schultz & Hernes, 2013: 1). While using the term *ongoing temporality*, they underscore the dynamic nature of organizational temporality—the continuous recombination of organizational pasts and futures (Schultz & Hernes, 2013).

4.1.2 Building the Sensed Continuity in Passing Time

From the phenomenological viewpoint, both past experiences and future anticipations are recreated in the ongoing present, in the emerging recombination of pasts and futures; they are anew at every moment. They do not represent the fixed, static, and objective past experience and future expectation projected based on the past in the continuum, as often presented in cognitive psychology (i.e., Eacott & Easton, 2012; Lind & Williams, 2012). "Time is not a line, but a network of intentionalities," claims Merleau-Ponty (2002: 484). This network of intentionalities includes the significance of both past actualized and not actualized possibilities and future possibilities as they are perceived in the present (Levine, 2006; Luhmann, 2018; Valsiner, 2011). For example, Levine (2006: 42) claims that for the Japanese, "What doesn't happen ... is often more important than what does."

Still, viewing us living in the continually passing (Merleau-Ponty, 2002) or perishing (Whitehead, 1929/1978) time raises two questions.

First, if we assume that things do not stay "the way they are" but "are constantly threatened with disappearance, at least in their present form" (Hernes, 2014a: 45), then how could our experience have a continuous, ongoing, and processual nature with internal coherence instead of being a single momentary frame or a fragmented backflash as experienced by the protagonist in Nolan's Memento? Second, irrespective of its conscious or unconscious nature, how does an ongoing configuration of three temporal dimensions take place?

A subjective experience *with* and *in* time allows us to describe temporality as "carving out of temporal existence (present, past, and future) from the passing of time" (Hernes, 2014a: ix). The expression "carving out of temporal existence" (Hernes, 2014a: ix) hints at existentialism. From the perspective of existentialism, subjective temporality is emerging from the perceived tension between the infinity of external time and our finitude. To manage this finitude-infinity tension and maintain our sensed continuity in the passing and perishing time, we need to be able, meaning, we need both ability and capability, to connect our pasts to our futures and keep these connections up. As hinted earlier, the continuous connection between our pasts and futures is vital for ensuring our mental wellbeing and ability to cope with the demands of our everyday life. These connections are not passive, static, and fixed but effortful, intentional, and temporal.

Our subjective temporality is directly linked to our existence, which is profoundly temporal and built on our relations to the past, present, and future, or perhaps more precisely, to the pasts, present, and futures (Mead, 1932/2002). As Heidegger asserts, "Dasein's Being finds its meaning in temporality. But temporality is also the condition which makes historicality possible as a temporal kind of Being which Dasein itself possesses, regardless of whether or how Dasein is an entity 'in time'" (Heidegger, 1927/1962: 41). Therefore, our being in the world is characterized by temporality, defined as a process that combines past, present, and future into an existential whole. Our subjective lived experience of time, our temporality as an ongoing configuration of three temporal modes, influences how we connect to reality, make sense, and create that reality (Heidegger, 1927/1962; Merleau-Ponty, 2002).

However, how exactly the past, present, and future are configured into an existential whole is not predetermined. Quite the contrary, "Temporality has different possibilities and different ways of temporalizing itself" (Heidegger, 1927/1962: 351). In other words, our subjective temporality has the power to dictate our experience. Once again, the ongoing configuration of temporal dimensions underlines the active effort, whether conscious or unconscious, required to create connections, on the one hand, across the pasts, present, and futures, and on the other hand, between the subject and the world. But based on what and how do actors create and maintain these connections?

Husserl explained the experience's extension in time through the notion of time-consciousness. Working from the perspective of phenomenology, Husserl introduced the idea of retention, protention, and presentation as elements unified in the processual structure of an internal time-consciousness. Where protention stands for the "indeterminate anticipation of what is yet to come," presentation for "primal or momentary impression," and retention for "retaining what has just been experienced as it slips away" (Fuchs, 2013: 77). In Husserl's approach, we have an impression of the present experience, but we sense the present as an extension from the past to the future. The sensed extension is achieved with the simultaneous synthesis of retention to the immediate past and protention to the immediate future. According to Husserl, retention and protention are conditions that make it possible for us to experience a process of unfolding time, to see something in motion. We cannot access the situation based on the snapshot alone, as the snapshot does not contain data to decide how something is evolving from one phase to the next or moving from one point to the next. Based on the snapshot or even the 15-minute frame, as Shelby experienced in *Memento*, we cannot assign or evaluate the meaning associated with the situation, event, or experience. Therefore, the synthesis of retention, presentation, and protention enables us to establish and sustain the coherence of our lived experiences, evaluate the possible and actual direction of movement, sense the movement through time and give it meaning.

Protention is the anticipation of "a range of possible futures" (Blattner, 2020: 16) or a "range of possible developments" (Blattner, 2020: 17), some of these more probable than others (Fuchs, 2013). Because we experience the future as open, then according to Blattner, "protention is far more indeterminate than retention," while "In retention, you retain what you have *in fact* experienced." (Blattner, 2020: 17 *emphasis added*). For example, in observing an object's movement or development, we are tacitly aware that an object at point B is actually an object "at point B-as-having-earlier-been-at-point-A" (Blattner, 2020: 16). Therefore, Blattner defines retention as the *recollection* of recorded experiences. A recollection of *recorder* past experiences could be erroneous and biased, but nevertheless, it provides the grounding for the present impression and pre-visioning the immediate future. Therefore, even if erroneous and biased, it is material for pre-visioning. Pre-visioning is essential for temporality as "Temporality temporalizes itself primordially out of the future" (Heidegger, 1927/1962: 380).

Pre-visioning is driven by our current momentary expectations structured by our internal protentions (Blattner, 2020). Protention opens up "a field of possibilities" (Fuchs, 2013: 85), a multiplicity of possibilities with different perceived probabilities. The seen possibilities and their respective likelihood are determined by the selective synthesis of retentions, impressions, and intentions in the current moment. In this selective synthesis process, protention works as preparation for the future by constantly inhibiting or dis-actualizing inadequate associations (Fuchs, 2013: 85). Therefore, protention works as a filter that helps us focus our attention and determines the perceived probabilities of the available possibilities. "If protention is disturbed, the disactualisation of unsuitable associations and impulses will also fail" (Fuchs, 2013: 86). Therefore, without protention as a filter we will simultaneously be equally open and equally unprepared to all possibilities regardless of their suitability, utility, and probability. Moreover, as in the case of disturbed protention, the experience is evaluated in the mode of conscious reflection, which means retrospectively, it is missing an intuitive and "spontaneous linking of the *primal impression* with protention and retention" (Fuchs, 2013: 87). Therefore, because retrospective and conscious reflection always comes too late compared to the temporal coherence of implicit temporality, disturbed protention tends to cause perceived fragmentation, disorientation, and delays.

Also, as the future with its protained "range of possible developments" is perceived as more open and undetermined than the past, the actual development or our future experience might fall outside the range of expectations. If the process unfolds outside the expected pre-visioned range of possibilities, we would be unable to make sense of the experience (Blattner, 2020). In that case, we may experience a disruption in the continuous flow of experience. The perceived fragmentation of the coherent temporality alerts us that we are in some (more or less existential) crisis.

An event or experience occurring outside the pre-visioned range of possibilities may create abrupt and unexpected interruptions in the sensed temporal continuity. It forces us out of the pre-reflective mode to conscious reflection. Fuchs distinguishes clearly between different temporal levels, "the basic or micro-level of *internal time-consciousness* (Husserl) and the extended or *life-history* level of personal temporality" (Fuchs, 2013: 76). He uses the concepts of implicit and explicit temporality. Implicit temporality refers to an intuitive, pre-reflectively lived experience, where we lose the sense of time while being completely immersed in the fluid and effortless performance of activity directed towards immediate goals. In this mode of being, temporality corresponds to the continuous flow. In the words of Husserl cited in Fuchs, it is an ongoing *passive* or automatic process of synthesis where protention, retention, and presentation are merged into a coherent whole, where "neither past nor future stands out" (Fuchs, 2013: 77). According to Fuchs, to be in the mode of implicit temporality, two conditions should be met—"the basic continuity of consciousness" (Fuchs, 2013:77) and "the basic *energetic* momentum of mental life" (Fuchs, 2013: 78); that is, a spontaneous drive to the future (see the model on the left in Fig. 4.1).

Explicit temporality, on the other hand, is consciously reflected temporal experience "produced primarily through a *disturbance or negation*" that interrupts "the steady duration of the primary *becoming*" (Fuchs, 2013: 79) by shock, disappointment, shame, amazement, break or loss. The disturbance or negation creates a rift and splits. Respectively, the disturbance splits the present from the past by disconnecting *now* from *no longer* and the future from the present by disconnecting *not yet* from *now* (Fuchs, 2013) (see the model on the right in Fig. 4.1). According to Fuchs (2013: 79), the disturbance "is experienced as closely bound up

4 Temporality—Endogenous and Subjective

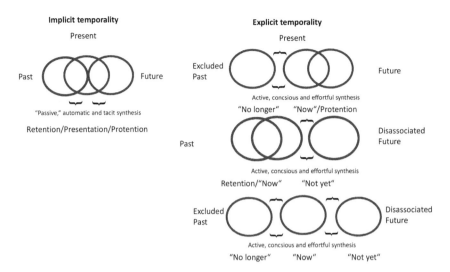

Fig. 4.1 Implicit and explicit temporalities

with certain time-specific emotions: the 'now' with surprise, astonishment or shock; the 'no longer' with regret, grief or remorse; the 'not yet' with desire, impatience, yearning or hope." Therefore, these experienced disconnections, irrespective of their direction, tend to create emotional tensions containing elements of displeasure and suffering (Fuchs, 2013).

Figure 4.1 presents coherent implicit temporality, where the past and future are merged in the present through the fluid and almost passive synthesis of retention and protention, and the three possible types of explicit temporality. In the latter case, the experienced time is divided into three dimensions of past, present, and future, which may appear as either the past or future disconnected from the present, or in the more severe case of temporal fragmentation, where *both* past and future are disconnected from the present. Both the terms, *excluded past* and *disassociated future* (Pulk, 2017), refer to situations where the perceived coherence and continuity are broken down and maintaining our endogenous temporality is challenged, for example, as could happen in the case of planned organizational interventions (see also Sect. 4.1.4). Bridging the gaps in the mode of explicit temporality requires an active synthesis of memories and expectations to overcome the fragmentation and restore to coherent continuity (Fuchs, 2013). A broken connection to the past and future could create confusion and disturbance, while restoring these connections could require substantial conscious effort.

4.1.3 Understanding Our Experiences and Ourselves in Time

Blattner (2020) amends Husserl's notion of protention and retention with Heidegger's tense and temporal aspect to explain the underlying dynamics of the protention-retention process. Blattner's explanation of the roles of tense and temporal aspect and the distinction in the way linguists and grammarians use the term *tense* is highly relevant. Blattner claims that in linguistics, the temporal position is expressed in *tense*.

In linguistics, according to Blattner, aspects signify different ways of viewing a situation's internal range of temporal choices. The perfect aspect stands for past experience, which has ongoing relevance. In contrast, the non-perfect aspect signifies a situation or experience that lacks continuous relevance. "The temporal character of the retention is not just that it retains the *past*, but that it retains the *past as relevant* to the present" (Blattner, 2020: 17 *emphasis in original*). This means, we constantly ignore a large amount of information by not paying attention to everything we are experiencing (Blattner, 2020). Instead, our attention is selective, meaning we do not randomly catalogue everything that takes place (Callender, 2017). Therefore, in the case of retention, the question is not simply about the past but about the relevant past, or more precisely, about the past seen as relevant in the present for the future. However, while distinguishing between relevant and non-relevant; that is, *Perfect* and *Non-perfect* elements of experience, we are moving "beyond tense to aspect" (Blattner, 2020: 18). According to Blattner, in *Being and Time* Heidegger "signals the centrality of the Perfect aspect" (Blattner, 2020: 19) as indicating *what* is relevant from the past.

In addition, Heidegger links action with future-oriented goal-directedness or with the *Telic* aspect. The *Telic* aspect expresses the result-orientation of the action, "for-the-sake-of-which" (Heidegger, 1927/1962: 119, 122). By adding the phenomena of relevance and direction to

Husserl's analysis, Heidegger emphasizes that we do not retain and protain everything but we select what we retain and protain and what do not retain and protain (Blattner, 2020). It could be said that while the *Perfect* aspect indicates *what* is relevant, the *Telic* aspect indicates *how* what is relevant is relevant; the *Telic* aspect shapes *how the past is relevant in the present for the future*. Therefore, as Blattner (2020) claims, temporal aspects do not denote duration or (dis)continuity related to occurrence, change, and development over time. Instead, temporal aspects allow us to reflect on more profound and more existential questions, like "questions about failing to face up to what already matters about the past and failing to respond to what we are called upon to do" (Blattner, 2020: 25). In other words, temporal aspects, although not directly tensed but still time-related, allow us to reflect on our authenticity.

To some extent, a similar idea is expressed by Schütz in his analysis of the temporality of human action. Schütz (1967), like Mead (1932/2002), views human action as intimately tied to the present. Schütz (1962/1982) distinguishes between *in-order-to* and *because-of* motives. As a rule, human action is future-oriented, and the relation humans have to things is mediated through future expectations and anticipations to achieve or accomplish something. Schütz (1962/1982) describes the drive to achieve something as *in-order-to* motivation. Schütz claims that in contrast to *in-order-to* motives with the extrinsic aim to accomplish something, event trajectories belong to the private domains of specific individuals and are informed by these individuals' biographies, which are the foundations for silent *because-of* motives (Schütz, 1962/1982). According to Schütz (1962/1982), the bodily internalized *because-of* motivation remains mostly an unconscious, background guide for directing our actions. Because the *because-of* motive is a part of our personal histories, an actor in his action is not necessarily aware of his *because-of* motives, which are giving direction to his actions (Pulk, 2016). Whether acknowledged consciously or carried on unconsciously, *because-of* motives could either inhibit or support our actions significantly. However, knowing our future-oriented *in-order-to* motives could explain only half of the story, as the hidden *because-of* motive, which carries the past relevance, completes the meaning of our actions.

Although the nature of the *because-of* motives in Schütz's theorization seems to be more implicit and unconscious than the relevance in Heidegger's *Perfect* temporal aspect, we can draw some parallels between Heidegger's temporal aspects and Schütz' motives. We can view the *because-of* motive as representing the *Perfect* temporal aspect and the goal-oriented *in-order-to* motive, the *Telic* aspect. The essential commonality between the views of Heidegger and Schütz is that they both see these temporal aspects or motives working simultaneously. That is to say, neither the temporal aspects—the *perfect* and *telic*—nor the *in-order-to* and *because-of* motives are ordered sequentially as tenses. Instead, both perform as pulling-pushing pairs working simultaneously in the present. Blattner (2020: 21), claims, "the *telic* aspect does not succeed the *perfect* aspect" and supports his claim with reference to Heidegger, who states, "The future is *not later* than having been, and having been is *not earlier* than the Present" (Heidegger, 1927/1962: 401 *emphasis in original*). Merleau-Ponty agrees with Heidegger that the past and future are always components of the present; they cannot exist somewhere else (Merleau-Ponty, 2002: 478). Therefore, if both past and future exist in the present, then instead of the sequence, the question is about the internal temporal coherence of the situation, event, or experience. In other words, the question is about the coherence of the *because-of* and *in-order-to* motives or the *perfect* and *telic* aspects about the relevance of the past directed to the future (Blattner, 2020).

Viewing the *Perfect* and *Telic* aspects working in pairs in the present and signifying what is relevant from the past for our current concerns and how, means, that either way, a shift in one goes hand-in-hand with a shift in the other. How some past event, situation, or experience is relevant to current or future concerns (the *telic* aspect) changes what is relevant in this past experience. Similarly, a shift in the *Perfect* aspect or what we have paid attention to as relevant changes how it is projected to the future. Therefore, "because the *Perfect* aspects of relevance and the *Telic* aspect of projecting forward are not directly tensed phenomena" (Blattner, 2020: 22), it is possible to change the trajectory of events or developments without changing the past but by changing the configuration of the *Perfect-Telic* aspects. As presented in Fig. 4.2, viewing temporal aspects (*Perfect* and *Telic*) being represented by the vertical axis and temporal

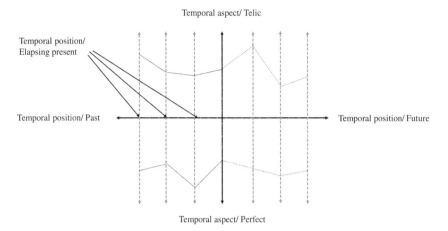

Fig. 4.2 The *possible shape* of our life as a combination of temporal aspects and temporal positions

positions (past, present, future) by the horizontal axis, it is possible to *visualize the shape of our life*. Although Fig. 4.2 is quite abstract, it helps us grasp how subjective temporality and the shape of our life, marked with the striped area, are forming in the combination of the temporal aspects and temporal positions. As Blattner (2020) explains, it is possible to make a mid-story shift and change what is relevant about the past and how it is relevant for the present and future without changing the past itself.

4.1.4 Temporal Continuity of and in Organizations

Fuchs's (2013) distinction between implicit and explicit temporality is also helpful in making sense of and understanding the nature of temporality in organizational settings (see Fig. 4.1 in Sect. 4.1.2). Implicit temporality helps us understand how organizational temporality could happen tacitly through the articulation of organizational meaning structures maintained by everyday ongoing activities and interactions (Hernes, 2014a). The expression *being in the flow* refers to experiencing coherent connections between an immediate past and an immediate future. On the one hand, explicit temporality could help us understand how different (un)planned interventions could lead to unexpected difficulties caused either by the *excluded past* or *disassociated future* (Pulk, 2016, 2017). Broken connections to the past or future bring time to the fore. To be able to move forward, they require effortful (re)creation of plausible connections across the past, present, and future through explicit temporality (Kaplan & Orlikowski, 2013; Weick, 1995). On the other hand, understanding the dynamics of explicit temporality is crucial in connecting either chronologically distant or qualitatively different pasts and futures in the present (see Fig. 4.1 in Sect. 4.1.2).

For example, the study conducted by Kaplan and Orlikowski (2013) focuses on the strategy creation process in an organization facing very high uncertainty about its future. In this sense, the coherence between past, present, and future was broken because the highly uncertain future created a fragmentation by standing to the fore and requiring active resynthesis across temporal dimensions. What is interesting about their study is the fact that although there were multiple options available for the future, the company had significant temporal struggles in resolving tensions related to the establishment of a new strategic direction. Kaplan and Orlikowski found that "a new view of the future could not take hold unless it is woven into a coherent, plausible, and acceptable strategic account that articulates *how such a future could emerge from a particular understanding of the past and a specific assessment of present concerns*" (Kaplan & Orlikowski, 2013: 967 *emphasis added*). Kaplan and Orlikowski (2013) demonstrate that the plausibility of a strategic account demanded that the temporal connections between past, present, and future were established and maintained. And only establishing and maintaining explicit temporality enabled organizational actors to construct an organizational future in a plausible manner and commit to working to achieve that future. Importantly, without creating a plausible strategic account, it was impossible to secure employee commitment to the strategic change (Pulk, 2017).

Kaplan and Orlikowski's study indicates that even when the explicit temporality does not cause a crisis, the situation may require serious effort to reflect and reconsider the circumstances and decide how to restore the continuity. However, it is important to note that a temporal crisis where the taken for granted implicit temporality is broken provides an opportunity to construct a new and different temporal direction of movement or temporal trajectory (Hernes, 2017). That is to say, while recognizing time is important, it is not sufficient, "*The trajectory also matters*" (Vedeler, 2015: 146 *emphasis in original*). Therefore, understanding how implicit and explicit temporality work could be helpful in attempts to intentionally redirect the course of an organization by purposefully reconfiguring the connections between the pasts, present, and futures (Schultz & Hernes, 2013) and synthesizing different narratives (Fuchs, 2013).

Surprisingly, Sutton (1987), with his study on dying organization, illustrates temporal coherence and its importance in an organizational setting. Sutton (1987) found that when an organization's death was announced in advance, employees increased their efforts for the dying organization, contrary to leaders' predictions. He stresses the advance announcement that organizational death will occur as a decisive turning point that enabled organizational members to interpret their organization as discontinuous (Sutton, 1987). As a result, although the organization itself was seen as discontinuous, the temporal continuity was maintained. The future, or to be more precise, the perspective of no future, was connected to the organizational present; it was not hard for employees to see that the end was coming and subsequently relate to that fact. Therefore, we can conclude that it is easier for organizational members to deal with the organizational change or rather becoming, which, despite the possible negative end results, is presented in a temporally consistent manner (Pulk, 2016, 2017).

On the one hand, in the organizational settings, actors operate in an ongoing present, where "the organization's future is continually enacted from past experience using materials available in the present" (Schultz & Hernes, 2013: 1). Materials about the past available in the present could be in different forms of memory, such as oral, material, or textual (Schultz & Hernes, 2013), which means that the continuous enactment of the organization's future using past experience available in the present is a somewhat conscious effort referring to explicit temporality.

On the other hand, Hernes (2014a) refers to organizational meaning structures as carriers of organizational tacit intentionality that in its entirety is available to organizational actors only through subsidiary awareness (Polanyi, 1962, 1967). Meaning structures are not "structures of representation, but as performative structures created and sustained through acts of articulation" (Hernes, 2014a: 110). Hernes adds that, as these are created and sustained through performativity, "the becoming of the meaning structure and this holistic impression can only be intuited. Intuition captures a sense of movement, the meaning structure in the making, about the meaning of the organization in the light of its movement through time, experienced in the present" (2014: 109). Intuition works smoothly without the need for explicit reflection and conscious reasoning. Therefore, implicit temporality works in organizations through organizational meaning structures.

Therefore, ongoing (organizational) temporality functions based on the same logic as subjective temporality, and it has similar types and structures. Furthermore, the claims that a richer reservoir of past experiences (extended span) enables greater flexibility in constructing hypothetical future scenarios and identities (e.g., Abram et al., 2014; Luhmann, 2018; Weick, 1995) are valid in organizational studies. For example, Schultz and Hernes et al. (2013), Hernes and Schultz (2020), and Hernes et al. (2021) show how focusing on a different set of past elements or possible future elements differing significantly from the present and *translating* these into the present, past and future respectively, makes it possible to create different new opportunities and realities.

Schultz and Hernes' (2013) study in the LEGO Group could serve here as an illustration of how the shift in the *perfect* aspect of the past; that is, what from the past is considered as relevant in the present for the future, makes a strategic shift possible without challenging the organization's core identity. In their study, Schultz and Hernes show how the LEGO Group successfully redefined their strategy by changing the configuration of the elements they had previously focused on from the past. The company defined its new strategic future by selecting a different set of elements from its past. Although not highlighted in the previous strategy, these new selected elements of the past were accessible to the actors in the LEGO Group belonging to the collective past of the organization.

4.2 Temporal Idealism, Endogenous Temporality and the Agency of Passing Time

Although I do not intend to go deep into the philosophical discussion about temporal idealism, relationism, or realism (Bardon, 2013), I think it is worth briefly mentioning them. In short, temporal idealism is the opposite of temporal realism (Bardon, 2013). Temporal realism claims that time exists independent of human experience as objective, actual, and real (see Chap. 3). From the perspective of temporal realism, past, present, and future are viewed as different and separate temporal categories defined either in dualistic terms or relative to one another. On the other hand, temporal idealism views time and temporality as a mental construct rooted in the human experience and interpretation. Said differently, temporal idealism claims that time and temporality are mentally constructed and they exist only in the realm of human experience (e.g., Simpson et al., 2020). Therefore, following the idea of temporal idealism, it can be concluded that outside the domain of human experience there is no time; time is just a pure intuition.

For example, Klempe (2015) points out that both Saint Augustine and Kant, although focusing on different aspects, one on actually experienced time and the other on ideal aspects of time, come to the conclusion that an ideal understanding of time is different from actual time. This difference stems from the fact that only an ideal understanding of time includes the concepts of past, present, and future. The expression *an ideal understanding of time* refers not to perfect time or perfect timing but to the idea of temporal idealism, according to which, time, including past and future, exists only in the human mind. We can track elements of temporal idealism in the works of Bergson, Mead, Merleau-Ponty, and Heidegger. For example, Blattner's (1999) book titled "Heidegger's temporal idealism" is a profound analysis of Heidegger's existential philosophy, where Dasein is a core concept. Dasein refers to the existential being of a human entity able to focus on its personal existence and question it. Thus, Dasein is an entity able to problematize its being or, in the words of Heidegger, "That entity which in its Being has this very Being as an issue" (Heidegger, 1927/1962: 68).

However, Rousse (2021) challenges Blattner's interpretation of Heidegger as a failed temporal idealist and claims that Heidegger's *deworlded time*, or *natural time* stands for "an endogenous sequentiality in which events are ordered independently of Dasein and the stand it takes on its being" (2021: 1). Based on Dreyfus (1991), in his interpretation of Heidegger, Rousse distinguishes the phenomenological world or the world where Dasein lives and the ideal time of that world from the natural or physical world evolving according to natural or real time. According to Rousse, "For Heidegger, the natural universe unfolds as an endogenously sequential ordering of events that Dasein can study through natural science and by which Dasein is constrained in its everyday activities" (Rousse, 2021: 2). Rousse concludes that Heideggerian "World-time turns out to be a co-production of Dasein's non-sequential originary temporality and the endogenous sequentiality of events in nature" (Rousse, 2021: 1).

Importantly, Merleau-Ponty highlights ideal time as an escape route from being imprisoned in the present. According to him, "Through the ideal nature of time, [the subject] ceases to be imprisoned in the present" (Merleau-Ponty, 2002: 481). Therefore, the ideal nature of time allows us to extend our being both to the past and to the future; it enables us to escape the present and sequential, spatial, and linear time.

However, instead of diving more deeply into this debate about temporal idealism versus temporal realism, I would recall the quote from Baars cited earlier that "we are always already living *in* time, and in some sense, we are always already *living* time," and in that sense, it could be helpful to keep our mind open to both these qualitatively distinctive times, their qualitative differences and different implications for our being and becoming in the world.

4.2.1 Endogenous Temporality—Expanding Beyond Temporal Idealism

From Baars' quote cited above, "we are always already living time. Although (*unlike stones or trees*) we can be aware of this" (Baars, 2012: 144 *emphasis added*), we can understand that although stones and trees are not aware of their temporality, they have temporality or, maybe more precisely, they are temporal as well. This implies that the pasts and futures of stones or trees or whatever objects or things are intrinsically connected despite their assumed unawareness of these connections. A similar idea, that is, the idea that *things* like stones and trees are temporal, is expressed by Merleau-Ponty (1999). He claims, "[Time] arises from my relation to things. Within things themselves, the future and the past are in a kind of eternal state of pre-existence and survival" (Merleau-Ponty, 2002: 478). Merleau-Ponty underlines that the past and future are always in things from the phenomenological perspective, and thus, things are temporal.[3] But it is somehow inappropriate to discuss subjective temporality in relation to *things* or mental and physical objects or entities. But there are still intrinsic connections to pasts and futures, which allows us to speak about their endogenous temporality.

Hernes et al. (2013: 2) have stated that temporality, in the broader sense, means "the ways in which the passing of time shapes the very being of things". First, this definition assumes that although the passing of time shapes and possibly changes the way things are or maybe even their nature, these things have duration or continuity in time. In other words, as they extend across past, present, and future, then irrespective of their awareness of time or temporality or lack of it, they are in the becoming. Second is, *things* that in one or another form move through time (Hernes et al., 2021: 367) are temporal. Therefore, we should not constrain ourselves with temporal idealism and view temporality as something that belongs to humans only or depends only on the experience of human actors. Instead, it could be helpful to pay attention and understand the temporality of *things*—relationships, ideas, events (for events, see Chap. 6), and activities (for activities, see the next chapter). That is, anything that resists instant vanishing together with perishing time but maintains its own becoming in passing time through some existing continuous pattern or structure either in the material or in the immaterial world around us. Mead, relying on Whitehead, explains:

---

[3] Referring to time as born in a relationship, one could claim that Merleau-Ponty argues for relationism, that is, "what we have to say about time has to do with our mode of organizing and relating events" (Bardon, 2013: 175).

Professor Whitehead interprets relativity in terms of events passing in a four-dimensional Minkowski[4] world. The order in which they pass, however, is relative to a consentient set. The consentient set is determined by its relation to a percipient event or organism. The percipient event establishes a lasting character of here and there, of now and then, and is itself an enduring pattern. The pattern repeats itself in the passage of events. These recurrent patterns are grasped together or prehended into a unity, which must *have as great a temporal spread* as the *organism requires to be what it is*, whether this period is found in the revolutions of the *electrons in an iron atom or in the specious present of a human being*. Such a percipient event or organism establishes a consentient set of patterns of events that endure in the relations of here and there, of now and then. (Mead, 1932/2002: 172 emphasis added)

From this quote, it appears that while temporality and passing time are closely related terms, the nature of passing time is relative. Furthermore, a temporal spread of events or organisms may vary depending on what is required for something to be what it is. Although a more detailed discussion of events and event-based time will follow in Chap. 6, it is worth underlining the idea expressed in the quote that a temporal spread of an event, just like a temporal spread of an organism, depends on what is required for an event to be an event. This quote answers the often-heard question raised from the chronometric perspective that "how long does an event last?" or "how long should an event last to count as an event?" Therefore, answering that question from the standpoint of endogenous temporality, the event's duration is as long as it takes for an event to be or become what it is. Finally, temporality applies equally to an iron atom and a human being. In other words, whether the entity or substance in passing time has a duration it also has temporality regardless of being consciously aware of its temporality or unaware of it. Having duration or persistence, in turn, requires a connection between the past and future in the present. In other words, temporality means connections across the pasts, present, and futures held up by the becoming entity or subject it constitutes. However, temporality is possible only in flowing or passing time. Time, perceived as continuously and simultaneously both as

---

[4] A more detailed description of specific characterization of Minkowski's time-space could be found, for example, in Callender (2017).

approaching and as passing, allows the emerging sensation of temporality. It cannot be temporality if time stays still. And time does not stay still; instead, time is productive (Callender, 2017:157).

4.2.2 The Agency of Time

To be productive presupposes agency. Indeed, various utterances or sayings express the agency attributed to time. For example, time is viewed as a healer—"time heals all wounds", indicates that our emotional pain, sadness, disappointment, or grief gradually diminishes as time passes. There is a saying, "time takes all and gives all", which adds some generosity to time but still with reservations. However, generally, the agency of time is related to its passing and perishing nature, as emphasized by the murderous aspect of the time. For example, expressions like "Time is a great teacher, but unfortunately it kills all its pupils" (Berlioz quoted in Callender, 2017: xx) or "Time is a big invisible thing that will kill you" (Callender, 2017: 1), reveals the agency of time in very dark colours. While these may sound a bit exaggerated, it is hard to deny the fatality of time for mortals such as humans. Hernes, in line with the principal idea expressed by these quotes, explains:

> A world on the move signifies temporal evanescence, or perishing of time, as Whitehead formulated it, of the world that surrounds us at present. Instead of assuming that things stay the way they are, they are constantly threatened with disappearance, at least in their present form. What influences the work of practitioners, and consequently those who analyse their actions, is the acuteness associated with the perishability. (Hernes, 2014a: 45)

However, the quote borrowed from Callender indicates that our relationship with time is not one-directional. Being a pupil of time reveals an interaction between the subject and time. Therefore, our relationship to time is not one-directional but we have a reciprocal relationship with time. Hernes emphasizes that the perishing aspect of time comes hand in hand with an emerging aspect. Passing time could be viewed in a less grim manner without diminishing the agency of time. Hernes claims, "the passing of time throws us continually into situations in which we recreate past and future" (2014: 45). Therefore, in making choices, we create time, while time as continuously emerging brings new situations that allows new experiences and enables and forces us to temporalize ourselves. By bringing new situations, emerging time opens new possibilities while eliminating previous ones. While changing things and the world around us and our relationships to these things and to the world (Merleau-Ponty, 2002), time also changes us "because we inescapably form part of a moving world, and as we observe the changes around us, we respond to them and anticipate others, and our reactions and anticipations become part of our experiential past" (Hernes, 2014a: 45).

Therefore, maintaining duration or continuity in passing time does not mean that something or somebody stays as it/he/she is. It could be that the phrase *to be what it is* is slightly misleading, as allowing *it* to be interpreted as something or somebody stays in a static state. Although, trying to remain as we are in passing time could be highly demanding, and in most cases simply impossible. Because perishing time exercises its agency and does its work by shaping everything and everybody in it, an alternative to the *to be what it is* could be to become what it could become. But what something or somebody could become has usually multiple options which change in time, as possibilities which were once open have disappeared with perishing time while the emerging time has brought new possibilities and opened new directions.

Although becoming is conditioned by past decisions and the contingencies of choices, its exact trajectory is undetermined. Viewing becoming as a form of being supplemented with temporal agency or, in the words of Hernes, "carving out of temporal existence (present, past, and future) from the passing of time" (2014: ix) on the one hand, and on the other hand, time as having agency paints the picture of the continuous duel or dance between the organisms' and events' becoming and their struggle to actualise their potentiality on the one side, and agentic emerging and perishing time on the other. Depending on the nature of becoming, this duel or dance between becoming and agentic time seems to be the source of almost endless creativity and creation. However, the main focus of the becoming is not to be continuous but to enable continuity in the continuously perishing time. In the words of Whitehead, "There is a becoming of continuity, but no continuity of becoming" (Whitehead, 1929/1978: 35).

4.2.3 Becoming, the Realization of Possibilities, and Actualization of Potentialities

Becoming is an emerging self-replicating process in the temporally tangled web-like world (Edwards & Jaros, 1994; Hernes, 2008, 2014). While the continuously passing character of time means that time is simultaneously emerging and perishing (Mead, 1932/2002; Whitehead, 1929/1978), the simultaneously emerging and perishing nature of time enables and even forces becoming. The concept of *becoming* (Whitehead, 1929/1978) presupposes temporality made possible by being in the flow of time. Becoming is an extension or *prehension* (Whitehead, 1929/1978: 18) in time. It is "embodied *birthing* of new elements" (Callender, 2017: 103). The main focus of becoming is not to be continuous but to enable continuity in continuously perishing time. Therefore, becoming is profoundly temporal.

Becoming is an activity characterizing the entire universe and everything in it. Therefore, becoming is not something reserved for humans only, but the natural way all things are—in the becoming. In the case of human beings, becoming could occur either through the implicit or explicit temporality discussed above. Implicit temporality indicates that becoming can happen smoothly, naturally, and almost unnoticeably. Everything evolves or degrades gradually and becomes different. Only when the "implicit time of pure becoming" (Fuchs, 2013: 79) is negated or somehow disturbed or hindered "the explicit experience of time arises" (Fuchs, 2013: 79), and with the explicit experience of time and temporality, conscious decisions and effortful leaps may demand our attention. Becoming is not predetermined, and thus it presupposes openness, the possibility to become. Heidegger, referring to human existentiality, claims that "Dasein is in each case essentially its own possibility, it can, in its very Being, *choose* itself and win itself; it can also lose itself and never win itself; or only *seem* to do so" (Heidegger, 1927/1962: 68).

Consequently, the becoming could be more or less intense, more or less visible, and dramatic. The less intense becoming is described by Helin et al. (2014) as "limited coping". Limited coping refers to realizing the possible; that is, to the realization of one possibility from multiple possibilities that are available to maintain the same course or trajectory. It is essential to keep in mind that trying to keep things as they are in passing time requires effort. Therefore, managing to stay the same could be viewed as an achievement. Therefore, *limited coping* does not necessarily signify something unimportant and somehow inferior, even though compared to the actualization of potentiality, it refers to something that is possibly less intense and dramatic than creating a *new* or transforming qualitatively.

Potentiality is the central thought in Whitehead's process theory (Whitehead, 1929/1978, Whitehead, 1938), reflecting that the world is constantly emerging.

> If the universe be interpreted in terms of static actuality, then potentiality vanishes. Everything is just what it is. Succession is mere appearance, rising from the limitation of perception. But if we start with process as fundamental, then the actualities of the present are deriving their characters from the process and are bestowing their characters upon the future. Immediacy is the realization of the potentialities of the past, and is the storehouse of the potentialities of the future. Hope and fear, joy and disillusion, obtain their meaning from the potentialities essential in the nature of things. (Whitehead, 1938: 99-100)

From the processual viewpoint, everything is in the process of becoming, and therefore how things are at the moment in their actual state; that is, in their actuality, does not represent their ultimate being. Heidegger shares this view in his conceptualization of Dasein's being as potentiality by writing:

> Dasein is not something present-at-hand which possesses its competence for something by way of an extra; it is primarily Being-possible. Dasein is in every case what it can be, and in the way in which it is its possibility. ... The Being-possible which Dasein is existentially in every case, is to be

sharply distinguished both from empty logical possibility and from the contingency of something present-at-hand. (Heidegger, 1927/1962: 183)

Following the quote from Heidegger, potentiality-for-Being is not necessarily obvious, prominent, or visible, does not necessarily follow any logical path, and therefore is not readily available. Instead, the actualization of potentiality is not *present-at-hand* but demands creative power. According to Helin et al. (2014: 9), "creation needs to be understood as the actualisation of the virtual, rather than as realisation of the possible." Although, it could be argued that in some cases, the actualization of potential could be based on both previous and current limited coping. Therefore, the realization of some possibilities may be more supportive of the actualization of potentialities than others.

However, as a counterpart to actuality, potentiality refers to something virtual, to something not yet here in the physical or actual form, and to something open as one of the multiple options to actualize (Helin et al., 2014). Hernes explains, "the two, potentiality and actuality, are mutually dependent, just as pronouncing a word depends on the existence of what is not pronounced, and presence depends on absence" (Hernes, 2014a: 126). As a counterpart to that which is, potentiality "involves imagination about how things *might become* in the light of the possibilities that lie ahead, but also about how things of the past *might be* perceived differently" (Hernes, 2014a: 5 *emphasis added*). Surprisingly, the importance of imagination or, respectively, lack of it, was highlighted in the letter of an eminent economist at London School of Economics (LSE) in their response to Queen Elizabeth. Namely, the Queen visited LSE in November 2008 and referring to the global financial crises asked why nobody saw it coming. The British Academy response letter, signed by LSE professor Tim Besley, a member of the Bank of England monetary policy committee, and the eminent historian of government, Peter Hennessy, concludes that the principal cause behind the failure to foresee the financial crisis and its magnitude was, "*a failure of the collective imagination of many bright people*, both in this country and internationally, to understand the risks to the system as a whole" (The British Academy, July 2009 cited in Rodriguez et al., 2016: 22 *emphasis added*). The letter confirms that even leading economists, usually prized for their rational models, acknowledge the utmost importance of imagination in seeing potentialities and the ways their actualization may shape our futures.

But in the abundance of possibilities (Hernes, 2014a), not all possibilities have an equal probability (Fuchs, 2013) of being selected for realization or of even being recognized (Kahneman, 2011). Therefore, not all potentialities have equal probability of being actualized. At every single moment, there are always more options open than we could to take. Meaning, at every single moment, what something "is (or was or will be), ... could also be otherwise" (Luhmann, 1995: 106). Therefore, there are multiple possibilities open to become otherwise and in their perceived taken for grantedness things could be much more fragile than we tend to think.

On the one hand, being available as one of the numerous options to actualize, there is no guarantee that a particular potentiality will be actualized. It could remain unactualized, and the possibility of its actualization may become lost in the irreversibly passing time (Kahneman, 2011). On the other hand, the capacity to actualize temporal non-actualities entails the risk of remembering inaccurately or having unsound anticipations (Luhmann, 1995: 46). Therefore, it could be highly desirable that some potentialities remain unactualized.

According to Hernes, "every act exhibits some potentiality for what may come, and even for what has been" (Hernes, 2014a: 37). "By actualizing the potentiality in the situation" (Hernes, 2014a: 199), actors can stabilize their being in perishing time. In other words, our action in the present situation both creates and constrains our future and past potentialities (Chia, 1999; Hernes, 2014a). By actualizing certain potentialities, actors could maintain their movement trajectories, even while the actualization of different potentialities could stabilize movement along different trajectories (Hernes, 2017). However, every act of stabilization includes the seed of destabilization, as illustrated by MacKay and Chia's (2013) study on the Canadian automobile industry. MacKay and Chia argue about what they call "unowned change" which emerged as the unintended consequences of some choices. However, these unintended consequences could be viewed as actualized potentiality resulting from the chain of possibilities realized earlier.

4 Temporality—Endogenous and Subjective 149

Thus, potentiality entails risk—the risk of remaining unactualized and the risk of becoming otherwise. Selecting a particular possibility from the range of available possibilities or just deciding between the options to act or not to act has consequences; some of these may have far-reaching implications—they can actualise undesirable potentiality. Meaning, potentiality stands both for the future opportunity and for risk, for something not actual or readily available in the present but potentially possible for better or for worse. The actualization of potential entails a shift in the existing trajectory. Put differently, it is not possible to actualize potentiality by keeping the same trajectory. However, it could also be the case that it is impossible to maintain the current trajectory even if we attempt to do so. The latter tends specially to apply to negative potentialities—a' la the climate crisis or accidents. But the potential is not something related only to the future. Every actuality has a potential to be otherwise. Therefore, there is potential for the present to become otherwise.

As showed by MacKay & Chia, 2013), the achieved stabilization could often be more fragile than we tend to think, meaning one careless act can activate a different trajectory or push us along a different trajectory. Interestingly, the past, in its openness, also has potentialities to become otherwise as illustrated by the recent discovery of numerous unmarked graves of indigenous children in Canada that prompted outrage leading to the destruction of statues of British Queens and several catholic churches. While some of the incidents date back more than a hundred years, they displayed the potential to create strong reactions with social consequences actualized, so to speak, today.

The possibility to become otherwise and the risks related to the actualization of potentiality is vividly illustrated in the interactive movie "Black Mirror: Bandersnatch" by Slade et al. (2018). While watching the movie, the viewer/player is requested to make a series of choices about how he/she would act in specific situations and which possibilities to realize. Depending on the viewer/player's choices, the movie has many endings, actually so many that even the producer, Russell MacLean, is not sure about the exact number. Based on the general patterns of choices some hard to reach *golden egg* endings are so hard to reach that some scenes remain unseen by some people. Perhaps that is how it tends to be in real-life. However, in the decisive moments, the viewer/player has ten seconds to decide which one from the available possibilities he/she will realize. If the viewer does not make his/her choice, a default decision will be made for him/her. There are numerous possible paths, and depending on the decisions made, the movie's length varies substantially (ranging from less than an hour up to two and a half hours). In most cases, the interactive design of the movie allows the viewer/player to go back and redecide the last critical decision—the one, which changes the course of the story decisively. Some paths, although developing differently, are equifinal, while some endings may stay unreachable due to the choices made earlier in the movie, and hence, require a complete restart.

Notably, like becoming, potentiality is not reserved only for human beings. For example, Wallack (1980, in Hernes, 2014a: 14) describes the Whiteheadian stone, its becoming as a stone through time, and its potentiality for affecting other stones, human perception, soil enrichment, animals, and plants both in the immediate and remote environments. But although material objects are temporal and have potentiality, "only human co-presence can bring about change in the sense of exploiting the potentiality of a situation because it has the ability to recall a different past as well as project a different future, which is what confers agency upon the present" (Hernes, 2014a: 83). Therefore, humans play an essential role in actualizing the potentiality of the world they inhabit and their relationships with that world.

For example, Mattila et al. (2019) analyse the potential of foods to become waste and possibilities to reduce the potentiality of household food waste. With their study, the authors aim to understand how temporal inter-relations in humans (consumers) and non-humans (foodstuffs and kitchen appliances) enhance or inhibit the potentiality of food becoming waste. Apparently, it is not easy to reduce household food waste as Mattila et al. conclude, "Food waste reduction, integrating time and temporality, human and non-human action, appears a complex phenomenon" (Mattila et al., 2019: 1641). Representing an inefficient use of the resource, attempts to reduce food waste are an integral part of general efforts in line with concerns about sustainability. While food's potential to become waste is an undesirable option, something worth the effort to reduce and avoid, the actualization of some other potentialities may entail the risk of being upfront hazardous. For example, a nuclear power plant entails the potentiality of a fatal catastrophe as happened in 2011 in Fukushima, due to the earthquake and tsunami. A more severe case is Chernobyl, which took place decades ago in 1986. The Chernobyl catastrophe is a vivid example of how the human factor could trigger the actualization of potentialities that are fatal.

4.3 The Present and Now

At the EGOS annual colloquium 2019 in Edinburgh, in the time and temporality sub-theme, somebody wondered about the ontology of the future while stating, "we know the ontology of the present." That statement caught my attention. Do we really know the ontology of the present? Do we know what the present is? A glance at the literature reveals that there is no universal interdisciplinary agreement about the ontology of the present. Therefore, it is hard to claim that we know what the present is, or that what we know or think that we know about the present is unproblematic. It seems that the present is something treated as taken for granted, something that does not require a clear definition and conceptualization. It seems to be with the present like other things we tend to take as for granted—as soon as we try to grasp it, it slips away. Different questions pop up, like how long is the present? When does the present begin or end? What does it mean that the present is in between the past and future? How did we get from the past to the present? How can we get from the present to the future? How does the future turn to the present? What does now mean, and how does it differ from the present?

Based on tests performed in experimental psychology, Cravo and Haddad conclude that we literally live in the past as "Every sensation we have was physically caused by an event that took place in the past and might even have ceased to exist" (Cravo & Haddad, 2015: 116). However, both Mead (1932/2002) and Schütz (1967) see human action as intimately tied to the present. They see the present as the locus of action or ontological reality. The present is real while the past and future are imaginative (Bakken et al., 2013; Mead, 1932/2002), and as such, extending beyond the real (Bakken et al., 2013). The interpretation of the imaginative past, like the imaginary and expected future, are both mediated through the present or happening in the present (Hussenot & Missonier, 2016). Therefore, actors never escape the present; the past and the future are continually constructed using the materials of the present (Mead, 1932/2002).

Callender tries to tease our understanding about the present with the question, "do we experience the present?" (Callender, 2017: 180). This question, while probably well justified in physics, could lack relevance in human life. I am leaving aside mindfulness training to concentrate on the moment and *feeling* the present. In everyday life, we do not judge the existence/non-existence of the present based on whether we experience the present as such, and thus, framing this question in that way does not matter. What matters is that *we can experience only in the present, which gives* to the present its significance. Mead stresses that "Our values lie in the present, and past and future give us only the schedule of the means, and the plans of campaign, for their realisation" (Mead, 1932/2002: 108). Still, following schedules and realizing plans can take place in the present only because "the present as the locus of reality" is marked by "its becoming and its disappearing" (Mead, 1932/2002: 35).

Luhmann asserts that the present is "not a brief interval between past and future" but "nothing other than the difference between past and future" (Luhmann, 2018: 124), having its actuality only as a difference between the two non-actualities. The present "*is* only in that *it is no longer and not yet*" (Luhmann, 2018: 124 *emphasis in original*); an actuality that differentiates one non-actuality (past) from another non-actuality (future). Therefore, non-actual past and future situations are mobilized to cope with current actual situations, while coping with current issues in the present moment shapes "how the current situation and previous and future situations relate to each other" (Griesbach & Grand, 2013: 65). Put differently, while coping with current issues, actors choose a particular possibility to realize from a range of possibilities. Depending on the possibilities chosen for realization, actors form their subjective time by creating temporal connections between the current, previous, and future situations.

However, the present, being a pure difference, is undetermined and new at every moment (Luhmann, 2018). The ongoing present (Schultz & Hernes, 2013) in "its becoming and its disappearing" (Mead,

1932/2002: 35) enables the experience of flow and provides a basis for exercising our agency to decide and choose which of the available possibilities to realize (Callender, 2017). Still, it is important to note that the qualitative features of the ongoing or elapsing present are not homogeneous. Some moments in the present could be more decisive than others. The present could offer an instant moment that could radically change the trajectories of events and may have far-reaching consequences for better or for worse. Still, the present falls into the past, which means that possibilities in the flow of time are not fixed or permanent but may vanish (Helin et al., 2014). These decisive moments appear as unpredicted possibilities for the actualization of potentiality.

Dreyfus (1975: 151) explains that these instant moments apply "to any occasion in human life when one makes a decisive choice, a commitment which gives a definite form to one's future and a retroactive meaning to one's past". Sato and Valsiner (2010) call these decisive moments bifurcation points. In bifurcation points, the choice between alternative possibilities is made, and the course for the future is set, including a new range of possibilities. In the organization studies literature, that kind of unique moment is referred to as a potentially decisive "window of opportunity" (Tyre & Orlikowski, 1994). In these unique and decisive moments, the entire past could be reassessed, enabling us to set a completely new focus for the future. Because in the elapsing present, a specific "window of opportunity" may close and disappear, not appearing again; Kaplan and Orlikowski call this instant moment a "fleeting now" (Kaplan & Orlikowski, 2013: 967).

However, now, locating "outside of the realm of science" (Carnap, 1963: 38), could be a problematic concept (Callender, 2017; Rovelli, 2017). As Carnap explains,

> I remarked that all that occurs objectively can be described in science: on the one hand the temporal sequence of events is described in physics; and, on the other hand, the peculiarities of man's experiences with respect to time, including his different attitude toward past, present, and future, can be described and (in principle) explained in psychology. But Einstein thought that scientific descriptions cannot possibly satisfy our human

needs; that there is something essential about Now which is just outside of the realm of science. (Carnap, 1963: 37–38)

However, Klempe, referring to Heidegger, states that "time is only real as long as it is experienced as being, which is in the moment of the now" (Klempe, 2015: 16). In that sense, the word game on the label of Yogi tea, "The time is now—now is the time," hits the point. Klempe adds, referring once again to Heidegger, that to understand *the now*, we also need *the then*, meaning that the primary way to understand actual existence is through a particular time. Particular time indicates that both the phenomenological present and *now* refers to an egocentric temporal viewpoint, not to the allocentric temporal viewpoint (Callender, 2017). Meaning, it refers to our specific *now* as actuality exposed to the particular given past and future as non-actual time horizons (Luhmann, 2018: 123). Therefore, the now corresponds to our specific temporal frame and not to universally and objectively valid temporal relationships (Callender, 2017). In other words, we can only understand our actual existence through a particular time as the temporality of *our lived experience* occurring in the present. Our becoming, either through realizing the possible or actualization of the virtual, could happen only through action in the particular present. We do not have an alternative option available. Even if we prefer to live in the past or the future, we cannot do that. We have no other choice than to live in our present, which is the locus of our action (Mead, 1932/2002) and our actuality.

Therefore, even if from an external allocentric temporal viewpoint, it could be true that our action is lagging behind being a response or reaction to the stimulus from the past (Callender, 2017; Cravo & Haddad, 2015) and maybe even carried out in the past, it does not matter. What matters is that our action occurs in our particular present and has consequences in our particular future when it turns to the present. We create our future in the present, in the current moment—now. There is a scene in the TV serial "Fargo" season four, episode nine (Uppendahl et al., 2020), where an older man paints writing on a billboard next to the highway. When Rabbi Milligan drives by, the unfinished sentence *"The future is…"* annoys him. The Rabbi expresses his frustration about the uncertainty emerging as a combination of this unfinished sentence and his own unknown future. It is almost as if the Rabbi expects the slogan on the billboard to illuminate his future. The older man does not rush, knowing that he will be out of a job as soon as he finalises the text on the billboard.

The next time when the Rabbi happens to drive by the old man has just finished his task, and the Rabbi can read from the billboard, *"The future is now."* The Rabbi is confused about this solution and turns once again to the older man demanding an explanation. The older man offers different possible interpretations of the message—a claim about the unreliability of time, a desire to use time wisely and not waste it, or the arrival of the feared future or the fulfilment of the prediction (Uppendahl et al., 2020). From his personal perspective, the older man interpreted the *now* as the feared future has turned into the present, and he has become unemployed (with this approach, he reveals his time-centric view, see Sect. 3.3.1). However, when using an egocentric perspective, the billboard's message could be interpreted that at this very moment, you are creating your future. What you are doing now sets the course to your future, and the future is not far away but very close, embedded in our ongoing action in the very moment. The action that is taking place in the present with the direction to the future is spontaneously responsive to the living surroundings at the current moment (Shotter, 2010).

Therefore, the inability of physics to explain now (Callender, 2017: 225) does not disturb us much in our everyday life. As Luhmann points out, the calculation "(Tuesday between Monday and Wednesday)+(Wednesday between Tuesday and Thursday) = x" does not make much sense because "there is no total today" and therefore "that x cannot be resolved" (Luhmann, 2018: 122). We do not need *a total today* or *objective universal now* when we are not talking about the universal and objective present but about the egocentric and particular present. Furthermore, despite maybe lagging in objective terms, we have the agency to form both immediate and even more remote future through our action in the perceived present. The ongoing present in "its becoming and its disappearing" (Mead, 1932/2002: 35) enables the experience of flow, ongoing temporality, and the associated perception of agency (Callender, 2017). Our sense of agency tied to the continually refreshing or ongoing present (Callender, 2017; Schultz & Hernes, 2013) refers to the active efforts of actors to make connections across past, present, and future within the flow of time.

4.4 Futures and Pasts

Callender (2017) claims that we are immersed in a temporally asymmetric world. He points out two temporal asymmetries influencing our perceptions of reality. First, knowledge asymmetry means that we do not know what will happen in the future, while (we tend to think) we know what has happened in the past. We have formed some memories about the past that we lack about the future. However, he points out that it is not that we know so much more about the past than the future, but the way we know the past is different from how we know the future (Callender, 2017: 259, 274). Describing this asymmetric difference in our knowing, Valsiner states that the "past contains the unilinear actualized trajectory, and frees itself from the non-actualized earlier possible trajectories. In contrast, the future entails a variety of equally potential (not yet actualized) trajectories" (Valsiner, 2011: 142). Therefore, the future in its possibilities and unactualized potentialities is ambiguous and uncertain. Second, there is causal asymmetry or counterfactual dependency. Based on that, the future depends on present action in the way the past does not. "It's a plain fact of life that *our actions are sometimes effective in bringing about future goals, but rarely or never effective in bringing about past goals*" (Callender, 2017: 273 *emphasis in original*). Said differently, we have a sense of agency towards the future; we believe we can change and control, shape and create it, but we do not have this sense of agency towards the past (Torre, 2011). Explaining the asymmetry of counterfactual dependence, Lewis states:

> In short, I suggest that mysterious asymmetry between open future and fixed past is nothing else than the asymmetry of counterfactual dependence. The forking paths into the future—the actual one and all the rest—are the many alternative futures that would have come about under various counterfactual suppositions about the past. The one actual fixed past is the

one past that would remain actual under this same range of suppositions. (Lewis 1979: 462 cited in Callender, 2017: 259).

Indeed, it is common to see the past as known, concluded, and closed. The future, by contrast, is seen as unknown, open to change, evolving to some extent according to our intentions while happening partly against our expectations (Luhmann, 2018). Although Lewis' citation may resonate with the common understanding about the multiple possible futures anchored in the singular and fixed past, a common feature of such process thinkers as Whitehead, Mead, and Heidegger is that they do not speak about the past and future but pasts and futures. Furthermore, they do not talk about somehow fixed or finalized futures and pasts. Instead, all three see both futures and pasts as undetermined and open, meaning we do not know what is behind more than what is ahead. The unpredictability and openness are caused by the unpredictable and open interconnections between the past, present, and future characterizing the emerging reality (Helin et al., 2014). Let's start with the future.

It is easy to agree that the future is open and unknown because this is how it is; we do not know what the future brings. But the open and unknown future in its ambiguity could make us nervous (Callender, 2017; Valsiner, 2011). From the present perspective, the future is constituted by a range of potentialities of existing actualities with different probabilities for realization. Therefore, the future, as non-actual, exists only in the form of vague and uncertain possibilities. However, facing a range of possibilities with an ability to choose between them and decide which one to realize nurtures our agentic beliefs that "whether we decide to do, we will do" (Callender, 2017: 260). Therefore, the unknown and open future gives us a sense of agency. Our temporal agency, with its intentionality, orients us towards the future. But the future, in its openness, is also a significant source of anxiety.

Heidegger emphasizes that our very existential being is future-oriented. He stresses that being, as always projected "towards its ownmost potentiality-for-Being" (Heidegger, 1927/1962: 236) is always ahead of itself oriented to the future. Heidegger adds, *"The primary meaning of existentiality is the future"* (Heidegger, 1927/1962: 376 *emphasis in original*). At the same time, being oriented towards the future means being oriented towards an unknown.

Following Merleau-Ponty, even if the future remains uncertain, we are not necessarily paralysed by that. We don't just float in wishful thinking waiting for something to happen. Instead, our intentions are driving us forward or in the words of Merleau-Ponty, "my world is carried forward by lines of intentionality which trace out in advance at least the style of what is to come" (Merleau-Ponty, 2002: 483). Luhmann stresses, "the difference that is placed in the future as purpose organizes foresight" (Luhmann, 2018: 126). This means attention is neither distributed evenly across possibilities nor is its focus on the most probable possibility. Instead, how we see possibilities and assess their probabilities depends on our future aim. Heidegger supports this thought when he argues from the perspective of authentic Dasein that "it projects itself not upon any random possibilities which just lie closest, but upon that uttermost possibility which lies ahead" (Heidegger, 1927/1962: 349) as the potentiality-of-Being. Therefore, it could be said that we are naturally or even existentially inclined towards the future, and not towards the past.

Our present action is intentional and oriented towards the expected and anticipated future (Schütz, 1967). "Since intentions and outcomes are very loosely coupled" (Fuchs, 2001: 27), there is no guarantee that the future will play out as expected and anticipated or our intentional actions will lead to the results we were aiming for; the future remains open. Callender claims, "one of the most basic facts of life is that we face great uncertainty in the future direction. Coupled with causal asymmetry, this adds up to one of life's principal predicaments: we're uncertain about many of the events we potentially can control" (Callender, 2017: 275). Therefore, based on Callender, it can be argued that although we cannot control everything about the future, there are still some aspects about the future we can control. Taking control presupposes making a decision; that is, deciding which of the available possibilities to choose. The unknown-ness and openness of the future are necessary conditions for decision-making (Luhmann, 2018) because there is neither the need nor the chance to decide anything about something known and determined. But making a decision may not be easy.

4 Temporality—Endogenous and Subjective 159

Still, it is the ability and capability of making decisions that allow us to see the future as a possibility constructed as a difference from the past and present. However, to become determined and decide, the purpose, as a currently non-actual difference between past and future, should have convincing value in the present (Luhmann, 2018: 129). Making a decision is selecting and committing to a particular possibility over others to achieve our purpose. Selecting one possibility from the available range and committing to it limits the future, which could otherwise feel intimidating in its open unknown-ness (Luhmann, 2018). Deciding is to subordinate the future to a specific purpose.

Interestingly, Luhmann states that "Decision-making is possible owing to an exchange of temporal determination. The past remains irreversibly determinate and the future indeterminate, but the decision postulates that it is not determined by the past and for this reason must determine the future" (Luhmann, 2018: 131), respectively leaving the past open as alternatives. Additionally, by choosing a possibility, we are committing to a particular future, and this particular future starts to shape and create the past, as it becomes it. Therefore, in decisive moments of now, the past is in our present as an open possibility.

Compared to the idea of an unknown and open future, the idea of an unknown and open past could be harder to agree with because we have some knowledge and memories about the past, which we lack about the unknown future. At least, that is how it seems to be. However, for example, Oakeshott's idea about the past runs against the idea of the known, fixed, and singular past. Oakeshott claims that "A fixed and finished past, a past divorced from and uninfluenced by the present, is a past divorced from evidence (for evidence is always present) and is consequently nothing and unknowledgeable" (Oakeshott, 1995: 107). Moreover, Oakeshott lists five different types of pasts—historical, practical, remembered, recalled (1995), and encapsulated pasts (1983)—none of these is seen as final and fixed. As presented in Table 4.1, historical past is neither the only past nor a complete and objective recording of past events, but a selection of events judged to have relevance. Therefore, the historical past is inferred past. Oakeshott distinguishes between the remembered and recalled or recollected pasts. He views the remembered past as an internalized past locating in the continuity of consciousness and memory,

Table 4.1 Different types of pasts based on Oakeshott (1983, 1995)

	Historical past	Remembered past	Recalled or recollected past	Practical past	Encapsulated past
The main feature	Always an inference; a product of judgement and selection	Always personal; internalized; part of our self-awareness	Past as a resource; an external reservoir of experience/knowledge	Known as our past as ours; inseparable from self-love	Embodied past
Consisting of	The world of ideas; not the course of events as a mere series of successive events, but a world of co-existent events	Consists of memories based on personal experiences	Consulting the past; conscious work with the past experiences/events/ideas as analogies relevant in the present; thinking, judging, (re)constructing the past experiences/events/ideas in the present	Designed to justify and validate practical beliefs about the world including the present and the future	Consists of our personal, genetic, and cosmic pasts, physical, cognitive, and mental processes, collective habits, and traditions.
'Location'	The present world of the historian	In the continuity of consciousness and identity; may or may not be historical	In different memory forms like material artefacts, written text, audio-visual recordings	In the service of politics or religion; may or may not be historical	Being our own past

Combined by Oakeshott, M. (1995). Experience and its modes. Cambridge: Cambridge University Press, pp. 99–110; and Oakeshott, M. (1983). On history and other essays. Oxford: Blackwell, pp. 15–16.

associated with our self-awareness and identity. It is important to stress that "The past in history is not the remembered past. The remembered past may be historical, but it is not historical because it is remembered" (Oakeshott, 1995: 102). Remembered past is always personal. The recalled past is viewed as an external resource at our disposal to consult as a way of informing the present action in the present. In other words, the recalled past is not a transfer of the fact from the past to the present. Instead, recalling is thinking, judging, and constructing in the present, meaning, the recalled past is constructed in the present.

Oakeshott (1995) distinguishes further between the practical past and encapsulated past. The practical past is influential in relation to the present and future; it could overlap with the remembered past, and it could be fancied. Oakeshott describes the practical past as that "which preceded the present, that from which the present has grown, wherever the significance of the past lies in the fact that it has been influential in deciding the present and future fortunes of man" (Oakeshott, 1995: 103). Furthermore, the practical past may or may not be historical. In general, the practical past serves either the interests of politics or the interests of religion and it may or may not be historical. The idea that the practical past is an influential tool in the hand of politics is supported, for example, by the attempts of the post-communist Russia to rewrite the history and to reinterpret of the Second World War (Zajda & Zajda, 2003; see also, for example, Hodge, 2020; Radchenko, 2020, Tyler, 2021). The encapsulated past (Oakeshott, 1983) is the total sum of experiences combining personal, genetic, and even cosmic past, the outcomes of physical, cognitive, and mental processes, collective habits and traditions, promises, expectations, failures, and so on. The encapsulated past is an embodied past. Oakeshott argues that we are our past irrespective of remembering or recalling that past. Moreover, to a large extent the encapsulated past is beyond direct recall (Oakeshott, 1983).

Indeed, for example, Mead is very clear and categorical in stating that "for all pasts are as essentially subject to revision as the futures, and are, therefore, only possibilities" (Mead, 1932/2002: 181). If the past, like the future, exists as possibilities (Mead, 1932/2002), we cannot be sure about the ultimate meaning of the past. As a possibility, the past is open to the imagination (Bakken et al., 2013; Hernes, 2020) and recreation (Helin et al., 2014; Hernes, 2014a). Hernes uses an even stronger expression and states that the "past is hostage to the imagination projected on it from the present" (Hernes, 2020: 34). Therefore, in contrast to the one fixed past proposed previously by Lewis, the past is not a static, stand-alone unit but something formed by our imagination in the ongoing present.

Notably, the hypothetical and imagined past is not limited to realized possibilities and actualized potentialities. The non-realized possibilities that remain as traces could be reactivated as elements of the past to be incorporated into constructing our temporal reality in the present moment (Valsiner, 2011). Therefore, the past, containing both realized and non-realized possibilities and actualized and non-actualized potentialities (Luhmann, 2018; Valsiner, 2011) with related anticipations of *what could have been different and how if we had decided differently*, is fertile soil for the imagination. Heidegger also underlines the past's indeterminacy. He describes Dasein as "*running ahead to its past, to an extreme possibility of itself that stands before it in certainty and utter indeterminacy. Dasein* as human life *is primarily being possible*, the Being of the possibility of its certain yet indeterminate past" (Heidegger, 1924/1992: 12E *emphasis in original*).

Consequently, the past is not fixed and dead. It "must not be defined in terms of the common concept of the bygone" where "the bygone is that of which we say that it no longer is" (Heidegger, 1982: 290). Heidegger insists that instead of the common concept of the bygone as what was but does not exist anymore, we should think about the past as "Being-as-having-been". In contrast to what was but gone by now, "Being-as-having-been" (Heidegger, 1927/1962, 1982) is still a part of our existence. As part of someone's or something's existence, the past actively constitutes both the present and the future (Valsiner, 2011). In the words of Heidegger:

> The past is not some occurrence, not some incident in my Dasein. It is *its past*, not some 'what' about Dasein, some event that happens to Dasein and alters it. This past is not a 'what', but a 'how', indeed the authentic 'how' of my Dasein. This past, to which I can run ahead as mine, is not some 'what', but the 'how' of my Dasein pure and simple. (Heidegger, 1924/1992: 12E *emphasis in original*)

4 Temporality—Endogenous and Subjective

Being-as-having-been (how) implies that the "excluded possibilities are retained as possibilities" (Luhmann, 2018:134). Disregarded interests could surface again and once lost opportunities could hold an acutely painful importance in the current moment. Opportunities not taken and lost are open to the what-if question—*what could have been otherwise, what could be otherwise and what could become otherwise*. These questions could reveal tensions between *what is, what could have been, what may become*, and *what is not yet*. Therefore, being continuously in a mode of "running ahead," we need simultaneously to coordinate two types of the past and two types of the future. We need to coordinate both with the past that happened and that which did not but could have happened. Alike, about the future, we need to coordinate with possibilities and potentialities. These two types of pasts and futures may easily consist of multiple options, changing dynamically in an irreversible time by adding extra complexity.

Figure 4.3 below visualizes the related complexities. Our subjective lived experience of time is marked at the top with the dotted arrows with the direction running from the past to the future. This is the direction that indicates the ego-centric view of time (see Sect. 3.3.1), and this is how we tend to perceive our movement through time equipped with a temporal agency (see Sect. 3.5). At the bottom of the figure, solid black

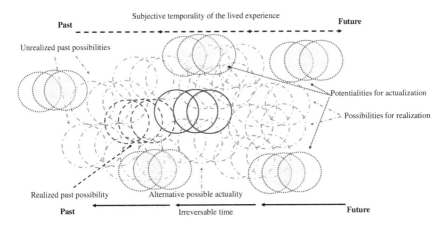

Fig. 4.3 Possibilities, potentialities and becoming in irreversible time

arrows represent the irreversible movement of time with the direction running from the future to the past marking the time-centric view and indicating the emerging and perishing nature of time and the agency of time (see Sects. 3.5.2 and 4.2.2). The connected circles show implicit temporality, for the sake of simplicity, explicit temporality is not included. The circles with the full line stand for current actualized implicit temporality. The circles with the dashed line show the past realized temporality, while the circles in light grey dashed lines stand both for the past and future unrealized possibilities. Finally, the light grey circles with the dotted lines represent future potentialities, the actualization of which in the current moment is open. The idea of this figure is to illustrate the general openness of the evolvement of endogenous temporality. As the figure represents dynamic *ongoing evolvement* not a static state, the trajectory of becoming is not determined but could move in various "directions", depending on which elements are included. Therefore, it can become otherwise.

The momentary stabilization in passing time achieved through the realization of selected possibilities is fragile, as things could have been otherwise, could be otherwise, and could still become otherwise (Luhmann, 1995). In some cases, while still impossible to re-do or undo what is done, it could be possible to "go back" and take corrective action. In that sense, sometimes it is possible to correct the course of events. But considering the irreversibility of time, that could not always be the case. Therefore, the acute awareness of lost opportunities could be burdensome. Additionally, the *because-of* motives hidden in our unconscious mind could successfully disguise the reason for questionable decisions or reactions or even direct self-sabotage.

Since our past contains both realized and unrealized possibilities and actualized and non-actualized potentialities, our relationship to the past is not necessarily straightforward and easy to track. More precisely, the past connection to the present and future could be complicated because our past contains decisions, events, and experiences that took place and those that did not but could have been. "Our pasts will vary with present situations and future prospects; in this sense, the past is never complete or transparent, but changes as time or life goes on" (Baars, 2012: 151). Although the past itself is out of our direct control and cannot be changed, its particular relevance and meaning are subject to redefinition (Mead, 1932/2002). Therefore, although we cannot live our past again as it was and repeat our *having-been-ness* exactly as it was, its meaning is open to reinterpretation in the present (Hernes, 2014a). That is to say, in the ongoing present also the meaning of the past is open to ongoing reinterpretation.

Hernes et al. (2020) questions the *factness* of the past and its closed nature by referring to its non-actuality. He claims, "If the past is no longer, it is gone forever, and can only be retrieved through the experience of the present" (Hernes, 2020: 34). As such, the past is a product of our *imagination in the present* (Hernes, 2020). We cannot access the past experience in its *pure* form; neither can we have an identical experience. Being filtered through the present, the past experience retrieved in the present is a new experience (Callender, 2017). We cannot be twice in exactly the same situation because as we move through time, we accumulate new experiences, and we recreate our memories continuously by reinterpreting the meaning and significance of our past and adjusting our purpose as a link between the past and future when we make decisions (Luhmann, 2018).

Figure 4.4 below presents ongoing temporality as it takes place in the actual present—*what is*. The model in Fig. 4.4 builds largely on the model of implicit temporality presented in Fig. 4.3. The arrows marked with a solid line at the top and bottom of the figure show agentic time moving from the future to the past. The arrows at the top stand, on the one hand, for lived experiences; that is, for the *things* that have happened. On the other hand, there are the future anticipations and expectations, images of how the future might be. The arrows at the bottom remind us that both the lived experiences and anticipations/expectations represent something not actual in the present moment. Therefore, they stand for non-actualities or possibilities. This sets the broader context of ongoing temporality.

Viewed from the perspective of the actor, ongoing implicit temporality evolves based on the actor's subjective lived experience that evolves from the past to the future. In the centre there is *now* as an immediate experience. However, the immediate experience in the *now* is constituted simultaneously by the relevance of the past as seen in the present moment

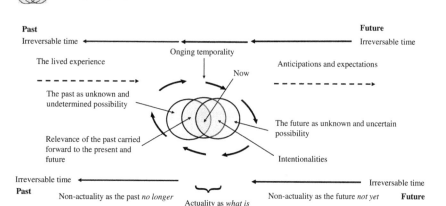

Fig. 4.4 The model of ongoing temporality

(from the centre one step to the left), and immediate future directed intentionalities (from the centre one step to the right). In addition to the known past and intended future, the experience of *now* is affected by the open and unknown past and future as mere possibilities. However, as we are dealing with ongoing phenomena, then the possibilities that are unknown at one moment may emerge to known-ness at the next. Consequently, ongoing temporality is vibrant and dynamic.

4.4.1 Issues Related to Memories

Being in the flow of time enables us to add experiences, expanding the range of identifiable possibilities through enriched memories (Luhmann, 2018). However, it is important to stress that while a longer and richer past contributes to an enriched memory, it does not provide more knowledge about the future. Moreover, our past, in the form of memories, is fragile; it is perishable. The perishing nature of time also erases the experiences and knowledge (Helin et al., 2014) available from the past as a material in the present. In its openness, the fragile and perishing past cannot be treated as unproblematic and taken for granted (Hernes, 2014a). As discussed in the previous chapter, we do not remember everything; we tend to forget, remember selectively, and sometimes choose to intentionally ignore our memories. While forgetting could be both good (trying to forget an unpleasant or traumatic experience) and bad (forgetting valuable experience or knowledge), it implies that our memories could be biased, incorrect, or even unavailable to us. However, Luhmann (2018) views forgetting as a normal process contrary to remembering, which he sees as exceptional. He highlights the role of memory in regulating what will be remembered and recalled and what will be forgotten:

> Memory is not a resource that is only occasionally used, activated when past occurrences are to be recalled. The memory serves rather to discriminate constantly between forgetting and remembering, between releasing operational capacities and constructing identities for repeated use. (Luhmann, 2018: 126)

Baars (2012) points to the quite common shortcoming of chronometric time in relation to memories. Namely, some experience dating back many years could be more readily available and proximate than another dating back a few months. Additionally, "memory as presence of the past does not just comprise what or how we want to remember. We only evoke a part of our memories consciously; another part evokes us or keeps asking for our attention, even when we might prefer to forget it" (Baars, 2012: 151).

Importantly, as we remember selectively and continuously recreate our memories, they do not necessarily represent our factual past. We may get trapped in believing the past we are lured into based on some memory cues. It turns out that knowing your past is far from self-evident and granted as our memories could easily play tricks on us. Our memories do not represent or equal our past. For example, Luhmann claims that memory *invisibilises the past* by occupying its place (2018: 126). According to Luhmann (2018), memory works as a filter that relieves us from processing abundant and redundant information and retains only what can be used in the present, making it known. He asserts that as decision and memory work as a pairs they determine one another through their reciprocal relationship (Luhmann, 2018: 127). Therefore, memory does not restore the past irrelevant for making decisions in the present, for choosing possibilities to realize. But while our conscious memories are biased and selective, our past, forgotten or covered from our conscious mind (Oakeshott, 1995), could still shape our decisions and actions unconsciously (Oakeshott, 1983; Schütz, 1967).

However, to keep past experiences and knowledge available, at least the selected part of that, the connection to the past needs to be maintained. Otherwise, the knowledge accumulated through past experiences tends to disappear due to forgetting (Argote, 2013). The availability of the distant past, either chronometrically distant or just significantly different from the present, requires maintained connections through memory cues. In organizations, memory is organized mostly in written documents and reports, which contain both information and decisions made, although they may lack the explanation for why a particular decision was made (Luhmann, 2018). Schultz and Hernes et al. (2013) have suggested that material and oral memory forms serve as important links to the past in addition to textual forms. By highlighting the term *memory form*, Schultz and Hernes (2013: 4) are emphasizing that the form in which memory "is evoked shapes the meaning of an experience". However, Luhmann warns that the organization's memory is highly selective, as "records *organize* not only remembering but also forgetting" (2018: 127), and as such, memory retains only a fraction of past experiences.

4.5 The Immanence of the Past and Future in the Present

Temporal process philosophy gives primacy to the temporal present (Mead, 1932/2002; Emirbayer & Mische, 1998; Hernes, 2014a, 2014b), viewing past and future as dimensions of the present (Deleuze 1994 in Hernes, 2014a) and different in terms of their degree of determinacy. That is to say, the past and future are not distinct elements of time, but they constitute the intrinsically ongoing present. At the same time, the ongoing present shapes and modifies the past and future. This mutual co-constituting is called immanence (Chia, 1999; Cobb, 2007; Hernes,

2014a; Hussenot et al., 2020; Hussenot & Missonier, 2016). According to the principle of immanence, each moment in its present actuality includes its non-actualities. That is, each actual present includes its not-anymore being as preceding moments when projecting itself to the not-yet possibility in the future. In the process, which takes place in the present, the future anticipation shapes both the past and present. Simultaneously, the future is formed by the present and past. The principle of immanence sees past, future, and present as co-constituting one another; there are not distinct detached temporal elements.

In bringing the past and future into the present, actors establish the making of the present. We can say that the non-actual past and future are not separated from the actual present. Instead, the non-actual past and future constitute the actual present. Simultaneously, the non-actual past and future form one another and are, in their non-actualities, formed by the actual present. The past, future, and present do not exist as three district units influencing one another with a specific, measurable, and calculable strength. Instead, the past, present, and future actively participate in *forming* one another as constitutive elements.

This implies that the current act is not just about anticipating what is to come, but the anticipation of what is to come actively shapes present action. Meaning, the workings of the future act that has not yet taken place are not just passively anticipated. Still, the anticipation of the future event shapes the making of the present act, as actors work with an *anticipatory sense* (Shotter, 2006) preparing themselves in the present for what is to come. For example, Lorino (2018: 46) describes how the anticipation of winter and the associated cold weather shapes the intentionality of current actions and directs them to prepare for the future by preparing logs to have the needed heating material. Although in this example, Lorino (2018) builds his argumentation up from the perspective of the semiotic mediation of pragmatism, his example also illustrates how the future, through anticipation, constitutes the present by shaping action carried out in the present. The principle of immanence helps actors to sense continuity both in the past and in the future (Hussenot et al., 2020) Whitehead also highlights the role of the future:

It is evident that the future certainly is something for the present. The most familiar habits of mankind witness to this fact. Legal contracts, social understandings of every type, ambitions, anxieties, railway timetables, are futile gestures of consciousness apart from the fact that the present bears in its own realized constitution relationships to a future beyond itself. Cut away the future, and the present collapses, emptied of its proper content. Immediate existence requires the insertion of the future in the crannies of the present. (Whitehead, 1933: 191)

Following this argumentation, neither the past nor future is something spatially or chronometrically distant; it is not something we can *travel* (i.e., Shipp & Jansen, 2021). Instead, the past and future are with us at every present moment enabling us to maintain sensed continuity through our subjective temporal experience in passing time. The past and future, viewed as a difference from the present, could be similar to or different from the present. But in either case, they are always with us in our present (Merleau-Ponty, 2002) by constituting it. With such a view, both the meaning of the future and the past are open (Helin et al., 2014; Hernes, 2014a; Schultz & Hernes, 2013). In other words, the present moment is assessed considering past experiences and future promises, while at the same time, the meaning of both the anticipated future, as well as the experienced past, are recreated (Hernes et al., 2013; Schultz & Hernes, 2013). As the dimensions of the present, we can hypothetically think about the experienced future and anticipated past. Therefore, instead of remembering the past and predicting the future, it can be that we are "remembering our plans" and not "forgetting to anticipate" (Baars, 2012: 155).

Therefore, the experience of being, as a becoming, is oriented to the future, while the beliefs about possible futures motivate current action (Hitlin & Elder Jr., 2007; Weick, 1995). At the same time, the ability to see different future possibilities, including more distant futures, depends on our grasp of the past. Through action, in the passing of time, experiences are accumulated, and the temporal span becomes longer (Hernes, 2014a), enabling more far-reaching future projections. That is, the temporal span into the future is rooted in the temporal span into the past. It is important to recognise that the "span indicates that our temporal markers are not *points* but stretches" (Bakken et al., 2013:18). Although not necessarily symmetrical, the longer span into the past enables a greater extension into the future (Hernes, 2014a; Kaplan & Orlikowski, 2013; Schultz & Hernes, 2013). Therefore, the past serves as an important resource for looking forward (Hernes, 2014a) and creating a sense of continuity (Zerubavel, 2003), while future expectations and anticipations reinvigorate the meaning of the present and past.

The past's meaning is changing based on present circumstances and future anticipations in the passing time. Oakeshott stresses that the past "varies with the present, rests upon the present, is the present" (Oakeshott, 1995: 107) and he adds, "There are not two worlds—the world of past happenings and the world of our present knowledge of those past events—there is only one world, and it is a world of present experience" (1995: 108). At the same time, future anticipations change based on our current circumstances and the relevance we ascribe to our past experiences. According to Baars, "questions about the meaning of the past also come from questions about the future when there is a need to clarify or find out something in the past before we can go on" (Baars, 2012: 152). He adds, "This presupposes an openness to have a future" (Baars, 2012:152). Similarly, Husserl (quoted in Adam, 1990: 31) stresses the reciprocal relationship of the past and future by claiming, "even a concern with short-term memory has to include fundamentally the future dimension."

Therefore, it could be argued that in order for us to be able to reinterpret our past(s), two necessary conditions need to be met. First, (re)interpretation of the past requires the future (Helin et al., 2014), meaning there should be a plausible perspective of the future within reach to be able to reinterpret the past(s). Reinterpretation of the past enables us to construct different histories (Bakken et al., 2013; Kahneman, 2011), and different identities, whether personal, organizational, or national (Zerubavel, 2003), which in turn, could open up a different future, something which was not considered before. Second, the future cannot be deterministic or wholly planned and scheduled. Instead, it should be open enough to enable different views of our past(s). Only with open future(s) can we exercise our agentic creative power to shape our being in the passing time and connections between our pasts and futures. As the meaning of the past is mediated through the future as it is seen in the present, there is no past without the future. Therefore, the influence occurs from a future point to a point in time (Hernes, 2014b). In this sense, the future creates the past.

Viewed like that, temporal agency—the ability to combine and recombine past and future possibilities in the present moment—is more important than specific qualities of the present moment per se. The immanence of past and future in the present as possibilities and potentialities, and our temporal agency as an ability to (re)combine pasts and futures, gives us the creative power to *create our time*. While exercising the creative power of our temporal agency, actors *create* their own time by forming particular temporal patterns in particular trajectories of becoming from the range of possibilities. Subjective time is like a process of knitting the fabric of time from which we are made. In that sense, the subject is time.

4.6 The Temporal Structure of Agency

Jaques (1982/1990) stresses that despite being contemporaries from the objective viewpoint; nevertheless, each of us *lives in a different time*. These various subjective times differ based on our personal lived experience of time, which in turn is affected by our temporal personality stemming from our temporal orientations and focus and continuously changing (living) linkages with past(s) and future(s). Said differently, the subjective times emerging from our temporal personalities vary in the same way as our appearance, fingerprints and desires, among other characteristics and traits.

Poetically speaking, choosing between and from the past, present, and future into different temporal patterns in the fabric of time presupposes agency. In the previous chapter, we discussed the importance of temporal agency. We defined temporal agency as our ability and capability to "construct and reconstruct the temporal conditions that shape [our] lives" (Orlikowski & Yates, 2002: 686) and exercise our creative power towards the future. In this section, we will discuss the temporal structure of agency. It is crucial not to confuse the temporal agency discussed in the previous chapter with the temporal structure of agency.

In their seminal paper, Emirbayer and Mische (1998) have created a theoretical model of the temporal structure of agency. Their theorizing is based mainly on Mead's (1932/2002) conception of the internal conversation, which shapes a person's reflections and attitude toward social context. Emirbayer and Mische define agency as a "temporally embedded process of social engagement, informed by the past (in its *iterational* or habitual aspect) but also oriented toward the future (as a *projective* capacity to imagine alternative possibilities) and toward the present (as a *practical-evaluative* capacity to contextualise past habits and future projects within the contingencies of the moment)" (Emirbayer & Mische, 1998: 962 *emphasis added*). They highlight how actors searching in their past may evoke activities that could shed new light on their future projections, shaping the present. The "chordal triad of agency" (Emirbayer & Mische, 1998: 970) represents the agency of the present (Emirbayer & Mische, 1998; Flaherty, 2003; Hernes, 2014a). By proposing the chordal triad of agency, Emirbayer and Mische emphasize that a person does not pick a point or even a range in the continuum (Ancona, Goodman, et al., 2001a: 513; Ancona, Okhuysen, & Perlow, 2001b: 645) as his/her temporal reference but grounds his/her action on three-dimensional agency.

The *iterational* element in the temporal structure of agency brings the past forward. The *iterational* element orienting towards past experience occurs through the "selective reactivation by actors of past patterns of thought and action" (Emirbayer & Mische, 1998: 971). The *projective* element "encompasses the imaginative generation by actors of possible future trajectories of action" (Emirbayer & Mische, 1998: 971). Emirbayer and Mische emphasize that projective agency is about giving *shape and direction* to future possibilities (Emirbayer & Mische, 1998: 984), and thus, it entails creative power. By projecting themselves onto the future; that is, projecting images of where they want to go and how they can get there, actors "move beyond themselves" (1998: 984). The projected images can be of varying degrees of clarity and present varying degrees of probability. The future, as well as the past can at any time be different both from now and before, and therefore the effects of projective decisions can never be precisely known. And finally, the *practical evaluative* element, which refers to the present, "entails the capacity of actors to make practical and normative judgments among alternative possible trajectories of action" (Emirbayer & Mische, 1998: 984).

Emirbayer and Mische argue that at every moment, human agency as "a temporally embedded process of social engagement" (1998: 962) is constituted by elements of iteration, projectivity, and practical evaluation. Said differently, at every moment, human agency is formed by a combination of the elements of past, present, and future in the present. The past and future elements are brought to the present, which is the locus of action (Mead, 1932/2002). In the present, the selection of past experiences and judgement of future possibilities takes place. While one temporal orientation is dominant, "each primary orientation in the chordal triad encompasses as subtones the other two while also showing how this *chordal composition* can change as actors respond to the diverse and shifting environments around them" (Emirbayer & Mische, 1998: 962). Notably, the dominant orientation is unstable, not fixed, allowing actors to recompose their multi-dimensional temporal focuses in their unfolding emergent contexts.

A "*chordal triad* of agency within which all three [temporal] dimensions resonate as separate but not always harmonious tones" (Emirbayer & Mische, 1998: 972) indicates that selecting past and judging future possibilities is not a straightforward and tensionless activity. Quite the contrary, a chordal triad of agency allows the occurrence of disharmony between the tones meaning there could be inconsistency and friction. There could surface temporal tensions. To solve these temporal tensions, actors need to distinguish what is relevant in the present from what is not in light of their current intentionality leading to the future. Depending on which element of the chordal triad prevails and which elements provide background support, and the degree of harmony versus tension between the elements, the nature of the social engagement of actors can vary. Therefore, the temporal structure of agency plays a critical role in the temporal relations of actors to their reality, to the world because it affects sensemaking (Sandberg & Tsoukas, 2020; Wiebe, 2010) and decision-making (Luhmann, 2018). Although Emirbayer and Mische's (1998) model of the temporal structure of agency is theoretical, several studies also drawing upon Mead (1932/2002) have applied their model and provide empirical evidence on how actors, in their situated activity taking place in the present, consider past and future together (e.g., Hussenot & Missonier, 2016; Kaplan & Orlikowski, 2013; Reinecke & Ansari, 2015; Schultz & Hernes, 2013).

Jaques stresses that although it may not be self-evident that "different people live in different time-scales, or in different *temporal domains,*" it does have "profound and far-reaching consequences for everyone" (Jaques, 1982/1990: 21), as our subjective lived experience of time influences the way we connect to reality and make sense of that (Heidegger, 1927/ 1962; Merleau-Ponty, 2002).

4.7 Conclusion

This chapter emphasizes that temporality and becoming are not something reserved for humans only. Quite the contrary, everything persisting in passing time is temporal. To highlight the temporality of entities, organizations, relations, ideas, activities, and so on, and to avoid being trapped in temporal idealism, I have used the term endogenous temporality. Endogenous temporality stands for an intrinsic configuration of the past, present, and future and applies to organisms and to physical and virtual entities. Endogenous temporality including subjective temporality has an ongoing nature. Subjective temporality of lived experience is a narrower concept applying to humans only and could be either implicit or explicit. The former refers to a passive effortless synthesis of past, present, and future, while the latter refers to conscious and effortful connections across temporal dimensions. Endogenous and subjective temporalities are the prerequisite for becoming. Becoming refers to the ongoing process of changing and transforming through the realization of possibilities or actualizing potentialities in passing time.

Passing time holds an agentic power by shaping everything and everybody in it. The agency of time stems from the idea of an irreversible, simultaneously emerging, and perishing time. The passing nature of time, which challenges every existing form and state, allows and even forces everything into becoming. Still, the becoming; that is, the realization of our possibilities or actualization of our potentialities in passing time could be challenging due to the perishing nature of time. Therefore, becoming could be a smaller or larger accomplishment, more or less intense and decisive. Becoming is like co-creation or a creative dance with the elements of a duel between the agency of time and our temporal agency. In this duel or dance, we create our subjective temporalities, our subjective pasts and futures. We shape our time while being shape by it. Importantly, our temporal agency has a tripartite structure. In other words, the temporal structure of our agency includes the past, present and future dimensions and at every moment our attention could be filtered more through iterations of the past, projections to the future, or practical evaluations in the present.

The literature shows that the basic logic of becoming and temporality holds both at the individual and organizational level. In both cases, the past, present, and future are seen not as distinct temporal elements but, in every moment, constituting one another, forming the united whole. How we connect to the world and time is shaped by our qualitatively different temporal reconfigurations of the past, present, and future. When trying to study someone's lived experience, we need to investigate his or her relationship with passing time and inquire about his or her temporal composition. The latter means how his/her pasts and futures form the existential whole of his/her temporality in the ongoing present. In these configurations, both the past and future remain open as possibilities giving us significant agentic freedom to create our time. However, the unity of the tripartite structure constitutes both the temporalities of human existence and the temporal structure of agency. In other words, our agency has a temporal structure including all three dimensions. The dominance of one temporal orientation over the others could influence how we exercise our agency; however, the dominant temporal orientation is not fixed and it may change from one moment to the next.

References

Abram, M., Picard, L., Navarro, B., & Piolino, P. (2014). Mechanisms of remembering the past and imagining the future—New data from autobiographical memory tasks in a lifespan approach. *Consciousness and Cognition, 29*, 76–89.
Adam, B. (1990). *Time and social theory*. Polity Press.
Ancona, D. J., Goodman, P. S., Lawrence, B. S., & Tushman, M. J. (2001a). Time: A new research lens. *Academy of Management Review, 47*, 523–549.
Ancona, D. G., Okhuysen, G. A., & Perlow, L. A. (2001b). Taking time to integrate temporal research. *Academy of Management Review, 26*(4), 512–529.
Argote, L. (2013). *Organizational learning: Creating, retaining and transferring knowledge*. Springer Science Business Media.
Baars, J. (2012). Critical turns of aging, narrative and time. *International Journal of Ageing and Later Life, 7*(2), 143–165.
Bakken, T., Holt, R., & Zundel, M. (2013). Time and play in management practice: An investigation through the philosophies of McTaggart and Heidegger. *Scandinavian Journal of Management, 29*, 13–22.
Bardon, A. (2013). *A brief history of the philosophy of time*. Oxford Scholarship Online. doi: https://doi.org/10.1093/asprof:oso/9780199976454.001.0001.
Bergson, H. (1910). *Time and free will: Essay on the immediate data of consciousness*. Kessinger.
Blattner, W. D. (1999). *Heidegger's temporal idealism*. Cambridge University Press.
Blattner, W. D. (2020). Temporality, aspect, and narrative: A Heideggerian Approach. In J. Reinecke, R. Suddaby, A. Langley, & H. Tsoukas (Eds.), *About Time: Temporality and History in Organization Studies* (pp. 15–28). Oxford University Press. https://doi.org/10.1093/oso/9780198870715.003.0002
Bluedorn, A. C. (2002). *The human organization of time: Temporal realities and experience*. Stanford University Press.
Callender, C. (2017). *What makes time special?* Oxford University Press.
Carnap, R. (1963). Carnap's intellectual biography. In P. Schilpp (Ed.), *The philosophy of Rudolph Carnap* (pp. 3–84). Open Court.
Chaudhary, N. (2015). Living with the belief in cyclical time: Collective and personal constructions of Hindu. In L. M. Simão, D. S. Guimarães, & J. Valsiner (Eds.), *Temporality: Culture in the flow of human experience* (pp. 333–351). Information Age Publishing.

Chia, R. (1999). A 'rhizomic' model of organizational change and transformation: Perspective from a metaphysics of change. *British Journal of Management, 10*, 209–227.

Cobb, J. B. (2007). Person-in-community: Whiteheadian insights into community and institution. *Organization Studies., 28*, 567–588.

Cravo, A., & Haddad, H. (2015). When is now: Measuring how we perceive instants in time. In L. M. Simão, D. S. Guimarães, & J. Valsiner (Eds.), *Temporality: Culture in the flow of human experience* (pp. 115–126). Information Age Publishing.

Dreyfus, H. L. (1975). Human Temporality. In J. T. Fraser & N. Lawrence (Eds.), *The Study of Time II* (pp. 150–162). Springer Verlag.

Dreyfus, H. L. (1991). *Being-in-the-World: A Commentary on Heidegger's Being and Time, Division I*. The MIT Press.

Eacott, M. J., & Easton, A. (2012). Remembering the past and thinking about the future: Is it really about time? *Learning and Motivation, 43*(4), 200–208. https://doi.org/10.1016/j.lmot.2012.05.012

Edwards, L. B., & Jaros, G. G. (1994). Process-based system thinking—Challenging the boundaries of structure. *Journal of Social and Evolutionary Systems, 17*(3), 339–353.

Emirbayer, M., & Mische, A. (1998). What is agency? *American Journal of Sociology, 103*(4), 962–1023.

Flaherty, M. G. (2003). Time work: Customizing temporal experience. *Social Psychology Quarterly, 66*(1), 17–33.

Fried, Y., & Slowik, L. H. (2004). Enriching goal-setting theory with time: An integrated approach. *Academy of Management Review, 29*(3), 404–422.

Fuchs, S. (2001). Beyond agency. *Sociological Theory, 19*(1), 24–40. https://doi.org/10.1111/0735-2751.00126

Fuchs, T. (2013). Temporality and psychopathology. *Phenomenology and the Cognitive Sciences, 12*(1), 75–104. https://doi.org/10.1007/s11097-010-9189-4

Griesbach, D., & Grand, S. (2013). Managing as transcending: An ethnography. *Scandinavian Journal of Management, 29*, 63–77.

Hatch, M. J., & Schultz, M. (2017). Toward a theory of using history authentically: Historicizing in the Carlsberg Group. *Administrative Science Quarterly, 62*, 657–697.

Heidegger, M. (1924/1992). *The concept of time*. Trans. William McNeill. Oxford: Basil Blackwell.

Heidegger, M. (1927/1962). *Being and time*. Blackwell Publishers.

Heidegger, M. (1982). *The basic problems of phenomenology*. Indiana University Press.
Helin, J., Hernes, T., Hjorth, D., & Holt, R. (2014). Process is how process does. In J. Helin, T. Hernes, D. Hjort, & R. Holt (Eds.), *The Oxford handbook of process philosophy and organization studies* (pp. 1–16). Oxford University Press.
Hernes, T. (2008). *Understanding organization as process: Theory for a tangled world*. Routledge.
Hernes, T. (2014a). *A Process theory of organization*. Oxford University Press.
Hernes, T. (2014b). Alfred North Whitehead. In J. Helin, T. Hernes, D. Hjorth, & R. Holt (Eds.), *Oxford handbook of process philosophy and organization studies* (pp. 255–271). Oxford University Press.
Hernes, T. (2017). Process as the becoming of temporal trajectory. In H. Tsoukas & A. Langley (Eds.), *Sage Handbook of Process Organizational Studies* (pp. 601–607). Sage.
Hernes, T. (2020). Events and the becoming of organizational temporality. In J. Reinecke, R. Suddaby, A. Langley, & H. Tsoukas (Eds.), *About Time: Temporality and History in Organization Studies* (pp. 29–43). Oxford University Press. https://doi.org/10.1093/oso/9780198870715.003.0003
Hernes, T., & Schultz, M. (2020). How actors translate between the on-going and the distant: A temporal view of situated activity. *Organization Theory, 1*, 1. https://doi.org/10.1177/2631787719900999
Hernes, T., Simpson, B., & Söderlund, J. (2013). Managing and temporality. *Scandinavian Journal of Management, 29*, 1–6.
Hernes, T., Feddersen, J., & Schultz, M. (2020). Material temporality: How materiality 'does' time in food organizing. *Organization Studies*. Advance online publication. https://doi.org/10.1177/0170840620909974
Hernes, T., Hussenot, A., & Pulk, K. (2021). Time and temporality of change processes. Applying an event-based view to integrate episodic and continuous change. In M. S. Poole & A. Van de Ven (Eds.), *The Oxford Handbook of Organizational Change and Innovation* (2nd ed., pp. 731–750). Oxford University Press. https://doi.org/10.1093/oxfordhb/9780198845973.013.27
Hershfield, H. E. (2011). Future self-continuity: How conceptions of the future self transform intertemporal choice. *Annals of the New York Academy of Science, 1*, 30–43.
Hitlin, S., & Elder, G. H., Jr. (2007). Time, self, and the curiously abstract concept of agency. *Sociological Theory, 25*(2), 170–191.

Hodge, N. (2020). Putin rewrites World War II history—and does battle over historical memory. *CNN*, June 18, 2020. Retrieved August 3, 2021, from https://edition.cnn.com/2020/06/18/europe/russia-putin-world-war-history-rewrite-intl/index.html.

Holman, E. A., & Silver, R. C. (1998). Getting "stuck" in the past: Temporal orientation and coping with trauma. *Journal of Personality and Social Psychology, 74*(5), 1146–1163.

Hussenot, A., & Missonier, S. (2016). Encompassing novelty and stability: An events-based approach. *Organization Studies, 37*(4), 523–546.

Hussenot, A., Hernes, T., & Bouty, I. (2020). Studying organization from the perspective of the ontology of temporality: Introducing the event-based approach. In J. Reinecke, R. Suddaby, A. Langley, & H. Tsoukas (Eds.), *About Time: Temporality and History in Organization Studies* (pp. 50–68). Oxford University Press. https://doi.org/10.1093/oso/9780198870715.003.0005

Husserl, E. (1964). *The phenomenology of internal time-consciousness.* (J. Churchill). Indiana University Press.

Jaques, E. (1982/1990). The enigma of time. In Hassard, J. (Ed.), *The Sociology of Time* (pp. 21–34). Macmillan.

Kahneman, D. (2011). *Thinking, fast and slow.* Farrar, Straus and Giroux.

Kaplan, S., & Orlikowski, W. (2013). Temporal work in strategy making. *Organization Science, 24*(4), 965–995.

Klein, S. B., & Nichols, S. (2012). Memory and the sense of personal identity. *Mind, 121*(483), 677–702. https://doi.org/10.1093/mind/fzs080

Klempe, S. H. (2015). Temporality and the necessity of culture in psychology. In L. M. Simão, D. S. Guimarães, & J. Valsiner (Eds.), *Temporality: Culture in the flow of human experience* (pp. 3–22). Information Age Publishing.

Levine, R. (2006). *A geography of time: The temporal misadventures of a social psychologist, or how every culture keeps time just a little bit differently.* Oneworld.

Lind, S. E., & Williams, D. M. (2012). The association between past and future oriented thinking: Evidence from autism spectrum disorder. *Learning and Motivation, 43*, 231–240. https://doi.org/10.1016/j.lmot.2012.05.004

Lorino, P. (2018). *Pragmatism and organization studies.* Oxford University Press.

Luhmann, N. (1995). *Social systems.* Stanford University Press.

Luhmann, N. (2018). *Organization and decision.* Cambridge University Press.

MacKay, R. B., & Chia, R. (2013). Choice, Chance, and Unintended Consequences in Strategic Change: A Process Understanding of the Rise and Fall of Northco Automotive. *Academy of Management Journal, 56*, 208–230.

Martin, W., Gergel, T., & Owen, G. S. (2018). Manic temporality. *Philosophical Psychology, 1*, 1. https://doi.org/10.1080/09515089.2018.1502873

Mattila, M., Mesiranta, N., Närvänen, E., Koskinen, O., & Sutinen, U-M. (2019). Dances with potential food waste: Organising temporality in food waste reduction practices. *Time & Society*, 28(4), 1619–1644. doi: https://doi.org/10.1177/0961463X18784123

Mead, G. H. (1932/2002). *The philosophy of the present*. Prometheus.

Merleau-Ponty, M. (2002). *Phenomenology of perception*. Routledge Classics.

Nolan, C., Todd, S., & Todd, J. (2002). *Memento*. Columbia TriStar Home Entertainment.

Oakeshott, M. (1983). *On history and other essays*. Blackwell.

Oakeshott, M. (1995). *Experience and its modes*. Cambridge University Press.

Orlikowski, W. J., & Yates, J. (2002). It's about time: Temporal structuring in organizations. *Organization Science, 13*(6), 684–700.

Polanyi, M. (1962). *Personal knowledge*. University of Chicago Press.

Polanyi, M. (1967). *The tacit dimension*. Routledge & K. Paul.

Pulk, K. (2016). *Making time while being in time: A study of the temporality of organizational processes*. PhD series, no. 43.2016, Copenhagen Business School [PhD], Frederiksberg.

Pulk, K. (2017). Perceived temporal discontinuity in organizational change processes—Risks and consequences. *Academy of Management Annual Meeting Proceedings, 2017*(1), 11776. https://doi.org/10.5465/AMBPP.2017.11776abstract

Radchenko, S. (2020). Vladimir Putin Wants to Rewrite the History of World War II. *Foreign Policy*, January 21, 2020. Retrieved August 3, 2021, from https://foreignpolicy.com/2020/01/21/vladimir-putin-wants-to-rewrite-the-history-of-world-war-ii/.

Reinecke, J., & Ansari, S. (2015). When times collide: Temporal brokerage at the intersection of markets and developments. *Academy of Management Journal, 58*(2), 618–648.

Reinecke, J., Suddaby, R., Langley, A., & Tsoukas, H. (2020). Time, temporality, and history in process organization studies: An introduction. In J. Reinecke, R. Suddaby, A. Langley, & H. Tsoukas (Eds.), *About Time: Temporality and History in Organization Studies* (pp. 1–14). Oxford University Press. https://doi.org/10.1093/oso/9780198870715.003.0001

Rodriguez, A., Turmo, J., & Vara, O. (2016). *Financial crisis and the failure of economic theory*. Routledge.

Roe, A. R. (2008). Time in applied psychology the study of "What happens" rather than "What is". *European Psychologist, 13*(1), 37–52. https://doi.org/10.1027/1016-9040.13.1.37

Rovelli, C. (2017). *The order of time*. Allen Lane.

Rousse, B. S. (2021). Retrieving Heidegger's temporal realism. *European Journal of Philosophy, 1*, 1–22.

Ryan, J. J., Kreiner, D. S., Seeley, J. S., & Paolo, A. M. (2015). Temporal disorientation base rates in Alzheimer's disease and Parkinson's disease. *Journal of Gerontology & Geriatric Research, 4*(3), 221. https://doi.org/10.4172/2167-7182.1000221

Sandberg, J., & Tsoukas, H. (2020). Sensemaking reconsidered: Towards a broader understanding through phenomenology. *Organization Theory, 1*, 1–34. https://doi.org/10.1177/2631787719879937

Sato, T., & Valsiner, J. (2010). Time in life and life in time: Between experiencing and accounting. *Ritsumeikan Journal of Human Sciences, 20*(1), 79–92.

Schultz, M., & Hernes, T. (2013). A temporal perspective on organizational identity. *Organization Science, 24*(1), 1–21.

Segal, P., Giarraputo, J., Juvonen, N., Golin, S., & Ewing, M. (2004). *50 First Dates*. Columbia Pictures, Happy Madison, Anonymous Content, Flower Films.

Shipp, A., & Jansen, K. (2021). The "Other" time: A review of the subjective experience of time in organizations. *Academy of Management Annals, 15*(1), 299–334. https://doi.org/10.5465/annals.2018.0142

Simão, L. M. (2015). Introduction: Time—Not always the same. In L. M. Simão, D. S. Guimarães, & J. Valsiner (Eds.), *Temporality: Culture in the flow of human experience* (pp. xi–xiv). Information Age Publishing.

Simpson, B., Tracey, R., & Weston, A. (2020). The timefulness of creativity in an accelerating world. In J. Reinecke, R. Suddaby, A. Langley, & H. Tsoukas (Eds.), *About Time: Temporality and History in Organization Studies* (pp. 69–88). Oxford University Press. https://doi.org/10.1093/oso/9780198870715.003.0006

Schütz, A. (1962/1982). *Collected papers I: The problem of social reality*. Natason, M. (Ed.). Martinus Nijhoff Publishers.

Schütz, A. (1967). *The phenomenology of the social world*. Heinemann Educational Books.

Shotter, J. (2006). Understanding process from within: An argument for 'withness'-thinking. *Organization Studies, 27*(4), 585–604.

Shotter, J. (2010). Adoption a process orientation...in practice: Chiasmic relations, language, and embodiment in a Living World. In T. Hernes & S. Maitlis (Eds.), *Process, Sensemaking, & Organizing* (pp. 70–101). Oxford University Press.

Slade, D., MacLean, R., & Brooker, C. (2018). *Black Mirror: Bandersnatch*. House of Tomorrow.

Sutton, R. I. (1987). The process of organizational death: Disbanding and reconnecting. *Administrative Science Quarterly, 32*, 542–569.

Torre, S. (2011). The open future. Philosophy. *Compass, 6*(5), 360–373.

Tyler, R. (2021). Why is Putin rewriting history? *Mace Magazine*, July 15, 2021. Retrieved August 3, 2021, from https://macemagazine.com/why-is-putin-rewriting-history/.

Tyre, M. J., & Orlikowski, W. J. (1994). Windows of opportunity: Temporal patterns of technological adaptation in organizations. *Organization Science, 5*(1), 98–118.

Uppendahl, M., Hawley, N., & Colston II, L. E. (2020). *Fargo* Season 4, Episode 9, "East/West". US: FX. November 15, 2020.

Vail, D. A. (2003). Book review: The human organization of time: Temporal realities and experience by Allen C. Bluedorn. *Contemporary Sociology, 32*(6), 768–769.

Valsiner, J. (2011). Constructing the vanishing present between the future and the past. *Infancia y Aprendizaje, 34*(2), 141–150.

Vedeler, D. (2015). Duration and experience: The temporality of development. In L. M. Simão, D. S. Guimarães, & J. Valsiner (Eds.), *Temporality: Culture in the flow of human experience* (pp. 129–214). Information Age Publishing.

Weick, K. E. (1995). *Sensemaking in organizations*. SAGE.

Whitehead, A. N. (1929/1978). *Process and reality*. New York: The Free Press.

Whitehead, A. N. (1933). *Adventures of ideas*. The Free Press.

Whitehead, A. N. (1938). *Modes of thought*. The Free Press.

Wiebe, E. (2010). Temporal Sensemaking: Managers' use of time to frame organizational change. In T. Hernes & S. Maitlis (Eds.), *Process, Sensemaking, and Organizing* (pp. 213–241). Oxford University Press.

Wong, T. (2001). Reviews: Heidegger's Temporal Idealism. *Politics and Culture*, 3. Retrieved April 14, 2021, from https://politicsandculture.org/2010/08/10/william-blattner-heideggers-temporal-idealism-c-2/.

Zajda, J., & Zajda, R. (2003). The politics of rewriting history: New history textbooks and curriculum materials in Russia. *International Review of*

Education / Internationale Zeitschrift Für Erziehungswissenschaft / Revue Internationale De L'Education, 49(3/4), 363–384.

Zerubavel, E. (2003). *Time maps: Collective memory and the social shape of the past.* University of Chicago Press.

5

Socially Constructed Time and Social Time as a Context

Berger and Luckmann refer to the intersubjectively available "standard time of everyday life" which is a combination of different types of times, such as clock time, rhythms of nature, and psychological or inner time.

> "The world of everyday life has its own standard time, which is intersubjectively available. This standard time may be understood as the intersection between cosmic time and its socially established calendar, based on the temporal sequences of nature, and inner time, in its aforementioned differentiations. There can never be full simultaneity between these various levels of temporality." (Berger & Luckmann, 1991: 40)

However, it is important not to confuse this intersubjectively available standard time of everyday life with the standardized clock time we discussed in Chap. 2; these times are not identical. In addition, as Berger and Luckmann indicate, these different types of time are not necessarily in harmonious relationship. Instead, we may expect to experience some tensions between them. In addition to the widely acknowledged opposition of objective and subjective time, tensions between subjective temporality and social time and between subjective temporalities are highlighted in the literature. Despite these tensions, Fuchs (2013: 76) asserts that our self-reference and sensed continuity in time requires either "implicit or explicit reference to the contemporaneous life of others." Baars (2012) expresses similar thoughts and paints a picture of a multi-layered and complicated tangle of temporalities. Baars (2012) points out that as we share the world with others, we are surrounded by the memories, fears, hopes and expectations of others. Our temporal perspectives interact with the temporal perspectives of others, creating a complicated and dynamic socio-temporal context (Baars, 2012: 155).

In other words, analysing subjective temporality without considering intersubjective temporality does not lead very much anywhere. Individuals in society are not isolated individual units holding their highly individualistic subjective temporalities. Instead, individuals in society are connected through ongoing interactions with others. This means that our subjective micro-time, shaped and constrained by intersubjective temporality (meso- and eso-time) could be less personal, *to a lesser extent our own*, than we tend to think. The subjective temporality discussed in the previous chapter never appears in isolation as purely individual. On the one hand, in our becoming, we are in continuous interaction with other individuals who hold their subjective temporalities and anticipated trajectory of becoming. In our ongoing interactions, we inevitably shape each other's temporalities and trajectories of becoming by enabling and supporting and also inhibiting and constraining the realization of each other's possibilities.

On the other hand, individuals are always participants in the broader social systems, which have their own measurable temporal rhythms and endogenous temporalities. Importantly, both the semiotic meaning of the perceived temporality of objective time, like the rhythms and pacing, and temporal dimensions of endogenous temporality; that is, the past and future, are socially created (Zerubavel, 1987, 2003). Therefore, the broader socio-cultural system or macro-time always shapes and conditions an individual's subjective temporality. Similarly, intersubjective temporalities are embedded in the temporalities of the epoch or era (Bakhtin, 1981), under the influence of macro-time. In short, "Time is never homogeneous, it is multi-faceted, and its aspects are distributed over its various contexts" (Cipriani, 2013: 25).

5 Socially Constructed Time and Social Time as a Context

Berger and Luckmann, quoted above, make it clear that the standard time of everyday life is a complex socially constructed phenomenon, which should not be confused with the *standardised time* discussed in Chap. 3, although the latter turned out to be socially constructed as well. Yet, there are more layers of complexity to add, like a plurality of social times and the multi-dimensionality of time viewed as a context. This chapter takes a closer look at the intersubjective nature of a socially constructed time and its implications for subjective time.

Temporality could be viewed either from the perspective of temporal realism and the ontology of time (Hussenot et al. 2020), as in Chaps. 2 and 3, or from the perspective of subjective lived experience, endogenous temporality (Hernes et al., 2020) and the ontology of temporality (Hussenot et al. 2020) as in Chap. 4. Therefore, temporality both at the societal and organizational level could be viewed as various temporal patterns ordering human activity through time or assuming "that the passing of time is an intrinsic quality of the world" (Hernes, 2014: 44). By conceptualizing time as a socially constructed phenomenon, the chapter covers the plurality of time reckoning systems. It reveals the importance of the temporal orientation of social activities, the possible collision between various social times, multidimensional time as a temporal context, and the socially created semiotic meaning of perceiving the temporality of objective time.

5.1 Intersubjective Temporality

In the previous chapter, I discussed subjective temporality as lived experience from the phenomenological perspective. However, it is important to highlight that from the perspective of phenomenology, it is not possible to understand the actions and experience of individuals in separation from their social context. The most fundamental principle of phenomenology is the intimate nature of the relationship between the subject and the world (i.e., Heidegger, 1927/1962; Schütz, 1962/1982; Merleau-Ponty, 2002; Polanyi, 1967). Consequently, the interpretation of our actions and intentionalities could only make sense if analysed together with the particular context we are embedded in. As the context for action, the world does not refer only to the spatial, physical world. Instead, the world is referred to as existing temporal relations forming the everydayness for an actor who is *thrown* into this temporal relational everydayness (Heidegger, 1927/1962). Smith highlights that "For Heidegger, we and our activities are always *in the world*, our being is being-in-the-world, so we do not study our activities by bracketing the world, rather we interpret our activities, and the meaning things have for us by looking to our contextual relations to things in the world" (Smith, 2013).

Among other *things*, we also interpret the meaning of time through our relations with and in the world; that is, our subjective time is less subjective and more intersubjective. According to Heidegger (1927/1962) Dasein always shares its being in the world with others, and therefore analysing an individual's experiences of time and temporality "must always take intersubjective temporality into account as well" (Fuchs, 2013: 76). Intersubjective time as the semiotic meaning of objective measures of time, and intersubjective temporality as the meaning of the past and future and their intrinsic connections in the present, are dialogical, "non-allochronic, non-schizogenic" (Cipriani, 2013: 7).

On the one hand, through the use of time and our subjective temporality, we take "possession of the world" and mould it to meet our expectations (Cipriani, 2013: 12). On the other hand, we are not entirely free in our opportunities to do that. Instead, we are operating in the limits and constraints imposed by a socially constructed multidimensional time as the context of temporal relations. Therefore, the world becomes a world of the making of the actor, which shapes the actor in turn. In this world, the personal experience of time is filtered through the socially constructed time as a temporal context, through the socially created meaning of past, present, future events. Our subjective time and our subjective temporality are formed in and by our context and ongoing interactions (Emirbayer & Mische, 1998; Lorino & Mourey, 2013).

Time remains outside our senses, and because of that, we are unable to perceive or recognize time directly (Elias, 1994). Either in spite of that, or because of that, there is a growing consensus among scholars across different fields that humans recognize time through events (i.e., Callender, 2017; Clark, 1985; Hernes, 2014; Jones, 2019; Sorokin & Merton, 1937; Whitehead, 1929/1978). (I will cover events in more detail in the next chapter). However, in social settings, the meaning of events is not universal and self-evident but socially constructed. For example, both Clark (1985) and Sorokin and Merton (1937) claim that the socially constructed importance of events makes time visible for humans. In line with that, Emirbayer and Mische (1998) argue that actors' social interaction strongly influences the personal experience of time—by "a temporally embedded process of social engagement" (Emirbayer & Mische, 1998: 962). But as social interaction and social, temporal relations vary, similarly, which events they recognize and what meaning they ascribe to these events also varies. Put differently, the plurality of social times entails a plurality of time reckoning systems.

5.2 Plurality of Social Times and Time Reckoning Systems

Lee and Liebenau (1999) argue that studies based on the assumption of objective time presume that all organizational members adhere to a linear time flow with a constant pace, like a straight arrow, and behave according to that belief. That kind of uniformity of understanding is questioned by several authors. For example, Klempe assumes that the hardly observable experienced time "would probably appear as diverse as life itself" (Klempe 2015: 4). Uniformity of organizational time is questioned also by scholars supporting social time. For sociologists, social time is a social phenomenon. However, it is important to recognize that there is no singular social time but a plurality of social times. For example, Gurvitch, 1990b has proposed eight different types of social time. Referred to by Hassard, Gurvitch's typology is "the most ambitious attempt to outline the qualitative nature of social time" (Hassard, 1996: 586). The eight types of social time in Gurvitch's typology—enduring, deceptive, erratic, cyclical, retarded, alternating, in advance of itself, and explosive (see Pulk, 2016, Table 1, pp. 60-61). With his typology, Gurvitch illustrates how distinct social times held by different social groups are often conflicting and competing with one another. Instead of viewing social actors as responding to pre-established temporal structures (see Sect. 2.3.2),

Gurvitch emphasizes creating temporal meanings based on a collective cultural experience and sensemaking. In other words, societies hold a plurality of qualitatively different time-reckoning systems.

Gurvitch (1964/1990a: 40) claims that social times can be understood only dialectically, and with eight types of times, he highlights the differences in the structural and astructural elements, continuity and discontinuity, and the contingency of social times (Gurvitch 1964/1990b: 69).

> "As a matter of fact, all the characteristics of time, always in degrees, can…be understood only dialectically: the 'discontinuous continuity' and the 'continuous discontinuity', the duration in succession and the succession in duration, the past, the present and the future, sometimes projected in one another, sometimes dominant over one another, and finally sometimes reduced to one another, the 'quantitative-qualitative' and the 'qualitative-quantitative' (quantity itself presented in the form of degrees of extensity and intensity), the homogeneous heterogeneity, and the stable-change and the changing stability." (Gurvitch, 1990a: 40)

As organizations are complex social systems, we can expect to see heterogeneous times and a plurality of time-reckoning systems within organizations. Time-reckoning systems have strategic importance in organizations because levels of profitability or perspectives for survival are directly dependent on the correct reading of the event and the subsequent decisions made in anticipation of the future (Clark, 1985). The plurality of time-reckoning systems raises some essential questions about their impact on organizational life. For example, questions about how different social times influence internal organizational affairs, business activities, events, and how these internal affairs, business activities, and events in turn affect social times. As the plurality of times, or more precisely, the plurality of social times, is a social phenomenon (Gurvitch, 1990a), not a subjective individual experience, then time reckoning systems at the personal level tend to be unhelpful at the collective level (Zerubavel, 1982).

Ancona et al. (2001: 519) refer to personal temporality as "the manner in which an actor understands and acts with respect to the temporal continuum". Gurvitch, in his typology, emphasizes continuity through discontinuity, where the discontinuity is seen as sudden configurational changes of past, present, and future. By challenging the idea of stable time-reckoning systems or stable social times (Clark, 1985; Hassard, 1996, 1990), Gurvitch emphasizes, "creating temporal meanings rather than responding to temporal structures" (Hassard, 1996: 586). Gurvitch argues that social sub-groups hold diverse, simultaneously coexisting, conflicting and constantly competing times. This argument is supported, for example, by the empirical research conducted by Reinecke and Ansari (2015). They analysed the collision between market and development temporalities and associated different temporalities with the different goals organizational subgroups hold. The mixture of colliding times creates the total social phenomenon described as vibrant and effervescent:

"…the pulsation of a total social phenomenon is manifested in a perpetual coming and going. All these levels permeating each other and struggling with each other are animated by the varied pulsations of continuity and discontinuity. Moreover, their accentuations change with each type of total social phenomenon, be it a We, a group, a class or a social society." (Gurvitch, 1990b: 68)

Being part of the total social phenomenon, words like 'pulsation,' 'perpetual coming and going,' 'permeating and struggling,' and 'change' indicate that social times are as vibrant and effervescent as the total social phenomenon described above.

5.2.1 Temporal Structures, Temporal Work, and a Collision of Times

Vibrant and effervescent social times in their plurality require coordination. In organizations, various temporalities and their interactions require organizing and coordinating, reducing possible temporal conflicts between various cycles of activities, and creating "a sense of concert in time" (Yakura, 2002: 958). To achieve that, organizations rely on temporal structures. In her study, Yakura (2002) shows how timelines based on the concept of standardized and context-free clock time, are used by different organizational subgroups to coordinate and synchronize their actions. She (Yakura, 2002: 956–959) defined timelines as boundary objects that enable different organizational actors to coordinate their work and to handle a plurality of social times existing concurrently. Yakura (2002: 957–958) shows the importance of timelines (artefacts representing clock time) as tools for managing different and possibly divergent subjective understandings about objective time, different occupational rhythms or cycles, and different experiences of urgency. It follows that, although timelines and deadlines assume standardized time, their meaning is interpreted differently based on the specific subgroup's approach to time (Dubinskas, 1988a). For example, concerning deadlines, Dougherty et al. (2013) found that the pacing of clock-time characteristic to managers emphasizes near future deadlines while scientists following the pacing of event-time could easily forget all the deadlines because events are unpredictable.

Orlikowski and Yates (2002: 684) use the term *temporal structures* to overcome the objective-subjective time dichotomy, understood as being simultaneously shaped by and shaping ongoing human behaviour. In organizations, for example, temporal structures—related to weekly meeting schedules, project deadlines, financial reporting, budgeting, and so on—influence the accepted code of conduct. Based on the work of Giddens, Orlikowski and Yates (2002) argue that the relationship between ongoing human action and temporal structures is reciprocal. This means that temporal structures shaped by ongoing human action are not independent of human action but shaped by it. At the same time, temporal structures are not fully determined by human actions because they, in turn, influence human action. Orlikowski and Yates (2002: 688) stress, "studying time in organizations requires studying time in use; that is, examining what organizational members actually do in practice, and how in so doing they shape the temporal structures that shape them".

Several scholars have pointed to the association between shared temporal structures and workgroups or teams and organizational performance (i.e., Abrantes et al., 2018; Orlikowski & Yates, 2002; Siren et al., 2020; Standifer & Bluedorn, 2006). Temporal structures, such as regular meeting schedules and deadlines (Orlikowski & Yates, 2002; Yakura, 2002), set the rhythm and timing for various activities for organizational

5 Socially Constructed Time and Social Time as a Context

actors. As mechanisms for coordination, temporal structures adjust "the creation, use, and influence of time in organizational life" (Orlikowski & Yates, 2002: 695), by providing "a form to daily life". Orlikowski and Yates (2002: 686) highlight that in their actions, people "routinely draw on common temporal structures that … have previously been enacted to organize their ongoing practices." Therefore, the shared temporal structures, "constituted in action" (Reinecke & Ansari, 2015: 640), are available coordination mechanisms (Claggett & Karahanna, 2018), which enable "people in organizations to experience time…in their everyday practices" (Orlikowski & Yates, 2002: 686).

However, viewed as readily available temporal coordination mechanisms established through recurrent activities, shared temporal structures seem to fall short in dealing with new emergent situations which require temporal coordination or the managing of conflicting temporal structures. Kaplan and Orlikowski (2013: 965) have highlighted the importance of intentional and purposeful temporal work leading to a *strategic account* that could enable a *concrete strategic choice and action*. With their study, Kaplan and Orlikowski (2013) show that organizations could face high uncertainty about the future even when multiple future possibilities are open to them or because of such possibilities. In other words, Kaplan and Orlikowski (2013) showed that resolving temporal tensions related to the establishment of a new strategic direction and creating a plausible strategic account requires purposeful and focused temporal work. Purposeful and focused temporal work is required to establish plausible connections between the past and future. Therefore, while temporal structures provide an almost taken for granted framework for coordinating everyday activities, there is a growing body of literature about active, either overt or covert, temporal work as a means to "constructing, challenging and defending time and temporality in organizations" (McGivern et al., 2018: 1025).

Temporal work in organizations may include attempts to merge different types of time. For example, attempts to merge clock time with event or social time (i.e., Dougherty et al., 2013; Huy, 2001; Orlikowski & Yates, 2002; Reinecke & Ansari, 2015; Yakura, 2002). Highlighting the complementarity of clock time and social time, Yakura (2002) and

Orlikowski and Yates (2002) have used the term *pluritemporality*, introduced first by Nowotny (1992), while Reinecke and Ansari (2015) have coined the term *ambitemporality* to describe how actors manage temporal tensions by bridging competing types of time through temporal brokerage. Studying the operational processes of different organizational units of Fairtrade, Reinecke and Ansari (2015) found that ambitemporality enabled the organization to handle nonlinear cyclical development activities in production in parallel with clock time based linear timelines that guided the activities in relation to consumer markets. Dougherty et al. (2013) found that pacing is a major source of conflict in the innovation process of pharmaceuticals. Depending on whether clock-time (managers) or event-time pacing (scientists) was used there were fundamental differences in how the entire process was understood and evaluated.

Temporal work in organizations may also include attempts to handle simultaneously short- and long-term temporal orientations referred to as *temporal ambidexterity* (Slawinski & Bansal, 2015). Studying the responses of oil-and-gas companies to climate change, Slawinski and Bansal found that compared to those organizations that polarized the short and the long term, organizations that "juxtapose the short-term and long-term" are "more likely to recognise the complexity of climate change and the need for integrated, multidimensional solutions" (Slawinski & Bansal, 2015: 531).

The notion of temporal work assumes that human actors have an agentic power and they *use* time intentionally. However, Gurvitch's typology of social times associates different social times with actions that are characterized by different qualities, including different temporal qualities (i.e., enduring, competing, fighting, being ahead of itself, being late, etc.). Consequently, Gurvitch suggests that activities have specific temporalities. If we agree that organizational activities have specific temporalities and "there is not a unitary organizational actor that acts, but the making of organizational actors through acting" (Hernes, 2014: x); in other words, action is what determines the actor and not vice versa, it is well justified to shift our focus from individuals and their temporalities, intentions and temporal work to the temporal orientation of the activities.

5.3 The Temporal Orientation of Activities

Adam, pointing out the importance of social time as a social tool for coordination, ordering, and regulation, claims, "social scientists view time as constituted by social activity" (Adam, 1990: 42). Her claim opens a new aspect of social time by attributing a central role to social activities as constituting social time. Adam's claim about the centrality of social activity in creating social time, including organizational time, is supported by several organizational scholars who have investigated temporal aspects of organizing (i.e., Ancona et al., 2001; Orlikowski & Yates, 2002; Reinecke & Ansari, 2015; Schultz & Hernes, 2013). In their attempts to overcome the distinction of objective and subjective time, these scholars promote the view of time as constituting and being constituted by established and institutionalized social practices (i.e., Bluedorn, 2002; Hernes et al., 2013; Reinecke & Ansari, 2017).

Somehow, surprisingly, the literature on temporal focus and temporal orientation concentrates on human actors, either individuals or groups. The role of time as a tool for ordering is drawn from the assumption that human beings act based on the temporal meaning they give to events and their own action. This view grants the main temporal agency to humans who evoke the past and project the future to orchestrate the temporal evolvement of activities. In principle, that makes sense. However, let's suppose that social practices and organizational activities as established and institutionalized patterns or routines that hold their distinctive temporalities occupy the central position in composing social and organizational time. In that case, we can expect that individual and even group time orientations are subsumed to the time orientation of institutionalized activity patterns (Granqvist & Gustafsson, 2016). Alternatively, we can assume that, at least in the organizational setting, the group's time orientation stems from the activities the group is occupied with, not from individual temporal preferences.

It seems unrealistic to assume that in organizations, groups of people with similar temporal *fingerprints* gather into groups to work together. To some extent, that may hold if we consider the concept of temporal fit (Levine 2006; Shipp & Cole, 2015); that is, the temporal match of the prevailing temporality of the individual, organization or team (Eldor et al., 2017; Shipp & Fried, 2014). It is easy to agree that working in the context of the vibrant temporality characterized by start-ups trying to scale up or the fast-paced working routines of flight attendants does not suit everyone (Whitelegg, 2007). Similarly, a very slow paced and highly predictable environment does not suit everybody. Nevertheless, the assumption that individual temporal preferences are subsumed to the temporality of organizational activities seems more plausible than the opposite, that the temporality of organizational activities is determined by individual temporal preferences.

According to Hernes, "organizing implies attempts at creating a meaningful and predictable order out of a tangled world. … It implies bringing together strands of a tangled whole within some selected and temporally evolving structures of meaning" (Hernes, 2014: 14). However, creating meaning and selecting strands into the evolving structures of meaning occurs based on experience (Hernes, 2014), while any experience is acquired through action. Organizations could be viewed as the nexus of activity streams (Thompson, 1967) or patterns (Luhmann 1995); that is, constituted by a range of different activity patterns (Luhmann 1995) or streams (i.e., Jarzabkowski et al., 2007; Lawrence & Lorsch, 1967). In that case, organizing also means among other things, ordering, coordinating, and negotiating between different streams of activities. This organizing, coordinating, and negotiating are not restricted to the entrainment of tempo, duration, frequency, etc., as the temporal dimensions of external time as discussed in Chaps. 2 and 3. Instead, different activity streams or patterns hold the specific temporal orientations (i.e., Dubinskas, 1988b; Lawrence & Lorsch, 1967) and endogenous temporality of the tasks, which does not necessarily conform to entrainment. Therefore, we can expect to see some clashes between different activity streams that hold endogenous, distinctive, intrinsic temporalities.

Despite the early studies of Dubinskas (1988a, 1988b) and Lawrence and Lorsch (1967) that focus on the relationship between organizational subgroup time orientation and their working tasks, the temporal orientation of activities tends to be overlooked. The exception is practice perspective, which emphasizes the future orientation of practices (Wenzel et al., 2020). To some extent, Emirbayer and Mische (1998), with their profound analysis of the temporal nature of human agency, could probably be blamed. However, besides analysing the temporality of human agency, Emirbayer and Mische state that "different temporal orientations of agency, *allowing us to examine forms of action that are more oriented (respectively) toward the past, the future, and the present*" (Emirbayer & Mische, 1998: 971 *emphasis added*). With that sentence, they hint that those different forms of action or activities could have distinct temporal orientations. In general, action is viewed as being oriented to the future (Schütz, 1967), and "Through its activity the living being carries itself forward, tends toward the future, creates it in front of itself" (Minkowski, 1970: 83). To do something is a future-oriented action, and our relations to things and the world are mediated through future expectations and anticipations to achieve or accomplish something in the future. However, as Emirbayer and Mische (1998) underline, action could be oriented not only toward the future, but also toward the past or present.

To claim that activities have future orientation could be interpreted as the objective time orientation of activities. As discussed in Chap. 3, there are a number of temporal aspects of objective time related to activities that are targets of planning, coordination, and entrainment. But activities need duration for their completion, which means that they are temporal (Mead, 1932/2002); they have their endogenous temporality or particular way to connect their past and future. In other words, during their existence, which is their duration, activities combine temporal elements from past, present, and future in a particular way. Although Mead (1932/202) stresses that the present is the locus of action, he also stresses that action stretches from the past to the future. Similarly, Schütz (1967) describes action as a process informed and conditioned by the past and driving to the future. Still, as Emirbayer and Mische (1998) claim, action, and thus activities, could be oriented more toward the past, the present, or the future, which means that activities, while sharing a general common future orientation, do not necessarily share the same temporal orientation.

Hernes and Schultz (2020) express a similar idea when claiming that most organizational activities are guided by temporal structures consisting of recurring actions and events with temporal orientation, that is to say, "events and activities are oriented into past and future" (Hernes & Schultz, 2020: 10). Therefore, the performance of organizational actors is conditioned and constrained by temporal structures, produced and reproduced by the recurring activities or practices "they and others have previously enacted to organize their ongoing practices" (Orlikowski & Yates, 2002: 686). These activities and ongoing practices have a temporal orientation. The temporal focus of actors may be less important than the temporal orientation of activities in determining the general course of action in organizations. Combining temporal orientation with temporal depth enables us to identify interesting variations in the temporal orientation of activities.

Dubinskas (1988b) introduces the distinction between closed and open-ended temporal orientations, which complicates things even further. He found that scientists applied an open-ended long-term temporal orientation in contrast to the short-term, closed temporal orientation of managers. However, Orlikowski and Yates clarify that in practice, "an open-ended or closed temporal orientation is not a stable property of occupational groups, but an emergent property of the temporal structures being enacted at the given moment by the groups' members" (Orlikowski & Yates, 2002: 691). An open-ended temporal depth emerges in situations where no event serves as an explicit mark of the provisional closure (Hernes, 2014). Therefore, an open-ended temporal depth has no fixed endpoint when stretching into the past or future. Openness could also refer to the range or selection of possible inputs or outcomes. In contrast to an open-ended temporal depth extending into the past or future without a fixed endpoint or preferred input/outcome, closed-ended temporal depth has a defined endpoint and rigidly defined input/outcome. It is worth emphasizing that although both Dubinskas (1988b) and Orlikowski and Yates (2002) consider closed or open-ended future orientation, closed and open-ended focus also applies to the past of activities.

For example, in their study in the ship design and construction company, Hernes and Pulk (2021) identified two activity streams with distinct temporal orientations. The product development activity stream consisted of long-distance open-ended future orientation as the primary orientation, or the dominant tone complemented by the short-term

5 Socially Constructed Time and Social Time as a Context   199

closed-ended past orientation. In addition to that, the design and production activity stream was characterized by a combination of an imminent closed-ended future orientation complemented with the short-term open-ended past orientation. Table 5.1 presents possible combinations of the temporal orientations of activities considering past-present-future orientation, long-short depth (including the long-present proposed by Kim et al., 2019), and closed or open-ended orientation. In principle, we could also add middle-term temporal depth. Still, I stick to a short-long divide here when considering temporal depth.

If we assume that activities as temporal durations have simultaneously both past and future orientations, then based on Table 5.1 we can draw sixteen temporal combinations as presented in Figure 5.1 below. Reaching only to sixteen combinations of temporal orientation presupposes that for the sake of simplicity and the size of the figure, we exclude the short/long divide of the present and keep the short present only. Considering the short/long divide of the present will double the number of possible combinations.

Our bodily experiences are acquired and accumulated through mundane everyday practices or activities, and our skills are maintained through performing these practices in a routinized manner. Routines, as mundane practices, are an important means for recalling the past, to draw on it, and consult the past for action (Oakeshott, 1995). When performed in a repeated manner, organizational routines help to maintain procedural memory (Hernes, 2014; Orlikowski, 2002) and organizational meaning structures (Hernes, 2014). Recognizing the temporal orientation of activities and understanding their dynamics in organizational settings could help to organize and entrain activities more efficiently. Understanding the temporal orientation of activities could also help to change temporal

Table 5.1 Temporal orientation of activities

Temporal depth	Temporal orientation			
	Past	Present	Future	
Short	Short closed	Short closed	Short closed	**Closed**
	Short open	Short open	Short open	**Open-ended**
Long	Long closed	Long closed	Long closed	**Closed**
	Long open	Long open	Long open	**Open-ended**

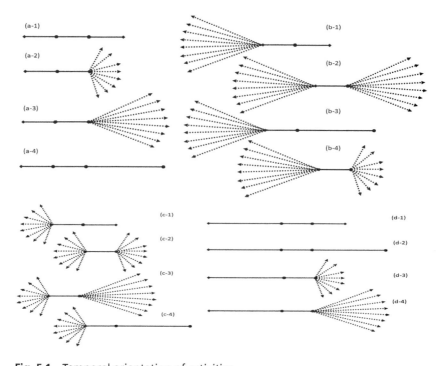

Fig. 5.1 Temporal orientation of activities
(a-1) Short-closed past/ Short-closed future, (a-2) Short-closed past/ Short-open future, (a-3) Short-closed past/ Long-open future, (a-4) Short-closed past/ Long-closed future, (b-1) Long-open past/ Short-closed future, (b-2) Long-open past/ Long-open future, (b-3) Long-open past/ Long-closed future, (b-4) Long-open past/ Short-open future, (c-1) Short-open past/ Short-closed future, (c-2) Short-open past/ Short-open future, (c-3) Short-open past/ Long-open future, (c-4) Short-open past/ Long-short future, (d-1) Long-closed past/ Short-closed future, (d-2) Long-closed past/ Long-closed future, (d-3) Long-closed past/ Short-open future, (d-4) Long-closed past/ Long-open future

structures if there is a need to do so. It would also help understand the challenges of the intended change implementation, difficulties in coordinating or entraining activity streams, etc. Combining the orientations of different activity streams may allow an organization to benefit from the utilization of the *window of opportunity* (Tyre & Orlikowski, 1994) and make either sudden changes in strategic direction or implement an unexpected innovation or both (Hernes et al., 2020; Hernes & Pulk, 2021).

In short, considering that organizations consist of activities and events, then being aware of their temporal orientations and recognizing differing temporal orientations could enhance our understandings of organizational dynamics and hopefully also improve the quality of management.

5.4 Social Time as a Multi-layered Context

Although Gurvitch is focusing on different types of social time, his typology also distinguishes between the different levels of social time. On the one hand, he introduces social times characteristic of groups (meso-time) and communities (eso-time). On the other hand, he highlights the social times characteristics of systems and institutions as macro-time (Hassard, 2001). These different levels enable us to view social time as a multi-layered context of temporal struggles. The levels with a higher aggregation have the asymmetrical power to constrain and condition levels with lower aggregation, while those at the same system level influence one another.

Sonnentag (2012) argues that temporal context is often viewed as a boundary condition in theorizing, which, according to her, is an overly limited approach. While in general, in psychological studies, time is considered as time experienced or perceived (Callender, 2017), Tateo (2015) disagrees with the idea of limiting time to experience. Tateo argues that experience is not creating time, but time is a context for the experience, and "the experience of temporality is possible only in time as context" (Tateo, 2015: 472). Tateo's viewpoint is supported by Bluedorn, who states, "Different temporal realities, different human experience" (2002: 47).

However, Bluedorn's statement could easily be shifted around to "different human experience, different temporal realities." In that sense, it is hard to agree that subjective and social time has nothing to do with experiencing time, providing only a socially constructed context. Viewing social time as a context only means that time is treated as external to human experience, which is not correct either and could easily lead to the chicken or egg problem. Instead of going into either-or choices, it is more helpful to view time as a social context and the human experience of time as parts of the symbiotic whole always shaping and forming one another in their reciprocal relationship.

According to Spradley and Phillips (1972: 526), the temporal social context plays such a significant role that in the context of the difficulties involved in acclimatizing to other cultures it occupies the second position right after language (see also Levine 2006). Following that, it seems well justified to analyse time as a social context. Therefore, let us return to Tateo and the two claims he puts forth. First, time as context is socially constructed, and second, temporality is possible only in time as context. Put differently, our becoming is possible only in the socially constructed time as a context. This does not mean moving to temporal idealism (i.e., Simpson et al. 2020). Instead, it means that humans need social context in their becoming to reach their potential. There are numerous examples of children who, while left socially neglected in their early developmental years, are unable to integrate into a social system later. Notably, human beings as social animals cannot reach their full potential without a supporting social context, and some social contexts are more supportive than others.

However, the plurality of socially created times often contradict and compete with one another, forming the context as temporal struggles. According to a phenomenological worldview, the world as the context for action does not refer only to the spatial, physical world. Instead, the world is referred to mainly as existing temporal relations forming the everydayness for an actor who is *thrown* into this temporal relational everydayness (Heidegger, 1927/1962).

While considering the phenomenological view of context as mainly temporal relations, Tateo (2015) develops his time-as-a-context model, distinguishing between different levels of temporal relations. Tateo (2015) uses four temporal dimensions and distinguishes between micro-time, meso-time, eso-time, and macro-time. Unlike Cipriani (2013), who uses micro-time, meso-time, macro-time, and mega-time as modalities to signify duration or span of time, and proposes that "If one wished to use a geometrical metaphor one might say that micro-time corresponds to a point, meso-time to a section, macro-time to a large segment of a straight line, mega-time to a straight line whose points of origin and conclusion are unknown" (Cipriani, 2013: 28), Tateo (2015) discards representing time as an arrow. Instead, he follows Merleau-Ponty, who, while referring to time, claims that "there are no principal and subordinate problems: all problems are concentric" (Merleau-Ponty, 2002: 477). Therefore, Tateo develops his concentric time-as-a-context model by following the concentric and four-layer structure of Bronfenbrenner's initial bioecological "development-in-context" model (Bronfenbrenner, 1979: 12).

The four environmental layers in Bronfenbrenner's model are microsystem, mesosystem, exosystem (or esosystem) and macrosystem. From the child development perspective (which could also be viewed as a becoming), the microsystem refers to our relationship with an immediate circle of parents, siblings, and peers. The mesosystem includes the extended interactions of microsystems, and exo- or esosystem refers to relationships with an extended family, neighbourhood, school boards, and parents' work environments. Finally, macrosystem stands for general social, cultural, historical, and economic systems (Bronfenbrenner, 1979). While Bronfenbrenner did not pay much attention to time in his 1979 book, time is integrated into micro-, meso-, and macrolevels in his later writing co-authored with Pamela Morris (1998).

In Tateo's (2015) reframing of Bronfenbrenner's "development-in-context" (Bronfenbrenner, 1979: 12), micro-time stands for the immediate and intimate individual psychological experience of temporality. It may also have its own unique rhythm and include ontogenetic and presemiotic time. Meso-time is an intersubjective construction of time, which, through communication, enables sharing and synchronizing individual experiences. Intersubjective meso-time is embedded in eso-time, a socially constructed consensual time at the societal level, and it includes time-related organizing and coordination norms, practices, and artefacts. Macro-time, including natural, historical, and phylogenetic time, represents the time of the era or epoch (Tateo, 2015). Tateo, based on identified time in Bronfenbrenner and Morris (1998), argues that there are at least three interacting layers simultaneously participating in the generation of temporal experience. These three layers are individual ontogenetic time (micro-time), intersubjective cultural/societal time (including both meso-time and eso-time), and natural, historical time (macro-time) (Tateo, 2015: 464, 467). All these layers or temporal dimensions are viewed to be in dynamic development against the irreversible

Table 5.2 Layers of social time as context

The layer of social time	Micro-time	Meso-time	Eso-time	Macro-time
Description of the social time layer	Pre-semiotic and ontogenetic/ Individual psychological experience of temporality	Intersubjective/ Communicated and intersubjective experience	Intersubjective/ Consensual, cultural, and societal	Natural, historical, and phylogenetic/ The evolution of the human species and civilization
The function of the social time layer	Intimate experience of time Individual psychological experience of temporality Individual temporal rhythms	Semiotic meaning of the temporal experience Makes individual time experience sharable Sets the immediate context for individual temporal experience	Sets the frame for experiencing the intersubjective experience of temporality Provides constraints and affordances for the development of the psychological experience Includes the social timing and institutional framing of life's course	Historical framing of human experience, time specific to epoch, or era

Based on: Tateo, L. (2015). Temporality and generalisation in psychology, pp. 477–478, and Marsico, G. (2015). Developing with time: Defining a temporal mereotopology, p. 31

one-directional time. The different layers with their short descriptions are presented in Table 5.2.

Tateo asserts that time as context "is constructed at different levels, corresponding to the progressive distance from the immediate individual experience" (Tateo, 2015: 463). Bronfenbrenner argues that to understand human behaviour, attention should be paid to the broader environment over a longer time. Tateo argues that to understand someone's temporal experience, attention should be paid not only to the immediate micro-time but also to all time layers with their interdependent and interconnected temporal relationships constrained by the irreversibility

5 Socially Constructed Time and Social Time as a Context

of chronological time (Tateo, 2015). Tateo's arguments are supported, for example, by Sonnentag (2012: 363), who argues, "Temporal context can have various layers, including the broader historical context, the economic context, the temporal context of the organization and of the broader organizational settings, as well as the temporal context of the team and of the individual." The idea of temporal embeddedness is also stressed by Lewis and Weigert (1981: 450), who claim that "Temporal embeddedness works as a mechanism making the experience of self continuity, a permanent identity across differing situations, plausible. Temporal embeddedness is a plausibility structure for the experience of the unity and continuity."

It is worth highlighting, that to describe his initial model, Bronfenbrenner uses the metaphor of Russian nested dolls for the multilayered ecological environment: "The ecological environment is conceived as a set of nested structures, each inside the next, like a set of Russian dolls" (Bronfenbrenner, 1979: 3). While this metaphor works well to highlight the concentric relationship of the layers in the model, it may give a false impression about the borders between the different layers. Namely, that the borders between the layers are rigid and close—each doll as a distinct, clearly defined entity without any more relationship with other layers than being embedded in the "upper" layer(s) or including a "lower" layer(s). With the Russian doll metaphor, Bronfenbrenner highlights the nested structure of the ecological environment and not the separateness of the layers. By contrast, in his book, Bronfenbrenner highlights the interconnectedness of the layers.

The idea of the concentric model is that an individual simultaneously experiences several time levels from the inner to the outer circle. Still, the question is what is going on at the borders between these qualitatively different but interconnected layers of time (Marsico, 2015; Tateo, 2015). On the one hand, macro-time as the time of an era or epoch sets the overall frame for societal eso-time, which in turn shapes affordances and constraints for the psychological experience of time both at the level of meso-time and micro-time. On the other hand, the individual psychological experience of micro-time shapes the intersubjective meso-time, which has its influence through eso-time on macro-time (Marsico, 2015; Tateo, 2015). However, the borders between the layers are ambivalent

(Marsico, 2015) and it is hard to imagine exactly how coordination and negotiation between different time levels occurs Marsico, 2015; Tateo, 2015). Still, Marsico (2015) points out that there is an additional complexity concerning temporality in addition to the coordination and negotiation between time levels. Namely, how the temporality of human beings is co-generated, on the one hand, by micro-, meso-, eso-, and macro-time, and on the other, by the recombination of past-present-future.

While the idea of coordination and negotiation between different dimensions of time taking place in a temporal border zone has some appeal if we look at the concentric cylinder presented in Fig. 5.2, it is incredibly challenging to transfer this idea to the social reality. Where and how can we draw these borders (marked with the dotted lines) between the temporal layers and how exactly does negotiation and coordination occur in the temporal border zone? It seems that although the concentric layers of social times are helpful in understanding and maybe also

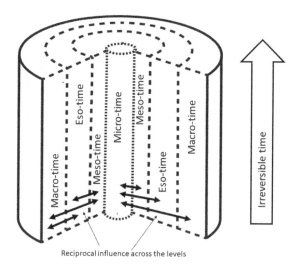

Fig. 5.2 Concentric model of social time as a context
Adapted from: Tateo, L. (2015). Temporality and generalization in psychology: Time as context. In L.M. Simão, D.S. Guimarães, & J. Valsiner (Eds.), *Temporality: Culture in the flow of human experience* (pp. 463–481). Charlotte, NC: Information Age Publishing

5 Socially Constructed Time and Social Time as a Context

analysing the multi-dimensionality of social time, we once again stumble upon the limitations stemming from a spatial representation of time.

While agreeing that distinguishing different temporal layers for analytical reasons could be helpful, I see that stumbling on the borders between these layers is unhelpful. I see the borders between these layers not so much as clear-cut borders but scattered transitions, and thus it is somehow hard to imagine negotiations happening at the borders. It seems that instead of focusing on negotiation taking place on the borders, it is tempting to speculate that it occurs across layers around or related to events. It makes sense to recall the number of scholars from fields as diverse as metaphysics (Whitehead, 1929/1978), physics (Callender, 2017), psychology (Jones, 2019), experimental psychology and neurology (Tulving 1983), sociology (i.e., Clark, 1985; Sorokin & Merton, 1937), and organization studies (Hernes, 2014), highlighting that humans recognize time through events. For example, according to anthropologist Michael Herzfeld, "Social time is the grist of everyday experience. It is above all the kind of time in which *events* cannot be predicted but in which every effort can be made to influence them. It is the time that gives *events* their reality because it encounters each as one of a kind" (Herzfeld, 1991: 10).

As the entire next chapter is devoted to events and event(s)-based time, I am running just slightly ahead of things by arguing that instead of viewing connections between layers taking place in a temporal border zone through negotiations and coordination, I would argue that different layers are connected through events; through the impact an event has on the different temporal layers. Therefore, if negotiation and coordination take place, it takes place around events not at the hypothetical borders. For example, Lewis and Weigert (1981: 433) point out that major events, whether natural, economic or social, could "have lasting effects on individual lives" and as "major points in social time enter the definition of human generations and are more useful sociologically than defining generations in physical, biological time (1981: 433–434). Moreover, viewing events as temporal elements of becoming that are internally connected and mirroring one another (Hernes, 2014) means that the influence of each event is reflected in all other events that are taking place across all the layers. Building on Tateo's time-as-a-context model, Figure 5.3 shows

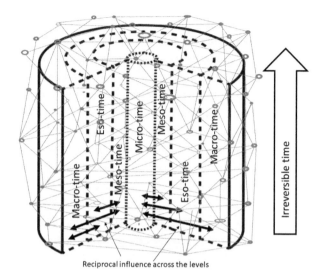

Fig. 5.3 A multi-layered concentric social time connected by events
Adapted from: Tateo, L. (2015). Temporality and generalization in psychology: Time as context. In L.M. Simão, D.S. Guimarães, & J. Valsiner (Eds.), *Temporality: Culture in the flow of human experience* (pp. 463–481). Charlotte, NC: Information Age Publishing

temporal layers or dimensions organized concentrically in irreversible time. At the same time, the network of events connects all layers of social time.

Before devoting our full attention to events (Chap. 6), let's have a look at the four proposed layers of social time, their reciprocal relations, and our relationships to and in these layers.

5.4.1 Micro-time and Meso-time

Micro-time stands for the immediate and intimate individual psychological experience of temporality; it may have its own unique rhythm, and it includes the subjective temporality of lived time, and ontogenetic and pre-semiotic time. Micro-times belong to the private domains of specific individuals and are informed by the biographies of these individuals and influenced by personal time frames leading to an unlimited number of diverse subjective times, as discussed in Chaps. 3 and 4. Individual time frames are affected by an individual's temporal orientation toward past, present, and future, and by their imagination of the future. "Through the use of time, the social subject takes possession of the world and moulds it to meet his or her expectations." (Cipriani, 2013: 12). Although, each micro-time has its unique temporality, connections, and combinations of past-present-future, micro-time never stands apart from its context but needs to consider the limitations imposed by social time. Therefore, those various subjective times are shaped by the intersubjective context (Clark, 1985; Hassard, 2002). In other words, different temporalities of various micro-times are coordinated in and by meso-time. As Bergman and Luckmann put it, "The temporal structure of everyday life confronts me as a facticity with which I must reckon, that is, with which I must try to synchronise my own projects" (Berger & Luckmann, 1991: 41).

Meso-time is an intersubjective construction of time, which, through communication, enables the sharing and synchronizing of individual experiences and time frames. Through communication and sharing experiences, people create memories, make sense of their current circumstances, and envision their futures. Meaning, through intersubjective time, people temporalize themselves. As discussed earlier, the intersubjective time frames are embedded in practices, group activities, and achievements (Sorokin & Merton, 1937). They are influenced by temporal reference to collectively recognisable events with relevance (Hernes, 2014). Holt and Sandberg (2011: 221) add, "we learn about things in relation to entire scenes of significance that rarely come into question" and "our primary relation with things in the everyday world is not that of detachment but absorbed coping." That is, our understanding of things is mediated through conscious or unconscious taken-for-granted assumptions about the temporal context we are operating in. Put differently, our subjective micro-time is influenced by our interaction with other micro-times that together shape the intersubjective meso-time, while at the same time being shaped by that. Therefore, the world becomes a world of the making of the actor, which shapes the actor in turn.

Organizational sociologists share this view, and although they agree that how actors understand time has far-reaching consequences and depends on their personal histories and time orientation, they point out that the person's social interaction influences the experienced personal time (micro-time) (Clark, 1985;Emirbayer & Mische, 1998 ; Gurvitch, 1990a, 1990b) embedded and framed both by the intersubjective (meso-time) and societal-cultural (eso-time) temporal context. Therefore, the time orientation of a decision-maker at the individual level tends to be overruled by the organizational temporal context and by the socially constructed discourse at the collective level. Still, the influence is not one-directional from top down. In his book titled *The Civilizing Process: Sociogenetic and Psychogenetic Investigations*, Elias (2000) describes how the bottom-up intentions of individuals and changes in their everyday habits directly influence the development of civilizations, and thereby, also the socio-temporal context.

As a result, it may be problematic to make a clear distinction between personally experienced time and social time peculiar to a social group. Moreover, sociologists disagree with the fingerprint metaphor (see Chap. 3) to the extent that it refers to the static, unchangeable nature of temporal personality (Emirbayer & Mische, 1998; Gurvitch, 1990a, 1990b). Instead, time orientation is viewed as a dynamic characteristic shaped by ongoing everyday interactions (Emirbayer & Mische, 1998; Lorino & Mourey, 2013).

In everyday interactions (Heidegger, 1927/1962), whether personal or organizational, the temporality of ongoing everyday interactions forms a background we are not necessarily consciously or cognitively aware of. As rooted in national and organizational cultures, temporal concepts (Rowell et al. 2017) are implicitly available to us through *subsidiary* or background awareness (Polanyi, 1967) that relates us to our surroundings and gives meaning to our actions and interactions (Rowell et al. 2017). Temporal concepts are elements of the organizational meaning structures (Hernes, 2014) that mould the background knowledge (Dreyfus, 1991), which is available to an actor at a subconscious level (Polanyi, 1962). Therefore, the efficiency of everyday interactions is achieved through a subsidiary (Polanyi, 1967; Tsoukas, 2003, 2009) or background (Dreyfus, 1991) awareness. Through the subsidiary or background awareness, the everyday copying or the everyday interactions are sensitive to operations (Weick et al. 2008), sensitive to their relational configuration and contextual inter-dependences (Becker 2004; Dreyfus, 1991). On the one hand, the implicit background knowledge includes temporal concepts that in turn guide temporal orientation and patterns. On the other hand, this background knowledge is not static information but bodily experienced temporal knowledge. That is, it incorporates past experiences while anticipating future happenings that are community or organization specific.

However, these relational configurations and contextual interdependences are not limited to meso-time. Holt and Sandberg (2011: 221) claim, "we live in an everyday world of instrumentality in which our intentional relationship with things, far from being individual and somehow private to us as mental beings, is governed by common human, social arrangements." The expression "common human, social arrangements" refers to a more general socially constructed consensual time at the societal level and includes temporal concepts, time-related organizing and coordination norms, practices, and values. Intersubjective meso-time is embedded in societal and cultural eso-time.

5.4.2 Eso-time

Gurvitch argues that it is not possible to separate social man from the total of social phenomena (and thus, from social time). He stresses that "This 'total man' cannot be reduced to mental life, not even to the collective consciousness. He is a body as much as he is a participant of societies, of classes of groups, of We-ness: all representing total social phenomena. And by this reciprocal participation, the total social phenomena participates in man as much as man participates in the whole" (Gurvitch, 1990b: 68). Following his quote, it could be argued that if "the total social phenomena participate in man as much as man participates in the whole" and social time is viewed as a part of the total social phenomena, then social time participates in man as much as man participates in social time (Elias, 2000).

Eso-time stands for a general social, cultural, and economic time. It is available to the whole society and includes public time frames produced and reproduced by all members of society. Eso-time conditions and constrains what happens in meso-time and micro-time and how; that is, how objective temporal rhythms at each level are entrained and the temporal relations of individuals, families, groups, and organizations relate to the world (see Chap. 2). For example, presenting a conflict between two radically different temporal orientations, Reinecke and Ansari (2015), in their study of Fairtrade Labelling Organization International, stress that different temporal orientations are associated with different worldviews (Reinecke & Ansari, 2015).

Referring to Heidegger and James, Tateo claims that "time enters the public sphere through acts of segmentation, measurement and semiotisation. Thus, socialized time enters the realm of interpretation and meaning, making possible the communication of time and coordination of collective activities" (2015: 465). Based on that, it could be argued that eso-time could be viewed as affecting the temporal context at least in five different ways.

First, both the conceptual definition and the semiotic meaning of temporal dimensions of objective time are embedded in a socio-cultural context. That is, the social coding mediated through length or duration, punctuality, frequency, and timing (Levine 2006; Zerubavel, 1987) varies "by eras, and within eras, by culture" (Bluedorn, 2002: 99). Depending on the particular eso-time, the definition of what punctuality is may vary (Levine 2006). Second, as a cultural time, eso-time reflects contemporary social values and norms and determines what is acceptable and what is not acceptable by and large. Using the fingerprint metaphor not for individual but the social temporal approach, Rifkin asserts, "Every culture has its own unique set of temporal fingerprints. To know a people is to know the time values they live by" (Rifkin, 1987: 1).

As "choices of strategy results from a combination of culture and personality" (Bluedorn, 2002: 48), the role of eso-time in choosing what possibilities to realize and what to leave unrealized, or even, which possibilities are recognized and which are not, is essential. Therefore, eso-time conditions and constrains social life; it sets the societal affordances (Gibson, 1986). Third, eso-time acts as an external pace giver (Zeitgeber) to different processes and activities in civil society. It entrains various cycles at the lower-level, operating as a time giver for individual micro-time and organizational meso-time. Fourth, temporal focus and temporal

5 Socially Constructed Time and Social Time as a Context

depth are rooted in eso-time[1] (Bluedorn, 2002), and fifth, eso-time determines, at the societal level, the *perfect* and *telic* aspects of the past (see Sect. 4.1.3) or the practical past (Oakeshott, 1995, see Sect. 4.4); in other words, what of the past matters and how it matters (see Chap. 4). The latter means that eso-time works as an instrument of power (Flaherty 2020; Levine 2006).

Eso-time stands for the era or epoch by giving its specific flavour or putting its stamp on everything taking place across all the different levels. From the societal perspective, for example, Bakhtin (1981) refers to the time of generations respectively as a specific unifying or dividing context. Members belonging to a particular generation share a similar temporal context, which leaves its mark on how they relate to the world, what possibilities they have open for realization, and what potentialities they could actualize. Eso-time for one generation could be significantly different compared to the preceding and following generations.

Eso-time could be a source of systematic constraints by suppressing those whose ambitions have not been confirmed with the existing norms. For example, the possibility of women getting educated, attending university programmes, or working as researchers and scientists is relatively recent, at least in a consistent manner. The availability of education in some vocational fields could be related to the gender discriminative value norms concerning particular professions. I am not sure about the current situation in the railway industry, but I remember that my best friend's older sister was dreaming of becoming a train driver as a child. Unfortunately, that was impossible because, in Estonia, only boys were accepted to the school that prepared train drivers.

Sometimes the eso-time has been a severe constraint to individuals who have been, so to say, "ahead of their (societal) time". For example, personal micro-time, as a temporal relation to the world, including things in the world and ideas about the world, could be well in advance of eso-time as futuristic inventors-creators like Nikolai Tesla, Jules Verne, or Leonardo da Vinci have shown. What they managed to envision was clearly outside the borders of their contemporary time. In this sense, their

---

[1] See Chap. 2 for the prevailing contemporary economic values and a general societal temporal focus, and Chap. 3 for a discussion of temporal depth.

contemporary time was not ready for them, and their ideas and ambitions. Probably, there was too great a gap between their ideas and the expectations of their contemporaries. As Harro Van Lente says in the interview with Benjamin Sovacool, "Expectations' analysis are not psychological but sociological: expectations provide a force that cannot easily be ignored" (Sovacool & Hess, 2017: 723). Arguing from the perspective of the sociology of expectations[2] (also known as the sociology of anticipations or expectations studies), a perspective that "assesses how visions or expectations about future benefits affect and structure technology" (Sovacool & Hess, 2017: 723), it seems to be possible to extend the role of social expectations also to ideas and ideologies.

For example, according to Gordon Walker, the sociology of expectation "gets into understanding the power of ideas and discourses, and how they become embedded in actions" (Sovacool & Hess, 2017: 723). In short, the sociology of expectations views expectations and promises, and emotions, like fear and hope, as formative forces (Sovacool & Hess, 2017). That is to say, expectations, promises, fears, and hopes at the societal level form the basis for recognizing new possibilities, a collective openness to new possibilities, and the readiness for their realization. It seems that, for example, society was ripe for the decisive church reforms initiated by Martin Luther early in the sixteenth century. Although Luther and his followers were convicted of heresy and expelled from the Catholic Church, they managed to avoid being burnt alive, and the church reform spread fast (Stern, 2020). While it was not Luther's purpose to initiate a new branch of Christianity but to just improve some habits within the Catholic Church, things became otherwise. It also seemed that the time was ripe for the dissolution of the Soviet Union around 1990–1992, which just happened almost organically to the great surprise of many.

Eso-time draws boundaries not only for micro-time but also for meso-time, as temporal relations to the world. For example, my grandmother—who was born during the Bolshevik revolution in 1905 and lived through the two world wars, witnessed both the German and Soviet occupation (the latter even twice) and both the first and second independent state of

---

[2] Also called 'the sociology of anticipations' or 'expectation studies' (Sovacool & Hess, 2017: 723).

Estonia—had quite different adulthood relations to the world compared to my parents. My adulthood relations to the world are quite different from my parents' adulthood relations to the world in Estonia under Soviet occupation between 1944 and 1991.[3] The societal time now and the societal time as I remember it from my childhood are significantly different. During the Soviet occupation, private entrepreneurship was prohibited in Estonia, and all organized economic activities were centrally controlled. Meaning, not only were economic activities controlled by the government but organizational time was also subordinated to the principles of central control. Through the organization time, family life was also affected by the societal eso-time. I remember that when I was still in kindergarten, I complained to my grandmother that my mom was waking me up in the middle of the night to take me to kindergarten. Although it was not necessarily true that mother had kicked me out of my bed in the middle of the night, it was neither completely wrong if we take into consideration that the working day started at eight in the morning. To be at work on time, she most probably woke me up around 6.20 am. Now, if we add that the clock in Estonia was set according to Moscow time, which is one hour ahead of the *natural zone time*, the time I was woken was 5.20 am. If we add that at such a time in the morning, there is complete deep darkness outside during most of the year, then we end up witnessing my childhood trauma—my mom dragging me out of bed and taking me to the kindergarten in the middle of the night.

From my school years, I remember that during the first two years from 1979 to 1981, I also had classes on Saturday because, at that time, the working week was six days long, reflecting the values of a proletarian society and the economic necessity of the post-war period. Therefore, the length of the school week reflected the length of the working week, and there was only one day per week for the family to be together. Only when the working week was shortened to five days, was the length of the school week also cut to five days. Therefore, the way society operated then reflected the underlying ideological values, much like the setup of the vast majority of contemporary societies underscore economic efficiency, commercialization, monetization, and short-termism in almost all

---

[3] The Soviet occupation in Estonia took place in years 1940-1941 and 1944-1991.

possible relations (see Chap. 2). Importantly, as Luhmann states, "An organization, thus, always finds society in a double sense: within itself and in its environment. What is special about organizations is how they organize this difference" (2018: 318). Meaning, according to Luhmann, the uniqueness of organizations is rooted in how they handle the temporal tensions between societal eso-time and organizational meso-time.

At the same time, social norms about something considered acceptable, unacceptable, or even criminal are considered *time-specific*. Still, they have significantly affected how individuals, families, and social collectives related to the world. Debates about the status of single mothers or rights of same-sex partners to be officially married are relatively recent, and the discussion on the latter topic is in many societies still ongoing. Being a girl with a child was considered so shameful that social contempt forced many young women to walk into the sea across different countries just a short century ago. On the other hand, even if Oscar Wilde had lived instead of in Victorian-era Britain, in post-war Soviet Estonia from the early fifties to the late eighties, he would have faced the same destiny—he would have finished in jail and his works would have been removed from sale as happened in Victorian era Britain. Therefore, some societal norms are so deeply rooted that they carry through centuries and across political regimes. However, their relative endurance does not mean that they are not subject to become otherwise.

Consequently, Jaques' observation, "In the form of time is to be found the form of living" (Jaques, 1982: 129), is highly valid. However, it is important to recognize the evolving nature of societal norms in the civil world. Cornejo and Olivares (2015: 99) insist that understanding every culture, including our own, should "be done under the principle that social life is always temporally in the process of becoming something else". Notably, culture as a semiotic system is in continuous change, but that applies to all social systems, to the entire set up of all societies, which means our being in the everyday world is highly temporal—not only because of the ongoing temporality of our sensemaking but also because of the ongoing evolving temporality of time-as-a-context.

5.4.3 Macro-time

Macro-time, in Tateo's model,[4] includes natural, historical, and phylogenetic time. Macro-time is a general background to all other layers or dimensions. As dilating "both backwards, towards what has already happened, and forward, towards what has yet to be" (Cipriani, 2013: 27), macro-time has an important role in supporting the maintenance of perceived temporal continuity at the level of eso-, meso-, and micro-time. Huy makes a valid point saying, "Since one cannot distinguish a figure without a background, the present does not meaningfully exist without a past" (2001: 191). Therefore, by including historical time, macro-time serves as an invaluable source for the future and the background to the present. The past provides a background to the present and makes the present visible through a comparison of the differences between the two. According to Saussure, "Difference makes character" (Saussure, 1959: 121), and so it could be argued that the difference between the past and present identified by comparing these two makes the character of both.

As the locus of human action and agency is the present (Mead, 1932/2002), then the focus is on understanding the present *with the help of the past*. In the words of Bluedorn, "the past provides a context, a frame, for the present, and the linkages with the past provide an explanation for the present by suggesting how the present came to be, which makes the present more understandable, more meaningful" (Bluedorn, 2002: 191).

However, as highlighted by Cipriani (2013), macro-time dilates not only backwards, but also forward, creating the future vision for society. There is a general agreement that the ability to project the future depends on the past, and respectively, the temporal depth to the future depends on the temporal depth to the past (i.e., Bakken et al., 2013; Bluedorn, 2002; Hernes, 2014; Kaplan & Orlikowski, 2013; Schultz & Hernes, 2013), and not the other way around. Because the past provides meaning

---

[4] For example, Zerubavel (1987) describes macro-time in a way that in Tateo's time-as-a-context model would classify as eso-time. Therefore, exact categories and the distinctions between them could be fluid and arbitrary, and it is important to pay close attention to how different categories are defined by different authors.

to the present and grounds to project to the future, it is hard to overestimate the role of the practical past (Oakeshott, 1995, see also Sect. 4.4).

Nevertheless, if individuals are selective about their past and their memories about the past are biased and distorted, there is no reason to assume that things are much different at the more aggregated level of social groups or societal systems. The manipulative presentation of the past is a common tool "at the macrosocial level of societal politics" (Zerubavel, 1987: 353). It could be in the interests of the ruling power to legitimize a particular interpretation of the past to control the future (Oakeshott, 1995). Therefore, it is no wonder that different regimes have suppressed some historical details and highlighted others, and we could expect to find numerous attempts to rewrite history (see also Sect. 4.4), as a rule, in favour of the ruling power or regime. Therefore, although standing for the highest level of aggregation, macro-time is neither objective nor neutral.

While in the time-as-a-context model, macro-time stands for the most stable and slowest changing layer, it is still changing. And it is changing not only because of the natural events "ordered in their own endogenous sequence" (Rousse, 2021: 2) in the irreversible passage of time, but also because of human (in)actions. This means that the relationships between the temporal layers of social time as a context are not one-directional, but all the layers are mutually co-constructing one another. This idea is expressed by Merleau-Ponty who states, "The civilisation in which I play my part exists for me in a self-evident way … I experience a certain cultural environment along with behaviour corresponding to it" (Merleau-Ponty, 2002: 405, 406). However, he underlines that all his perceptions are standing "out against a background of nature" (Merleau-Ponty, 2002: 404), meaning the natural and cultural environments are not in isolation from one another or from the behaviour of individuals.

Thus, in the phenomenological view of Merleau-Ponty, the personal, natural, and cultural realms merge into the coherent context, and each cultural environment, including its temporal relations and their semiotic meaning, is experienced according to understandings specific to environments. Simultaneously, as we all play our part in the existing civilization, we are all affecting nature through the symbiotic relationship between nature and culture. It is agreed, by and large, that fast changes with significant ecological consequences like climate change, ocean acidification, habitat destruction, extinction, and wide-scale natural resource extraction, are taking place. These changes that are shaping planet Earth with accelerating speed are caused by human activities such as carbon dioxide emissions, agriculture, urbanization, deforestation, and a general pollution. As a result, although not yet uniformly agreed, numerous convincing signs support the view that the Earth has entered a new geological epoch called the Anthropocene.

Viewing social time as a temporal multi-layered context where all the layers influence one another from top down and bottom up (Elias, 2000), then we might expect to see events in macro-time mirrored (Hernes, 2014) in events in other layers of the social context and *vice versa*. Therefore, all the layers are together in their becoming and constituting one another, which means that in conjunction with the changes in macro-time, changes are expected in eso-, meso-, and micro-time. As Nowotny states, "The future of our children is no longer predominantly interpreted in individual terms—as the desire for social advancement and well-being—but as a question of collective survival. It is the *time* of the next generation which is being argued about now" (Nowotny, 1992: 52 *emphasis added*).

5.4.4 Temporality of Time-as-a-context

An economic historian, North (1999) is concerned about time as a missing dimension in political sciences. North (1999) is convinced that without time being added to the equation, it is impossible to understand and explain the long-term developments in economic performance and change at the societal level. North is concerned with the *becoming* of ideas, beliefs, and institutions that influence the becoming of societies through economic performance. He expresses his conviction that without that, we cannot achieve a position as a prominent political scientist:

> "For an economic historian, time has always been something that is fundamentally disturbing, because there is no time in neoclassical theory. The neoclassical model is a model of an instant of time, and it does not therefore

take into account what time does.... I will be blunt: Without a deep understanding of time, you will be lousy political scientists, because time is the dimension in which ideas and institutions and beliefs evolve." (North, 1999: 316)

North's concerns related to "a model of an instant of time" are addressed, for example, by Heidegger (1927/1962: 474), who points out that *now-time* is based on the view that each case has its own *now-time*. In the framework of *now-time*, where time is seen as a pure succession, it does not have significance (Heidegger, 1927/1962).

On the one hand, from the perspective of an individual, the *intentional relationship with things* indicates that the meaning of things (i.e., their significance to human actors) is being-ready-to-hand in order to do something with the thing (Heidegger, 1927/1962). According to Heidegger (1927/1962) 'being-ready-to-hand' requires experience-based bodily knowledge from the actor, that they know how to handle a thing or tool and for what the specific thing or tool is or could be used for. Experiences need to be repeated before they are internalized into bodily knowledge (Polanyi, 1962). That is, to establish relationships to things, including the world, requires time. The claim that the properties of things are pre-set or "governed by common human, social arrangements" (Holt & Sandberg, 2011: 221) indicates that the everyday world, into which humans are thrown, is based on internalized knowledge and established (taken-for-granted) social arrangements. Both internalized knowledge and established social arrangements have an ongoing temporal nature. They are what they are in the specific temporal context. The relationship of things and common social arrangements is temporal; this relationship has a past. It is evolving into the future, tying the meaning of things temporally to human arrangements that are also temporal, not permanent.

On the other hand, our subjective lived experience of time influences the way we connect to reality and make sense of that (Heidegger, 1927/1962; Merleau-Ponty, 2002). Therefore, in organizations, we can expect to encounter various subjective times (note the plurality here). Those various subjective times are context-specific (Clark, 1985; Hassard, 2002), and this context includes both meso- and eso-times. Still, sharing an organizational and societal context does not mean the sameness of the

5 Socially Constructed Time and Social Time as a Context 221

micro-time. While several micro-times share meso- and eso-times, they each still have their unique individual temporalities, the connections and combinations of past-present-future. However, as Holt and Sandberg (2011: 221) claim, our "relationship with things, far from being individual and somehow private to us as mental beings, is governed by common human, social arrangements". Broader governing social arrangements that are in the dynamic process of becoming (Cornejo & Olivares, 2015) form the basis for a culture. Therefore, our being in the everyday world is highly temporal, not only because of the ongoing temporality of our sensemaking but also because the ongoing evolving temporality of time-as-a-context.

The ongoing temporality across the layers of social-time-as-a-context means that time-reckoning systems in their plurality are not fixed and static but evolving and changing in the flow of time due to the ongoing interactions across different temporal layers. In this sense, people create social times as much as social times create people. This idea is not something revolutionary and new. In their introduction to Italian political philosopher Giambattista Vico's third edition of *The New Science of Giambattista Vico*, Bergin and Fisch refer to Aristotle when stating that "The question of the nature of man is a question of becoming; there is nothing more natural than becoming; and the becoming of the *polis* is as natural as that of man, because these are not two becomings but one" (Bergin & Fisch, 1961: xxvii). Therefore, Aristotle already saw the becoming as an essence of both human existence and civil society. Moreover, he shows them as one united process of becoming instead of two separated processes. In other words, we can say that the becoming of social actors, processes, and systems is one process that combines different temporalities, possibilities, and potentialities into one unified evolution. This "evolutionary achievement of meaning" is irreversible, it is "grounded in the irreversibility of time" (Luhmann, 2018: 450).

Although Vico's work dates back to the first half of the eighteenth century, his thoughts are fresh and resonate with a process theory and temporal perspectives that are gradually establishing themselves in organization theories through current publications. It is easy to imagine Vico as one of the keynote speakers at the *Symposium on Process Organization Studies*. Being a political philosopher, Vico is interested in the very essence and principal laws of civil society. He builds his argumentation on the assumption of genesis or becoming; viewing nations as following an ontogenetic pattern of birth, development, maturity, decline, and fall. Notably, Vico did not see change in institutions as an adaptation to external forces but as their becoming fuelled by internal drives and stresses. Opening Vico's views, Bergin and Fisch emphasize that,

"a nation is identified not merely in cross section by a set of institutions shared by a group of people at a given time, but genetically by a system of institutions continually changing, whose changes are due not to external influences but to internal stresses, … There is not only an original and individual birth of new institutions within it, a continual transformation of old institutions, even a rebirth of the nation after death" (Bergin & Fisch, 1961: xxiii).

Vico states straightforwardly, "The nature of institutions is nothing but their coming into being *(nascimento)* at certain times and in certain guises. Whenever the time and guise are thus and so, such and not otherwise are institutions that come into being" (Vico, 1744/1961: 22). He argues that because civil society is manmade, its principles are manmade too, reflecting the ideas of humans as resulting from the "robust ignorance" of "corporeal imagination" (Vico, 1744/1961: 75), which Vico contrasted to the purest intelligence of God indicating that humans, in their corporeal imagination are unable to see the actuality with all its related potentialities. Additionally, Vico points out that humans create their realities by making choices, but "Human choice, by its nature most uncertain, is made certain and determined by the common sense of men with respect to human needs or utilities," however, "Common sense is judgment without reflection, shared by an entire class, an entire people, an entire nation, or the entire human race" (Vico, 1744/1961: 21).

In other words, men, when creating a civil society, are led by common sense ideas and corporeal imagination. As such, they lack "the purest" divine intelligence, which means knowing things profoundly, including both their positive and less positive potentialities with respective probabilities to actualize. The tendency to follow common sense without reflection refers to functional stupidity, a term coined by Alvesson and Spicer

(2012). As Alvesson and Spicer (2012) stress, functional stupidity as the unreflective conformity to existing ways of operating could make general coordination easier and establish provisional stability in highly dynamic environments if that provisional stability is suboptimal. Although Alvesson and Spicer (2012) discuss the occurrence of functional stupidity in organizations, it is easy to extend it from the socio-temporal context of organizations to the socio-temporal contexts of families and societies. However, "commonly held temporal assumptions and beliefs *exert* systemic influences over social action" (Cuganesan, 2021: 2). Not surprisingly, as a rule, commonly held temporal assumptions are aligned with the views of those in power (van de Scott, 2020). On the other hand, people "can become active agents reconstructing their own social relations" (Benson, 1977: 5), including their temporal relations and relations to time. People can challenge common sense ideas, including prevailing social time with its taken-for-granted ideologies (van de Scott, 2020) by reflecting and communicating their reflection back to context. Although that kind of initiative could easily be seen as rebellious action against the existing power, and thus, not welcome, history shows that human ideas and ideologies, including temporal norms, are not permanent and fixed but evolving.

It is easy to agree with North's (1999) claim that focusing only on the current circumstances without considering the agency of time or *what time does* and what it possibly could do, it is hard to become a superior political scientist. It is tempting to add that understanding neither the intersubjective nature of social time nor social time as a multi-layered context, where different layers of social time are forming each other and co-generating the temporal reality, and informing each other and co-generating the temporal experience, it is impossible to become a superior practitioner either.

5.5 Conclusion

As this chapter reveals, the standard time of everyday life is not the same as standardized clock time. Compared to the standardized clock time, which is also socially constructed, the standard time of everyday life is much more complex and complicated. One possible approach is to view the standard time of everyday life as a vibrant constellation of various social times in their plurality held by different individuals and social groups. Having their specific relations to the past and future and emphasizing either continuity or discontinuity, social times have different temporalities. In their ongoing interactions, social times collide and create challenges for one another while continuing the ongoing transformation. Viewed as consisting of a diversity of micro-times and intersubjectively shared temporal experiences moulded by broader social expectations and historical background, all of which are temporalized while evolving through irreversible time, makes social time a multi-layered and dynamic temporal reality.

Although individuals may have their psychological time and personal temporality, their individual time is never purely psychological but always also social. In the organizational context, the time orientation of individuals seems only to play a secondary role, as the time orientation of individuals tends to be over-ridden by the temporal orientation of activities as shared social forms to accomplish something. In other words, individual human beings are in an ongoing interaction with the broader social context with its multiple layers and ongoing temporalities. Therefore, the multi-layered social system forms a person, who in turn, shapes the social context. In that sense, people create social times as much as social times create people.

However, in qualitatively different time-reckoning systems, the meaning of time and temporality could vary significantly. These differences include the semiotic meaning ascribed to duration, sequence, pace, frequency, punctuality, and the meaning of the past and expected future. Therefore, the existing possibilities are seen and evaluated in the context of social time; that is, in the context of existing temporal expectations and beliefs.

References

Abrantes, A. C., Passos, A. M., Cunha, M. P., & Santos, C. M. (2018). Bringing team improvisation to team adaptation: The combined role of shared temporal cognitions and team learning behaviors fostering team performance. *Journal of Business Research, 84*, 59–71.

Adam, B. (1990). *Time and social theory*. Polity Press.

Alvesson, M., & Spicer, A. (2012). A stupidity-based theory of organizations. *Journal of Management Studies, 49*(7), 1194–1220. https://doi.org/10.1111/j.1467-6486.2012.01072.x

Ancona, D. G., Okhuysen, G. A., & Perlow, L. A. (2001). Taking time to integrate temporal research. *Academy of Management Review, 26*(4), 512–529.

Baars, J. (2012). Critical turns of aging, narrative and time. *International Journal of Ageing and Later Life, 7*(2), 143–165.

Bakhtin, M. (1981). *The dialogic imagination: Four essays*. University of Texas Press.

Bakken, T., Holt, R., & Zundel, M. (2013). Time and play in management practice: An investigation through the philosophies of McTaggart and Heidegger. *Scandinavian Journal of Management, 29*, 13–22.

Benson, J. K. (1977). Organizations: A dialectical view. *Administrative Science Quarterly, 22*, 1–21.

Berger, P., & Luckmann, T. (1991). *The social construction of reality: A treatise in the sociology of knowledge*. Penguin Books.

Bergin, T. G., & Fisch, M. H. (1961). *Introduction for The new science of Giambattista Vico*. Ancor Books Doubleday and Company.

Bluedorn, A. C. (2002). *The human organization of time*. Stanford University Press.

Bronfenbrenner, U. (1979). *The ecology of human development: Experiments by nature and design*. Harvard University Press.

Bronfenbrenner, U., & Morris, P. A. (1998). The ecology of developmental process. In W. Damon & R. M. Lerner (Eds.), *Handbook of child psychology: Vol. 1. Theoretical models of human development* (pp. 939–991). John Wiley.

Callender, C. (2017). *What makes time special?* Oxford University Press.

Claggett, J. L., & Karahanna, E. (2018). Unpacking the structure of coordination mechanisms and the role of relational coordination in an era of digitally mediated work processes. *Academy of Management Review, 43*(4), 704–722.

Clark, P. (1985). A review of theories of time and structure for organizational sociology. In S. B. Bacharach & S. M. Mitchel (Eds.), *Research in the sociology of organizations* (Vol. 4, pp. 35–79). Bingley.

Cipriani, R. (2013). The many faces of social time: A sociological approach. *Time & Society, 22*(1), 5–30.

Cornejo, C., & Olivares, H. (2015). Living and observing: Two modes of understanding time. In L. M. Simão, D. S. Guimarães, & J. Valsiner (Eds.), *Temporality: Culture in the flow of human experience* (pp. 95–114). Information Age Publishing.

Cuganesan, S. (2021). Investigating how the clock–event time dialectic shapes the doing of time in organizational change. *Organization Studies, 1*, 1–23. Advance online publication. https://doi.org/10.1177/01708406211006252

Dougherty, D., Bertels, H., Chung, K., Dunne, D. D., & Kraemer, J. (2013). Whose time is it? Understanding clock-time pacing and event-time pacing in complex innovations. *Management and Organization Review, 9*, 233–263.

Dreyfus, H. L. (1991). *Being-in-the-World: A commentary on Heidegger's Being and Time, Division I*. The MIT Press.

Dubinskas, F. A. (1988a). Cultural construction: The many faces of time. In F. A. Dubinskas (Ed.), *Making time: Ethnographies of high-technology organizations* (pp. 3–38). Temple University Press.

Dubinskas, F. A. (1988b). Janus organizations: Scientists and managers in genetic engineering firms. In F. A. Dubinskas (Ed.), *Making Time: Ethnographies of High Technology Organizations* (pp. 170–232). Temple University Press.

Eldor, L., Fried, Y., Westman, M., Levi, A. S., Shipp, A. J., & Slowik, L. H. (2017). The experience of work stress and the context of time: Analyzing the role of subjective time. *Organizational Psychology Review, 7*, 227–249. https://doi.org/10.1177/2041386617697506

Elias, N. (1994). *Reflections on a life*. Blackwell Publishers; Polity Press.

Elias, N. (2000). *The civilizing process: Sociogenetic and psychogenetic investigations*. Blackwell Publishing.

Emirbayer, M., & Mische, A. (1998). What is agency? *American Journal of Sociology, 103*(4), 962–1023.

Fuchs, T. (2013). Temporality and psychopathology. *Phenomenology and the Cognitive Sciences, 12*(1), 75–104. https://doi.org/10.1007/s11097-010-9189-4

Gibson, J. J. (1986). *The ecological approach to visual perception*. Psychology Press.

Granqvist, N., & Gustafsson, R. (2016). Temporal Institutional Work. *Academy of Management Journal, 59*(3), 1009–1035.

Gurvitch, G. (1964/1990a). The Problem of time. In Hassard, J. (Ed.), (1990) *The sociology of time* (pp. 35–44). Macmillan.

Gurvitch, G. (1964/1990b). Varieties of social-time. In Hassard, J. (Ed.), (1990) *The sociology of time* (pp. 67–76). Macmillan.

Hassard, J. (1996). Images of time in work and organizations. In S. R. Clegg, C. Hardy, & W. R. Nord (Eds.), *Handbook of Organization Studies* (pp. 581–598). Sage.

Hassard, H. (2001). Commodification, construction and compression: A review of time metaphors in organizational analysis. *International Journal of Management Review, 3*(2), 131–141.

Hassard, J. (2002). Essay: Organizational time: Modern, symbolic and postmodern reflections. *Organization Studies, 23*(6), 885–892.

Heidegger, M. (1927/1962). *Being and time*. Blackwell Publishers.

Hernes, T. (2014). *A process theory of organization*. Oxford University Press.

Hernes, T., & Pulk, K. (2021). How actors effect shifts in strategic trajectories: The role of temporal nexus events. *Academy of Management Annual Meeting Proceedings, 2021*(1), 11898.

Hernes, T., & Schultz, M. (2020). How actors translate between the on-going and the distant: A temporal view of situated activity. *Organization Theory, 1*, 1. https://doi.org/10.1177/2631787719900999

Hernes, T., Simpson, B., & Söderlund, J. (2013). Managing and temporality. *Scandinavian Journal of Management, 29*, 1–6.

Hernes, T., Feddersen, J., & Schultz, M. (2020). Material temporality: How materiality 'does' time in food organizing. *Organization Studies, 1*, 1. https://doi.org/10.1177/0170840620909974

Herzfeld, M. (1991). *A place in history: Social and monumental time in a Cretan Town*. Princeton University Press.

Holt, R., & Sandberg, J. (2011). Phenomenology and organization theory. *Philosophy and Organization Theory, 32*, 215–249.

Huy, Q. N. (2001). Time, temporal capability, and planned change. *Academy of Management Review, 26*, 601–623.

Jarzabkowski, P., Balogun, J., & Seidl, D. (2007). Strategizing: The challenges of a practice perspective. *Human Relations, 60*(1), 5–27. https://doi.org/10.1177/0018726707075703

Jaques, E. (1982/1990). The enigma of time. In Hassard, J. (Ed.), (1990) *The sociology of time* (pp. 21–34). Basingstoke: Macmillan.

Jones, M. R. (2019). *Time will tell: A theory of dynamic attending*. Oxford University Press.

Kaplan, S., & Orlikowski, W. (2013). Temporal work in strategy making. *Organization Science, 24*(4), 965–995.

Kim, A., Bansal, P., & Haugh, H. (2019). No time like the present: How a present time perspective can foster sustainable development. *Academy of Management Journal, 62*(2), 607–634.

Lawrence, P., & Lorsch, J. (1967). Differentiation and integration in complex organizations. *Administrative Science Quarterly, 12*(1), 1–47. https://doi.org/10.2307/2391211

Lewis, D. J., & Weigert, A. J. (1981). The structures and meaning of social time. *Social Forces, 60*(2), 432–462.

Lorino, P., & Mourey, D. (2013). The experience of time in the inter-organizing inquiry: A present thickened by dialog and situations. *Scandinavian Journal of Management, 29*, 48–62.

Luhmann, N. (2018). *Organization and Decision*. Cambridge University Press.

Marsico, G. (2015). Developing with time: Defining a temporal mereotopology. In L. M. Simão, D. S. Guimarães, & J. Valsiner (Eds.), *Temporality: Culture in the flow of human experience* (pp. 23–40). Information Age Publishing.

McGivern, G., Dopson, S., Ferlie, E., Fischer, M., Fitzgerald, L., Ledger, J., & Bennett, C. (2018). The silent politics of temporal work: A case study of a management Consultancy Project to Redesign Public Health Care. *Organization Studies, 39*(8), 1007–1030.

Mead, G. H. (1932/2002). *The philosophy of the present*. Prometheus.

Merleau-Ponty, M. (2002). *Phenomenology of perception*. Routledge Classics.

Minkowski, E. (1970). *Lived time: Phenomenological and psychopathological studies*. Northwest University Press.

North, D. C. (1999). In anticipation of the marriage of political and economic theory. In M.L.A.E.O. James E. Alt (Ed.), *Competition and Cooperation: Conversations with nobelists about economics and political science* (pp. 314–317). Russel Sage Foundation.

Nowotny, H. (1992). Time and social theory. Towards a social theory of time. *Time & Society, 1*(3), 421–454.

Oakeshott, M. (1995). *Experience and its modes*. Cambridge University Press.

Orlikowski, W. J. (2002). Knowing in practice: Enacting a collective capability in distributed organizing. *Organization Science, 13*(3), 249–273.

Orlikowski, W. J., & Yates, J. (2002). It's about time: Temporal structuring in organizations. *Organization Science, 13*(6), 684–700.

Polanyi, M. (1962). *Personal knowledge*. University of Chicago Press.

Polanyi, M. (1967). *The tacit dimension*. Routledge & K. Paul.

Pulk, K. (2016). *Making time while being in time: A study of the temporality of organizational processes*. PhD series, no. 43.2016, Copenhagen Business School [Phd], Frederiksberg.

Reinecke, J., & Ansari, S. (2015). When times collide: Temporal brokerage at the intersection of markets and developments. *Academy of Management Journal, 58*(2), 618–648.

Reinecke, J., & Ansari, S. (2017). Time, temporality, and process studies. In A. Langley & H. Tsoukas (Eds.), *The SAGE Handbook of Process Organization Studies* (pp. 402–416). SAGE Publications. https://doi.org/10.4135/9781473957954.n25

Rifkin, J. (1987). *Time wars: The primary conflict in human history*. Holt.

Rousse, B. S. (2021). Retrieving Heidegger's temporal realism. *European Journal of Philosophy, 1*, 1–22.

Saussure, F. D. (1959). *Course in general linguistics*. Philosophical Library.

Schultz, M., & Hernes, T. (2013). A temporal perspective on organizational identity. *Organization Science, 24*(1), 1–21.

Schütz, A. (1962/1982). *Collected papers I: The problem of social reality*. Martinus Nijhoff Publishers.

Schütz, A. (1967). *The phenomenology of the social world*. Heinemann Educational Books.

Shipp, A. J., & Cole, M. S. (2015). Time in individual-level organizational studies: What it is, how it is used, and why isn't it exploited more often? *Annual Review of Organizational Psychology and Organizational Behavior, 2*(1), 237–260.

Shipp, A. J., & Fried, Y. (2014). Time research in management: Using temporal ambassadors to translate ideas into reality. In A. J. Shipp & Y. Fried (Eds.), *Time and work, Volume 1: How time impacts individuals* (pp. 1–10). Psychology Press.

Siren, C., Parida, V., Frishammar, J., & Wincent, J. (2020). Time and time-based organizing of innovation: Influence of Temporality on Entrepreneurial firm's performance. *Journal of Business Research, 112*, 23–32.

Slawinski, N., & Bansal, P. (2015). Short on time: Intertemporal tensions in business sustainability. *Organization Science, 26*(2), 531–549.

Smith, D.W. (2013). Phenomenology. *Stanford encyclopedia of philosophy*. Retrieved April 12, 2021, from https://plato.stanford.edu/entries/phenomenology/.

Spradley, J. P., & Phillips, M. (1972). Culture and stress: A quantitative analysis. *American Anthropologist, 74*, 518–529.

Sonnentag, S. (2012). Time in organizational research: Catching up on a long neglected topic in order to improve theory. *Organizational Psychology Review, 2*(4), 361–368. https://doi.org/10.1177/2041386612442079

Sorokin, P. A., & Merton, R. K. (1937). Social Time: A Methodological and Functional Analysis. *American Journal of Sociology, 42*(5), 615–629.

Sovacool, B. K., & Hess, D. J. (2017). Ordering theories: Typologies and conceptual frameworks for sociotechnical change. *Social Studies of Science, 47*(5), 703–750.

Standifer, R. L., & Bluedorn, A. C. (2006). Alliance management teams and entrainment: Sharing temporal mental models. *Human Relations, 59*, 903–927.

Stern, R. (2020). Martin Luther. *The Stanford Encyclopedia of Philosophy* (Fall 2020 Edition), Edward N. Zalta (ed.). Retrieved June 20, 2021, from https://plato.stanford.edu/archives/fall2020/entries/luther.

Tateo, L. (2015). Temporality and generalization in psychology: Time as context. In L. M. Simão, D. S. Guimarães, & J. Valsiner (Eds.), *Temporality: Culture in the flow of human experience* (pp. 463–481). Information Age Publishing.

Thompson, E. P. (1967). Time, work-Discipline, and industrial capitalism. *Past and Present, 38*, 56–97.

Tsoukas, H. (2003). Do we really understand tacit knowledge? In M. Easterby-Smith & M. Lyles (Eds.), *The Blackwell Handbook of Organizational Learning and Knowledge Management* (pp. 410–427). Blackwell.

Tsoukas, H. (2009). A dialogical approach to the creation of new knowledge in organizations. *Organization Science, 20*(6), 941–957.

Tyre, M. J., & Orlikowski, W. J. (1994). Windows of opportunity: Temporal patterns of technological adaptation in organizations. *Organization Science, 5*, 98–118.

van de Scott, L.-J. K. (2020). Temporal front and back stages: Time work as resistance. In M. G. Flaherty, L. Meinert, & A. L. Dalsgård (Eds.), *Time Work: Studies of Temporal Agency* (pp. 83–101). Berghahn Books.

Vico, G. (1744/1961). *The new science of Giambattista Vico*. Anchor Books Doubleday and Company.

Wenzel, M., Krämer, H., Koch, J., & Reckwitz, A. (2020). Future and organization studies: On the rediscovery of a problematic temporal category in organizations. *Organization Studies, 41*(10), 1441–1455.

Whitehead, A.N. (1929/1978). *Process and reality*. The Free Press.

Whitelegg, D. (2007). *Working the skies The fast-paced, disorienting world of the flight attendant*. New York University Press.

Yakura, E. K. (2002). Charting time: Timelines as temporal boundary objects. *Academy of Management Journal, 45*(5), 956–970.

Zerubavel, E. (1982). The standardization of time: A sociohistorical perspective. *American Journal of Sociology, 1*, 1–23.
Zerubavel, E. (1987). The language of time: Toward a semiotics of temporality. *The Sociological Quarterly, 28*(3), 343–356.
Zerubavel, E. (2003). *Time maps: Collective memory and the social shape of the past.* University of Chicago Press.

6

Events, Time, and Events-Based Time

Events play a central role in how we understand temporality and time. We do not remember an abstract past, neither do we anticipate or direct our intentionality towards an abstract future. Instead, we remember the past in the form of events, and we anticipate the future as events occur. The centrality of events in recognizing time and making it visible to humans is emphasized by several authors across different streams of literature. For example, events are central in Whitehead's metaphysics, in the phenomenological philosophy of Heidegger (1927/1962) and Merleau-Ponty (2002), in Mead's philosophy of pragmatism (1932/2002), in Luhmann's (1995, 2018) theory of organizations as autopoietic social systems, in Hernes' (2014a) process theory of organization, in psychology as argued by Jones (2019) and in the theory of memory in cognitive neuroscience by Tulving (1983). This list is far from exhaustive, presenting only a few names from a few fields.

The notion of the event has found its way to organization studies. Although there is agreement about the tight connection between events and time and general agreement that "the world is a world of events" (Mead, 1932/2002: 1), understanding the exact nature of this connection and the conceptualization of time and events varies. In organizational studies, the connection between time and events is addressed at least in four conceptually different ways. Importantly, time and events are also conceptualized differently across these approaches. *First*, Luhmann (1995) describes the complex systems in organizations as creating opportunities by selecting temporal elements, like events, and selecting the relation between these elements. Luhmann emphasizes that the way elements relate to one another does not exist as a given and prefixed in any complex system. He stresses that relating elements is always a selective process through which organizations produce and reduce their range of options. The selection occurs through structure and process. These two forms, while mutually presupposing, differ in their relation to time (Luhmann, 1995).

The *second* approach is rooted in anthropology and views *time as reckoned in events* or events as signifiers of time (Clark, 1985; Sorokin & Merton, 1937). Events are what make time visible, and without events, humans lack the ability to *see* or perceive time.

According to the *third* view, time is seen as a *signifier of an order of events* (Barnett, 1949). Events are viewed as finished, discrete, and arranged sequentially in time. The sequential view of events in time is the most common approach, sometimes also referred to as the chronological view.

The *fourth* view is an *events-based time*, advocated, for example, by Hernes (2014a) and Hussenot and Missonier (2016), and accounts for an active view of time, that is, time with agentic power (Emirbayer & Mische, 1998; Hernes, 2014a). According to that view, actors are neither observing time in events nor arranging events sequentially in time. Instead, actors are in events, and in events, they take part in the ongoing construction of events, including the one they are in (Pulk, 2016).

It is important to recognize that these approaches differ in how events, time, and their mutual relationships are conceptualized. See Table 6.1 for a quick comparison.

It is crucial to pay attention to how events are understood because, as Hernes (2021: 29) stresses, "the understanding of events is closely tied to how we define time itself." For example, Hussenot and Missonier (2016: 531) define an event as a moment "in which the activity and its organization are concrete and tangible." However, considering that according to

Table 6.1 Comparison of the conceptualization of events and time in organization studies

	Structure/process framework	Events as signifiers of time	Time as a signifier of the order of events	Events-based time
Ontology Events	Temporality Temporal elements formed by realized possibilities pre-selected based on their confirming/ deviating and probable/ improbable nature	Time Events as having a clear prior meaning and significance Events signify the trajectory of a development of the situation.	Time Events as discrete, closed, and sequentially ordered	Temporality Active and agentic events in the becoming
Time	The patterns of events constitute time	Time is in events. Events make time visible.	Linear time contains sequential events. Events are in time.	Events are time

Whitehead (1929/1978), the duration of an event is whether it is required for an event to be what it is, the word *moment* could be misleading. Coming in *all shapes and sizes* (Hernes, 2020: 35), events are seen as temporal elements, including not only natural events, like volcano eruptions, and social events, like business meetings (Hernes, 2020) but also communicative episodes and decision-making (Luhmann, 1995, 2018) and a healthcare crisis like the COVID-19 pandemic.

6.1 Structure, Process, and Events

As through including temporal norms, social structures provide a temporal reference system (Adam, 1990; Zerubavel, 1982) or framework (Berger & Luckmann, 1991). Although clock time and calendars serve as instruments to build up the temporal structure of our lives and serve as a tool to orient in the context of multiple temporalities (i.e., Berger &

Luckmann, 1991), Chaps. 2 and 3 warn us that we could easily become trapped in time as an external and *real* structure that we inhabit. However, Luhmann (1995) hints that being trapped in the structure of time is not an inevitability but could be our choice or inability to see or create other possibilities. Luhmann,[1] who is interested in how organizations navigate in and organize the surplus of possibilities, argues that it is possible to alter our relation to time by shifting our focus from structure to process. Put differently, how organizations create and reduce their possibilities, and most importantly, how organizations are making their selection from the range of possibilities. Luhmann distinguishes two mutually presupposing forms—structure and process—that "differ through their relation to time" (1995: 44). He argues that, while keeping our attention simultaneously on both is probably too demanding, the system can create and maintain its selective relations through the "*reflexivity of the process of selection*" (Ibid), that is, by shifting its focus either to structure or to process. By doing that the system changes its relation to time. According to Luhmann:

> Structures capture the reversibility of time because they hold open a limited repertoire of possibilities for choices. One can negate structures, or change them, or with their aid gain security for changes in other aspects. Processes, by contrast, mark the irreversibility of time. They are composed of irreversible events. They cannot run backwards. (Luhmann, 1995: 44)

Therefore, following Luhmann, we can make quite an intuitive conclusion that structure could be both constraining and supporting. On the one hand, the acceleration and time pressure discussed in Chap. 2 confirms that the structure of everyday life, based on exogenous clock time and calendars, could be stressful. On the other hand, most people prefer an established temporal rhythm of daily life to the random evolution of days. Consequently, although a very tight and rigid structure could be stressful, the lack of any temporal structuring could be just as stressful. The latter is illustrated by the recent worldwide experience of the

---

[1] Although Luhmann (1995: 38) excludes human beings from systems, at the general level, his explanation about the selection process and its elements seems to apply also to individuals.

COVID-19 lockdown described from the perspective of people who were forced to stay isolated in their homes (and not from the perspective of the front-line medical personnel who were under extreme pressure). All of a sudden, everyday life lost its otherwise highly structured temporality. The lack of social activities caused by the COVID-19 lockdown created challenges for many in structuring their time, as without events there was not much to structure. The perceived uneventfulness during social isolation made it challenging to recognize time, order it, and distinguish between the days.

The inability to distinguish between the days is vividly expressed by a meme, circulating in the social media during the COVID-19 lockdown in Winter 2020/2021, where the names of the weekdays were changed to *Thisday, thatday, otherday,* etc. In other words, time as a structure loses its meaning without events as processes that require some structuring. There is not much use for calendars as temporal structures if there are no events to organize and schedule according to these structures. Moreover, structure, as an external negotiated frame for organizing and measuring events against expectations and norms, is changeable. In other words, expectations and measurement systems based on clock time could shift to event time or cyclical time, but despite that, it remains a structure albeit with different characteristics in the time-events relationship.

However, structure alone is like an empty *house* waiting to be filled with the process of life in the form of events. Whether this *house* is built up by clock time, solar or lunar time, tides, seasons, or the time it takes to cook a cup of rice is negotiable and changeable. Deroy and Clegg (2011), grounding their argumentation on Gilles Deleuze's work, share the view of structure's changeable nature by stating that "any event *can potentially deform* the structural regularities in which it is embedded" (Deroy & Clegg, 2011: 639 emphasis added). On the other hand, any event can potentially reinforce the existing structure. While the type of time selected to build up the expected temporal structure has importance, its importance is not primary because it is just a structure. There should be something meaningful to write into a calendar or schedule according to the clock, something that matters and is significant. Therefore, the question is how to vitalize the structure, understand what is going on, and make that meaningful. Understanding what is going on and how what is going on is meaningful requires reflexivity. It requires time to reflect and think and "reinforce its selective relations" (Luhmann, 1995: 44).

Estonian sociologist and philosopher Ülo Vooglaid (2018: 165, 190) has raised the question of what is the time unit of life? Following the line of MacBeath's theorization (1993 cited in Callender, 2017), he proposes that the time unit of life is an event for individuals. Based on this, events could serve as a valid alternative to chronometric time not necessarily to measure but maybe to evaluate life. Vooglaid's belief that the unit of human life is not necessarily seconds, minutes, days, and months, but events, resonates with Luhmann's view. Luhmann asserts that events are components of the process; they are the temporal elements of the process called life. Events are what vitalize the otherwise lifeless structure of time. While seconds and minutes and days and months (or cycles of the sun or moon or the seasons, or tides, or the time needed to boil rice) are helpful tools for organizing activities and coordinating social activities, events give the structure meaning. Therefore, chronometric time provides just a background structure and tool for measurement, but we do not measure or experience our life in chronometric time. Neither do we view being constituted or even shaped, except maybe ageing in general, in terms of years, months, or hours. Instead, we readily agree with the importance of events both in shaping our life and in constituting our essence of being. Put differently, it is easy to agree that we are the *outcome* of the events that have happened and our responses to these events that have happened, while it is hard to agree that we are the outcome of x number of years and months (or x number of circuits the sun has made or cups of rice boiled). We may even think about ourselves as events in their becoming.

According to Luhmann, structures aim to reduce the complexity created by the number of open possibilities by narrowing pre-selected possibilities based on their sensed validity. Pre-selection based on existing preferences, customs, predictability, and so on, acts as a filter to help handle the variety of open options by reducing the number of options considered viable (Luhmann, 1995). Therefore, eso-time and meso-time, as discussed in the previous chapter, that set demands on our everyday lives, stand for social structures. These social structures include temporal structures, which means that "Our attachment to everyday reality; that is, our concern with living and acting, necessarily narrows our vision; it obliges us to 'look straight ahead in the direction we have to go' (Bergson, 1946, p. 137) at the expense of peripheral vision. This happens because, in action, we are less interested in the things themselves than in the use we can make of them. We normally look at the categories things belong to, rather than things per se" (Tsoukas & Chia, 2002: 572). Therefore, temporal structures have instrumental valence to help us focus on the direction we *need to go*.

Social structures serve as *expectational structures* that include temporal norms (see Sect. 5.4.2), and as such, they order the pre-selection of possibilities by constraining the range of available possibilities (Luhmann, 1995: 292). Flaherty supports this idea by stating that "Temporal norms are evident in any given society," and "Within any particular society, …, there is typically enormous uniformity: most people do most things at appropriate times" (2020: 14). Therefore, what is seen as possible and when it is seen as possible, at the societal, organizational, or family level, is guided largely by expectational structures. For example, the temporal expectations of social norms dictates at what age children go to school, when it is a proper time to go to university or enter working life, when it is time for young men to go to military service, from what age could we expect to retire, buy alcohol and tobacco, or be allowed in casinos or become sexually active and marry, when it is time to have a family dinner, and what is the latest time that teenagers should be home in the evening. While expectational structures do not determine all possibilities, they constrain possibilities. As a rule, deviating from expectational structures at any level, whether in families, organizations, or societies, tends to come at least with some kind of fight (Flaherty, 2020). However, as mentioned, the structure needs to be vitalized, and according to Luhmann, this happens through processes. Luhmann explains that:

> Processes (and this defines the concept of process) result from the fact that concrete selective events build upon one another temporally, connect with one another, and thus build previous selections or predictable selections into individual selections as premises for selection. The pre-selection of what can be chosen is experienced as validity in the case of processes. (Luhmann, 1995: 44–45)

Luhmann concludes that structure and process work complementary to one another, and "A system that controls its own structures and processes can assign all elements that it produces and reproduces to these forms of amplifying selectivity. This means that, with regard to structures, we must reckon with confirming and deviant events, and, with regard to processes, with probable and improbable events" (Luhmann, 1995: 45).

Therefore, both negotiable and changeable structures as temporal frameworks and the irreversible process made up by events are mutually reinforcing and both are related to time, but their relationship with time differs, and it differs ontologically. The structure-time relationship follows the ontology of time, and the relationship of events (as processes) to time follows the ontology of temporality (Hussenot et al., 2020), which represents a process view (Hernes, 2020; Reinecke & Ansari, 2017). Therefore, as a process, internally connecting events form irreversible time. Luhmann asserts that "Events present the irreversibility of time within systems" (1995: 449). Table 6.2 presents the components of Luhmann's structure/process approach to events and organizational time.

As Table 6.2 indicates, analysed from the perspective of structure, possible events could be confirming or deviating. While when analysed from the perspective of process, possibilities are evaluated as probable or improbable. Importantly, what is highlighted by Luhmann is that while all four types are possible, these four types do not work as standalone criteria, but each selection incorporates both pairs. The pre-selection of possibilities entails evaluating the consequences of the choices to further event formations, their probabilities, and conformation of existing expectational structures. This means that each selection has at least four alternative options, and these four options are the bare minimum. Selection could be confirming/probable or confirming/improbable events (see Table 6.3). Alternatively, selection could be deviating/probable or deviating/improbable event. Four is a bare minimum because each event type could have multiple open possibilities, and thus, nothing is granted but "could also be otherwise" (Luhmann, 1995: 106).

Considering that organizations are complex social subsystems with their own energy that create their own time (Callender, 2017; Luhmann, 1995), their internal event trajectories may not necessarily sync either

Table 6.2 Temporal elements of structure/process based on Luhmann's reflexive selection process framework

Temporal form	Structure	Process
Content	Social expectations, norms, time measurement framework, rules, beliefs, and so on	By building upon one another temporally and by connecting internally with one another, events build premises for selection based on previous selections and predictable selections
Relation to time	Ontology of time: Time is reversible, negotiable, changeable, external, measurable	Ontology of temporality: Irreversible time, internal connection of events, endogenous temporality
Selection of events	Confirming events Deviating events	Probable events Improbable events
Pre-selection criteria	Validity of expectations, norms	Validity of a process, continuity of a process

Source: Based on Luhmann, N. (1995). *Social systems* (pp. 40–44). Stanford University Press

Table 6.3 Possible selection criteria for events

Possible combinatory pairs for events selection	Structure	Process
1	Confirming	Probable
2	Confirming	Improbable
3	Deviating	Probable
4	Deviating	Improbable

with the expectational structures of the broader social context or with the social context's event trajectories. Instead, an organization could select a possibility that makes perfect sense, which is highly probable when following the endogenous temporality of events. At the same time, that selection may deviate from the expectational structures and, because of that, could seem like an unexpected or unlikely choice. Similarly, although seen as possible, confirming events could be viewed either as probable or improbable from the perspective of previous internal connections of events—the temporal trajectory of events (Flaherty, 2020; Hernes, 2017).

Because of the structure-process complementarity, focusing predominately on one of these narrows our understanding about the open possibilities for the formation or activation of event trajectories.

Therefore, it is possible to argue that assuming that time is in events, and at every moment there is a surplus of possible events, selecting an event means selecting or creating time. For selecting an event, a subsystem requires energy; therefore, time presupposes energy. If the subsystem lacks energy, it is unable to select an event. Without the power to select an event, it cannot create its time and temporalize itself. In that case, the subsystem dissolves into its context. Callender (2017) claims that time emerges in a local, contextual subsystem that has its energy. A subsystem is always relational—sub to something or in relation to something. Distinguishing itself from its context, the subsystem needs to maintain its own temporality and its temporal boundaries in relation to context, which means it needs to create its own time/temporality. But to maintain its own ongoing temporality and to create its own specific time in the passage of perishing time requires energy and effort.

Importantly, Luhmann (1995) emphasizes that events, as temporal elements, constitute the system and the system could not exist separately from its temporal elements, which are events. Therefore, it is not possible to distinguish between the two. Citing MacIver (1942: 64 in Luhmann, 1995: 48), Luhmann assures that the event "is separate not from the whole, but in the whole," and therefore, theoretical distinction between event and structure or event and process is inappropriate. Instead, the distinction should be made between event and relation (Luhmann, 1995). That is to say, what requires attention and analysis is how multiple events, as temporal elements of the organization as a system, relate to one another as well as their own past and future as non-actualities. While Hussenot and Missonier claim that "there is no other reality than the actual event" (2016: 528), I argue that the actual event that is our reality also contains non-actualities and either realized or unrealized possibilities or unactualized potentialities (see Chap. 4). Therefore, these non-actualities that participate in the constitution of our reality include the past occurred and experienced events alongside past unrealized possibilities and anticipated future events. As none of the events as temporal elements can endure but they all pass, maintaining organizational time requires an ongoing constellation of events (Luhmann, 1995).

An organization's time may not sync with broader social time. Therefore, confirming/deviating and probable/improbable events of the system (society or economy) and its subsystem (organization) may not sync. The discrepancy between these layers of time offers the organization opportunities and entails risks (Blagoev & Schreyögg, 2019; Luhmann, 1995). Therefore, recognizing and reckoning time in events (Clark, 1985; Sorokin & Merton, 1937) is strategically important at the societal and organizational levels.

6.2 Events as Signifiers of Time

Vooglaid (2018), by proposing that the time unit of human life is an event, argues further that the duration of life's time unit is equal to the period between significant events. The longer the period between significant events, the slower the pace of time, and the shorter the felt duration of life when evaluated retrospectively. And vice versa, the shorter the individual's time unit of life, the faster goes time, and the longer the perceived length of our life. Therefore, the faster the pace of events in our life, the faster time is perceived to run, and if we look backwards, our life is perceived to be longer. For example, Vooglaid describes the presence of his grandmother as short, even though she lived to 80 years. Her life was short because her days were similar, lacking significant events. According to Vooglaid, a major event for his grandmother was when the cat had kittens (Vooglaid, 2018: 165–166). For sure, Vooglaid exaggerates with this evaluation, as there had been other and more important events in his grandmother's life in addition to the cat having kittens. For example, getting married, giving birth to her children, becoming a grandmother, etc. Strauss cited in Zerubavel (2003: 27) reminds us that: "there are … periods where … numerous events appear as differential elements; others, on the contrary, where … (although not of course for the men who lived through them) very little or nothing took place." Still, viewing events as time markers means that lacking significant events in our life could be considered to be living an uneventful or even empty life that when looked back on may look short.

Vooglaid's line of thinking is supported by the empirical results achieved in psychology, which confirm the tendency of faster-moving stimuli resulting in longer perceived durations (Bueti & Macaluso, 2011). For example, like in the Armageddon experiment discussed in Chap. 3, Wearden (2005) found that people who experienced more salient events to remember and anticipate evaluated the felt duration up to ten per cent longer than people who experienced uneventful boring duration. However, the objective duration was the same for both groups. Compared to an uneventful and boring duration, salient events may not necessarily represent something exciting and entertaining. They could be outstandingly intense and dense in a more demanding or negative way. For example, my colleague described how in April 2020, without any warning, the end of her marriage of 25 years just fell upon her. By claiming that *so much happened*, she described at some length how "feelings, emotions, and real circumstances changed not by the month or the year but by the hour, if not by the minute." Given the volatility of such circumstances and related extreme feelings and emotions, she felt as though instead of three days three years had passed by. (For more on the perceived temporality of objective time, see Chap. 3.) What seems to matter is not so much whether the event is perceived as being a positive or negative, but its intensity and density, and its significance in terms of its contingencies for both present and future.

On 21 June 2021, at the Estonian Business School master students' graduation ceremony, Liia Pjatakova posed an intriguing question in her Valedictorian Address. "If you could be a superhero, what would you choose to be your superpower?" (Pjatakova, 2021). After throwing out options like being able to fly, being invisible, indispensable, or able to travel through time, she agrees that "teleportation, super strength and the ability to read minds are awesome," only to state that none of these would be her choice. Revealing her somehow surprising choice, she says that "If I could choose, I would want my superpower to be the ability to recognise important moments in life as they happen." In her address, Pjatakova stressed that we often experience seemingly regular moments, the decisive importance of which becomes visible only later. Therefore, she wished for a superpower to recognize these moments and recognize these decisive events. She wished for the ability to recognize time in events.

In organization studies, the idea of events as of time is highlighted, for example, by Clark (1985). Clark (1985), like Sorokin and Merton (1937), claims that events and their perceived (socially constructed) importance enable humans to recognize time. That is, events and their perceived importance make time visible for humans. Importantly, as Levine points out, "Event time and clock time are not totally unrelated. But event time encompasses considerably more than the clock. It is a product of the larger gestalt; a result of social, economic, and environmental cues, and of course, of cultural values" (Levine, 2006: 91). The main assumption in viewing time as reckoned in events is that time becomes *visible* in social activities and is observable in events defined by social actors (Adam, 1990; Clark, 1985).

Clark emphasizes that "time is *in* events," and "events are defined by organizational members" (Clark, 1985: 36 emphasis in original). It is worth highlighting that those events are *defined by social or organizational actors*, meaning they may not be readily available for external observers. Therefore, events are not necessarily visible in objective observations conducted by outsiders. Even when we can register that something (an event) happened, the meaning of what happened and the direction it is pointing may still remain covered. At the same time, we always perceive things in connection to events (Holt & Mueller, 2011). Therefore, if time is in events and events are defined by organizational members, we can conclude that organizational members define time in organizations, and therefore, time in organizations is socially constructed and organization-specific.

6.2.1 Time Reckoning Systems

In addition to events as signifiers of time or tools that make time visible, events could be viewed as signifiers of a change in the course of development or event trajectory. For example, Clark (1985: 36) insists that for sociological analysis, time should be viewed as a social construction, an "organizing device by which one set or trajectory of events is used as a point of reference for understanding, anticipation and attempting to control other sets of events." The meaning ascribed to observed time in events allows social actors to construct event trajectories over time and expectations about what kinds of events will follow and when. Following the idea of time in events, Clark (1985) points out the importance of well-performing time reckoning systems—the ability to read events as signs of the nature of time. Malinowski (1990: 203) argues that a time reckoning system "is a practical, as well as a sentimental, necessity in every culture, however simple. Members of every human group have a need to coordinate various activities, of fixing dates for the future, of placing reminiscences in the past, of gauging the length of bygone periods and of those to come."

Social activities provide specific qualities to the periods of time they belong to, and "the social life of the group is reflected in time expressions. The names of days, months, seasons, and even years are fixed by the rhythm of social time" (Sorokin & Merton, 1937: 619). The rhythm of social life is expressed, for example, in the Estonian "old people's calendar," which does not refer to elderly people, but to the ancient people, or "rural people" because Estonia was a society structured through agriculture. In this calendar, the names of the months were related to specific farming activities usually performed at that time or expected tasks. There is "künnikuu" referring to April when it was time to plough fields; "heinakuu" referring to July when it was time to make hay; "lõikuskuu" referring to August when it was time to collect the harvest, and so on. These periods indicate the approximate timing and duration of one or another activity. The exact start and duration of a specific activity depended on the weather conditions. Therefore, it was important to reckon the correct time for the specific event in the surrounding events, which leads to time reckoning systems (Clark, 1985).

It is important to highlight that event-based time reckoning systems are not reserved for *primitive people* (Sorokin & Merton, 1937: 619) or societies. The importance of event-based time reckoning systems as tools for organizing social life and understanding ongoing and anticipated events in modern societies is highlighted, for example, by Adam (1990, 2004). In organizations, time reckoning systems have strategic importance because the levels of profitability or perspectives for survival are directly dependent on the correct reading of the event and the subsequent decisions made in anticipation of the future (Clark, 1985). The

6 Events, Time, and Events-Based Time 247

reading of events in organizational settings may include, for example, recognizing market trends or understanding economic cycles or attitudinal changes in societies related to generational shifts or the consequences of new technologies. While Clark (1985) stresses the strategic importance of the ability to reckon time in events, in contrast to Luhmann (1995), he does not pay attention to actively constructed temporal time through which some possibilities are actualized as events while other possibilities remain as non-events (Kahneman, 2011). The following examples try to illustrate both the importance of reckoning time in events and the power of non-events.

Two textbook cases demonstrating the failure to recognize time in events are the fall of Kodak and Nokia. Both companies were market leaders in their industries. Kodak held the market leader position as a producer of film cameras and film and Nokia as a mobile phone manufacturer. However, both companies lost their grasp of the market and ceased to exist. Although both companies recognized the looming threats—digital technology and the iPhone, respectively—they interpreted these as threats from competing companies, not as shifts in event trajectories (Pulk, 2016). Even more intriguing is the fact that both companies developed the technology that became fatal to them, meaning they had an opportunity to react and respond, but they missed it. Concerning Kodak, the Kodak engineer, Steve Sasson, invented the digital camera in 1975 (Veltri, 2017). Still, the management was unwilling to recognize it as "a point of reference for understanding, anticipation and attempting to control other sets of events" (Clark, 1985: 36). The management of Kodak was so focused on one specific event trajectory, and that was film-based development, that in response to Sasson's invention of filmless photography, they said, "that's cute—but don't tell anyone about it" (Veltri, 2017: 98).

Therefore, Kodak management failed to see this newly invented technology as a turning point from an existing trajectory to the new emerging event trajectory (Hernes, 2017) and adjust their business models accordingly. Instead of shifting to the new trajectory, Kodak stayed committed to the existing one through investing heavily (Veltri, 2017). That is, Kodak tried to maintain the trajectory they had despite of the market's changing trajectory. For Kodak, their rigid focus and uncompromising commitment to the film-based projected trajectory and their inability and unwillingness to read time in events correctly become their stumbling block.

The triangle of Nokia, Apple, and Väänänen opens at least as fascinating a story as the story of Steve Sasson and Kodak. While it is well known that with the iPhone, Apple conquered the smartphone market and Nokia somehow missed an opportunity, the story behind the smartphone technology is even more adventurous. Väänänen (2016) tells maybe a less well-known story of smartphone technology and its path to the consumer market in his book, *The Smart Device*. Namely, Finnish inventor Johannes Väänänen invented modern smartphone swiping technology and offered his MyDevice prototype first to Nokia as his first choice. Nokia missed its big opportunity when, in 2002, they declined the offer Väänänen made to them. However, Väänänen's story includes several exciting events. Like, for example, the spoiled business meeting with representatives of Samsung, the bankruptcy of F-Origin in 2005, a company that was a successor to MyOrigon and which held smartphone patents that Väänänen had worked out, how the touchscreen and swiping technology together with the first prototype reached into the hands of Apple, and even the prediction that the technological advancement Apple will introduce with the next-generation iPhones could be the Virtual Mirror technology. The patent of the Virtual Mirror technology was sold to US company after the F-Origin filed for bankruptcy. The Virtual Mirror technology means that by tilting and moving the device like a pocket mirror, it is possible to browse even a large web page from a very small screen without touching the screen with the fingers at all (Väänänen, 2016).

Johannes Väänänen's story is a fascinating example of how things could become otherwise (Luhmann, 1995) for both Väänänen and Nokia, but also Apple and Samsung. If Nokia had only decided to cooperate with F-Origin and Väänänen, it could still be the most powerful and successful Finnish company. If only F-Origin's partner had not blocked the entrance to the F-Origin office exactly on the day the Samsung delegates arrived in Oulu, it could easily be that instead of Apple's smartphone success story there is one about Samsung. The realization of either of those alternatives would have meant fortune and fame also for Väänänen. The potential was there; the virtual new idea offered the possibility to shift the event trajectory. Nokia failed to recognize this as an opportunity, as a potentiality with game-changing power.

However, like Kodak, Nokia did not sit around doing nothing. Instead, like Kodak made heavy investments to further develop film-based photo technology, so Nokia took a similar path. However, in organizations, where so many things that all require instant attention are happening at the same time, recognizing the critical opportunity or potential threat or shifting trends among multiple simultaneously evolving events is not a self-evident or easy task. Indeed, we could consider it a superpower (Pjatakova, 2021). As discussed in the previous chapter, possibilities with different probabilities for realization and mutually exclusive potentialities with different probabilities for actualization guarantee that becoming is never taken for granted or easy to predict and control. Following these stories, we should agree with Clark (1985) about the strategic importance of reading events, reckoning time in events, and adjusting our decisions and activities accordingly.

Two quite extreme examples of events, where the time in events was read in favour of all of humanity, although, maybe against the expectational structures at the time, could illustrate the broader importance of recognizing time in events and *see* a possible shift in event trajectories. First, Vasili Arkhipov, vice admiral on the Soviet nuclear-armed submarine during the Cuban Missile Crisis in 1962. When the US Navy spotted soviet submarines, Arkhipov disagreed with the captain and vetoed the captain's order to launch the nuclear torpedo[2] (The Future Life Award, 2017). In 2017, the *Future of Life Institute*[3] honoured Vasili Arkhipov posthumously with its award "for single-handedly preventing a Soviet nuclear attack against the US in 1962" (https://futureoflife.org/future-of-life-award). In the following year, the *2018 Future of Life Award* was awarded to Stanislav Petrov, who was a lieutenant colonel in the Soviet Air Defence Forces. On 26 September 1983, Petrov decided to ignore the Soviet early-warning detection system that had detected five approaching American nuclear missiles (The Future Life Award, 2018). Fortunately, Petrov chose to follow his gut feeling and ignore the algorithms, as it

---

[2] The episode of the documentary "Secrets of the Dead: The Man Who Saved the World" by Nick Green is available at https://www.youtube.com/watch?v=4VPY2SgyG5w.

[3] I am proud that one of the founders of the Future of Life Institute, Jaan Tallinn, sat next to me in elementary school. Jaan is also one of the founders of Skype.

turned out later, the alarm was erroneous. By doing that, he prevented a US-Soviet nuclear war and became the subject of the documentary film *"The Man Who Saved the World"* (Anthony & Staberg, 2013). Unfortunately, Petrov received his award posthumously, as he passed away in 2017.

In both these incidents, the main actors—Vasili Arkhipov and Stanislav Petrov—recognized the possible and dramatic shift of the course of events or, in their cases, the course of the entire human race. They recognized the time in events, and they managed to evaluate its significance. But once again, things could have happened otherwise. These examples also show how unplanned and unpredicted events with almost tangible potentialities to meltdown human civilization became highly probable. Furthermore, these examples show how such events can give enormous power to and put considerable responsibility on the shoulders of single individuals and how highly significant and decisive events as micro-level decisions could have a huge impact on macro-level affairs. Micro-time decisions could almost lead to the end of macro-time (see the previous chapter) and maybe even mega-time in the blink of the eye.

Of course, we could analyse these cases in light of Luhmann's structure/process-based reflexive selection process framework. This analysis could be quite fascinating as all the actors participating in these episodes performed under different assumptions and incomplete information (Anthony & Staberg, 2013), meaning that very different confirming/deviant and probable/improbable possibilities could have been drawn. The only limitation on applying Luhmann's reflexive selection process framework stems from the fact that there was no time for the reflexive selection of possible events. Because of the urgency of the event and its potentially fatal consequences, that is a critical limitation. In other words, recognizing time in events is strategically and, in some cases, even existentially important.

In the world today, we can witness sharply changing event trajectories; for example, in the fur farming industry, where in several European countries, due to the efforts of animal rights activists, either the fur farms are wholly prohibited or the sales of fur is partially banned. We can see the gradually spreading trend of investment funds avoiding industries and projects that do not consider issues related to sustainability. Hopefully, we still have time to avoid a complete ecological collapse despite the fact that we have already entered a new geological era caused by human activities, the Anthropocene. I hope there is still a possibility to seriously do something despite *greenwashing*, which has emerged as a new term referring to sustainability-related window dressing in both policy making and business.

6.3 Time as a Signifier of an Order of Events

Time as a signifier of an order of events refers to a sequential or periodic view of time. Following this view, episodes or events have identifiable start and end points that enable us to create a chronology of events and timelines by following the logic of the spatial linearity of time and ontology of time (Hussenot et al., 2020). While referring back to Chap. 2, sequential time has a central role in entrainment theory in organizing and coordinating activities, including their order of occurrence. The sequence of events plays a role at personal, organizational, and social level. Bergren and Luckmann (1991: 41) point out that "Both my organism and my society impose upon me, and upon my inner time, certain sequences of events that involve waiting. I may want to take part in a sports event, but I must wait for my bruised knee to heal. Or again, I must wait until certain papers are processed so that my qualification for the event may be officially established." Studying the sequence and order of events is used to understand the organizational processes (Van de Ven & Poole, 1990). Schematically, it states that $event_1$ occurs or occurred at time t_1, $event_2$ at t_2, $event_3$ at t_3, and $event_y$ at t_y. In other words, a sequential or periodic view of time sees events occupying a specific position in space-time, and this position does not change (Hernes et al., 2021). Therefore, if $event_z$ happened at the time t_z, it will stay that event that took place at that time forever (McTaggart, 1908), and so a sequential view of time sees the past as closed.

A periodic view of time is also widely used in organizational studies to compare *before* and *after* conditions and develop some specific condition over time, for example, studies where the conditions or states of something are measured, respectively, at points in time—t_1, t_2, t_3, and t_y (e.g., Allen et al., 1995; Van Oorschot et al., 2013). A periodic view of time is most often used to compare the specific state or condition between different periods of time or events (Hernes et al., 2021), while treating these periods or events as discrete. Therefore, a sequential view of time fixes both the nature of events and their occurrence in time. Events in time are viewed as *accomplished entities* (Hernes, 2020: 29) not as pre-selected possibilities as presented by Luhmann (1995) above. As accomplished entities, events are distinguished by their importance or unimportance and centrality or strength (Morgeson et al., 2015), while also assessed, for example, as good or bad (Van Oorschot et al., 2013), macroscopic or microscopic (Hernes, 2020), past or future (Hernes, 2014a; Hussenot & Missonier, 2016), chronometrically distant or near (Bluedorn, 2002; Hernes & Schultz, 2020), or qualitatively distant, that is, as opposed to the (immediate) past and present (Augustine et al., 2019; Hernes & Schultz, 2020).

A sequential time corresponds to McTaggart's B series time (McTaggart, 1908), where "time appears through the isolation of events in series; one event can occur before, at the same time, or after another event" (Bakken et al., 2013: 14). The perspective of a sequential or B series time affords "distinctions between causes (before) and effects (after), and the possibility of efficiency gains when isolated events, things, and activities are sequentially rearranged so that workflows can be coordinated and compacted along linear axes of time" (Bakken et al., 2013: 14). A prerequisite for causality is a temporal separation between events. As "a causal relationship can only hold between events if they are separated temporally so that a light signal, or anything slower, can pass between them" (Adam, 1990: 57), seeing the past, present, and future outside of each other enables us to construct causality between events. Consequently, when the focus is on establishing casual links, the past and present are seen as separate discrete events, instead of temporally extending events, with a directly observable and measurable causality.

The worldview led by assumed causality based on fixed laws tends to neglect the surplus of possible alternatives—how things could have turned out instead of how they actually turned out. Assumed causality means that the world is seen as a predictable outcome of confirmed laws in action (Kahneman, 2011). Predictability tends to overlook the fact that other possibilities exist as a-causal developments enabled by temporal extension. Although non-events "affect the psychological passage of time" (Levine, 2006: 41), Kahneman (2011: 200) claims that "the human mind does not deal well with non-events." Instead, for the human mind, it is more convenient to ignore "the myriad of events that would have caused a different outcome" (Kahneman, 2011: 200), as in, for example, the case of Arkhipov and Petrov discussed above.

However, ignoring the diversity of possible events does not mean that these non-events do not exist. For example, Luhmann (1995, 2018) and Valsiner (2011) insist that non-events as non-actualities may still enter the process of temporalization, affecting event trajectories by affecting decisions. Therefore, chronological time for measuring linear motion and sequential time for measuring before and after states are inadequate to capture "the problems that systems have in time and with time" (1995: 41–42). That is to say, the sequential view of time focuses on development over time but ignores the struggles that actors may experience with time and being in time.

Moreover, a sequential view of time, while allowing us to follow a specific evolvement in the event course, largely ignores that "the present is composed of events simultaneous with one another" (Callender, 2017: 50). Although these simultaneous events are achronal, meaning that "no two events in the now are such that one is in the causal past of the other" (Callender, 2017: 50), in their manifold, they struggle for their emergence and endurance (Shotter, 2006). That is, in their becoming, simultaneously evolving events are affecting one another. Although not being one another's causal past either in the present or in a future predicted based on past causal relations, they may participate in one another's formation. Furthermore, nothing guarantees that they will become one another's causal past in the future. To a large extent, the sequential view of time assumes that the *ceteris paribus* (everything else being equal) condition holds. However, the possibility of new emergent relations runs contra to the predictability based on fixed laws and rules assuming the ceteris paribus condition holds. In the complex, interdependent, and intra-acting social world, the ceteris paribus condition is fictional because we are not dealing with discrete but intertwined processes (Stake, 2006) which are co-constituting one another in their becoming.

Snowden (2003: 25) stresses the "phenomenon of retrospective coherence" or "retrospective illusion" by arguing that "the current state of affairs always makes logical sense, but only when we look backwards. The current pattern always seems logical. However, it is only one of many patterns that could have formed, any one of which would be equally logical." The message from Snowden (2003) is that causal links could be established so that the past serves as an explanation to the present. Therefore, with hindsight it is possible to explain the *existing* causal relationship (Kahneman, 2011). However, as stressed in Chap. 4 and the examples of Kodak and Nokia above, the current situation is only one of a range of possibilities, and at every phase, events could have happened otherwise or they could *have-been-also-otherwise-possible* (Luhmann, 1995: 296). That means, by focusing on causal relationships or sequential order between events, alternative possibilities are overlooked. Moreover, there may be no clear temporal separation between the events, but one event extends over or prehends to another without a clear temporal separation in the flow of time. For example, Mario Puzo (1990), in his fictional novel, *The Forth K*, tells a story which constitutes several seemingly unrelated storylines. However, at one point, these seemingly unrelated storylines get tangled and, by merging unpredictably together, create unexpected twists and turns, forming a new storyline.

Allowing to draw causal connections between events, a sequential view of time has attracted a lot of attention, and it is widely used in management and organization studies. For example, the Academy of Management Review 2001 special issue devoted to time and temporality (Ancona et al., 2001) implies a sequential view of events. Similarly, the *Academy of Management Journal* 2013 special issue dedicated to processual research (Langley et al., 2013) portrays sequential, discrete events (i.e., Jay, 2013; Gehman et al., 2013; van Oorschot et al., 2013) and focuses on the causal relationship between events over time. The ability to remember events and recognize their sequence is considered "a basic precondition to being able to perceive time" (Watzlawik, 2015: 226). However, it is important to highlight that the causal analysis in the sequential view tends to work better in relatively simple contexts. In complex systems, relationships become more complicated and less straightforward being influenced by "mistakes, null values, and disappointments" (Luhmann, 1995: 40). Therefore, the increasing complexity tends to weaken the relationship between the sequential order of events and direct causality between these events.

While signifying an order of events is a crucial role of time, it is not sufficient to explain the relations between time and events, which tend to be more complex. By ignoring complexity, interdependence, and intra-actions, it is easy to end up with an overly simplified world view (Stake, 2006). Whitehead (1925/1985, 1929/1978), referring to the inadequacy of Newtonian physics to explain, for example, a-causal temporal connections found in quantum physics, has warned about this kind of oversimplification, referring to the "fallacy of misplaced concreteness" and "simple location" (Whitehead, 1929/1978: 7, 137). According to Whitehead, both these terms refer to the tendency to ignore "the degree of abstraction involved" (Whitehead, 1929/1978: 7) and view entities as occupying a definable point in space-time. Once again, the ceteris paribus assumption is based on an oversimplification of existing complexities (Stake, 2006), which may lead to the unjustified sense of control over the world and some severe and unexpected consequences. Consequently, assuming that you have control and possessing the ability to predict the causal sequence of events could lead to misconceptions or even fatal errors (Clark, 1985) because by temporal bracketing, the sequential view of time overlooks the time embedded in the events, the internal endogenous connections between events. While the latter will be covered under an events-based view of time, let us continue with temporal bracketing.

6.3.1 Temporal Bracketing

The power of temporal bracketing is its capacity to identify the recurrence of specific theoretical mechanisms over time (Langley et al., 2013). Temporal bracketing serves as a tool to construct events and activities as progressive and "separated by identifiable discontinuities in the temporal flow" (Langley et al., 2013: 7). Although a periodic view sees the past stages in the change process as influencing the present stages and the present stages in turn as influencing the future stages, the past is treated as finished (Hussenot & Missonier, 2016) or accomplished (Hernes, 2020). Therefore, a periodic view of time discards the openness of the past and its potentially changing nature. Together with that, it discards the openness or changing nature of past events. It builds on the assumption that active construction in the present is based on selectively chosen memory cues (Schultz & Hernes, 2013), not on intrinsic connections of endogenous temporality.

Temporal bracketing cuts off the event from its endogenous temporal relations and its past and future connections. According to Hernes (2014a: 37–38), "This suggests that the present experience may be compared to previous experience as if they are distinct temporal units that can be held up against one another." Events viewed as discrete are seen as temporarily related through the successive order, through the structure seen as logical causal outcomes of previous events while still separate from those previous events. Viewed as separated, events are seen as not constitutive (Hernes, 2014a; Hussenot & Missonier, 2016).

Temporal bracketing assumes that discrete events are locating in time by following a fixed temporal order with a one-directional influence between these discrete events, meaning the past event influences the present event and the present event influences the future event. The relationship between events is strictly one-directional, meaning that the reverse possibility, that the future event is influencing the present or past event or the present event has some influence on the past event, is ignored. In other words, while having one-directional causal influence with a direction from the past to the future, events do not constitute one another. When viewed as lacking constitutive power, the agency of events is restricted to a one-directional influence, that is, from the past to the present and from the present to the future. However, when claiming that time is in events, then by robbing events of a two-directional temporal agency, time is left with limited agency only. Therefore, periodic analyses tend to overlook the temporal complexity of events and the agency that events may have in recreating the meaning of past events and their influence on the trajectories of future events.

The consequences of bracketing or cutting off an event from its temporal connectedness are stressed by philosophers with processual orientation (e.g., Heidegger, 1927/1962; Polanyi, 1967; Schütz, 1967; Whitehead, 1929/1978). The bracketing off ignores the intertwined messiness of the world (Heidegger, 1927/1962; Holt & Sandberg, 2011) and focuses on distinctions. These distinctions are something to which Whitehead (1925/1985: 61) refers as *simple location*. With simple location, Whitehead refers to separation or bracketing out, resulting in the view that objects or events occupy a unique location in the space-time, being here and now (Hernes, 2008: 37–42). As Chia (1999: 219) explains, "simple location emphasizes the inherent locatability of all experienced phenomena in space-time. For causal analysis to succeed, it must first be possible to locate and isolate both causal factors and their effects." Heidegger (1927/1962: 474) points out that *now-time* is based on the view that each case has its own *now-time*. As a result, "the ecstatical constitution of temporality" which is a foundation of datability and significance, is levelled off (Heidegger, 1927/1962: 474). That is, if events lose their agency, their power to influence other events in the present, past, and future, then also time, when viewed as being in events, loses its agency. In the framework of *now-time*, where time is seen as a pure succession, it does not have significance (Heidegger, 1927/1962).

Furthermore, Clark (1985: 70) states that over time analysis tends to present everyday life as "being significantly shaped by the historical past," while the historical past is seen as passive and inert, relatively unitary, clear, coherent, and fixed. That type of analysis is lacking the "plurality of varied *chronological codes*" (Clark, 1985: 69), which is the concern of historians when reconstructing a chronological account of events (Oakeshott, 1995). Therefore, periodic analysis, whether viewed as a chronological or before-after comparison, denotes the orderly succession of discrete events and acts in time (Schultz & Hernes, 2013). By focusing on causal relationships between the distinguishable stages of change, a periodic view assumes a spatial and temporal separation of events. Consequently, it allows us to analyse change in state, not becoming. Importantly, by assuming either a before and after or a sequential and serial view of organizational change, theorizing under a periodic view is still based on time as an external framework (Clark, 1985) informed by the ontology of time, not by the ontology of temporality (Hussenot et al., 2020).

6.4 Events-Based View of Time

The events-based view of time in organizational studies, promoted by Chia (1999), Cobb (2007), Hernes (2014a, 2014b, 2020), Hernes et al. (2021), Hussenot and Missonier (2016), and Hussenot et al. (2020), follows the conceptualization of events as presented in the work of Alfred North Whitehead. Whitehead does not constrain his theorization with temporal idealism; he does not view time as a construction of the human mind. Instead, he sees time as being in nature and emerging from events (Hernes, 2017). An events-based view of time is rooted in process theory (Hernes, 2014a, 2020), and its central idea is that events are not accomplished entities but "always in the state of becoming" (Hernes et al., 2021: 732). Events are what constitute time (Hernes, 2014a). Therefore, events are neither in time nor do they signify time, but *events are time*. As such, an events-based view disagrees with Merleau-Ponty's claim that "temporal relations make possible the events in time" (2002: 481). Furthermore, these are not temporal relations that make events in time possible, but events, through their becoming, form the temporal dimensions of time through their endogenous temporality. That means that like time is ongoing so are events in their becoming; not accomplished, finalized, and discrete entities, but always in the process of becoming otherwise. The importance of an events-based view of time is that it enables us to move beyond sequential ordering and see reality as an open field of emerging possibilities and developments. The idea of events-based time follows the ontology of temporality (Hussenot et al., 2020).

Whitehead's idea that time is emerging from events means that events are not ordered in time, instead, "events *are* time and define the very meaning of being in time" (Hernes, 2020: 31, emphasis in original). An events-based view of time sees time residing in events, not events residing in time (Hernes, 2014a, 2017). In other words, events constitute time instead of marking "mere happenings along a timeline" (Hernes, 2017: 602) as seen in traditional organization theory. Seeing time in events allows us to view events as ordering time; through their internal connecting, events order time. That is, an events-based view sees "the events that people are part of as connecting, rather than the people connecting. People are in events, but they are not constitutive of those events" (Hernes, 2017: 602). With that, an events-based view ascribes to events an agentic power.

> The power of an event, rather than being reliant on who were present, lies in its power to connect to other events, as it is the connecting power between events in time that provides organizations with their temporal

existence. Moreover, it is the power of the event to connect to other events while creating itself that confers agency upon an event. (Hernes, 2017: 605)

Notably, the events-based view of time is not restricted to humans or social systems only. Therefore, it makes it possible to go beyond reflexive selection of possibilities in social systems (Luhmann, 1995) or time reckoning systems (Clark, 1985). However, applying an events-based view of time to organizations does not deny the role and agency of human actors while participating in organizational events. However, according to the events-based view of time, "Events are not to be thought of as decisive events or marker events, but as basic building blocks of organizational life" (Hernes, 2017: 604). Therefore, we can view an organization as a structure of events (i.e., Hussenot et al., 2020; Luhmann, 1995).

The agentic power of events does not mean that human actors are left without agency. Being in events means that actors are in the ongoing present (Schultz & Hernes, 2013), where past events and expected events are enacted simultaneously. Based on that view, actors are not observing time in events (Adam, 1990; Clark, 1985), and neither do they arrange events sequentially (e.g., Jay, 2013; Langley et al., 2013; Van Oorschot et al., 2013). Instead, they are in events, and in events, they take part in the ongoing construction of events, including the one they are in (Hussenot & Missonier, 2016). The simultaneous enactment of the past and expected events in the ongoing present (Schultz & Hernes, 2013) allows the transcendence of events (Griesbach & Grand, 2013; Hussenot & Missonier, 2016). While participating in events, human actors can, through their actions, influence the becoming of events.

Both the examples of Vasily Arkhipov and Stanislav Petrov and Kodak and Nokia discussed above could serve as illustrations here as well. As the examples of Arkhipov and Petrov show, human actors, while being in the events they have not created, still have the power to influence how events evolve. It could be that an attempt to influence the trajectory of the event, even if it remains just an attempt, could, at least in some instances, be a moral responsibility of human actors. However, despite the possible role of humans in events, they do not constitute events, and the connecting is done by the events, not by human actors (Hernes, 2017).

6.4.1 Becoming of Events

According to Mead (1932/2002), the emergence of events is the real source of time. As neither the emergence nor becoming of events is predetermined, and events are time, so is not time predetermined. Events have the potential to become otherwise or lead to something else, and as events are time, time has the potential to become otherwise. The becoming of events signifies qualitative time-based changes bounded by the irreversibility of time (Luhmann, 1995; Valsiner & van der Veer, 2013). In their becoming, events, as temporal elements (Hernes, 2017; Luhmann, 1995), are actively participating in making, unmaking, and remaking temporal trajectories. Through their internal connecting, events, creating themselves, and through their ongoing becoming, they create both the sense of continuity and the irreversibility of time, which could be viewed as a perceived flow of time. Importantly, events are not triggered or connected by people but by other events.

An events-based view applied to organizations does not view the organization "as a social or an economic entity, but instead as the very process of co-definition and configuration of events by which people can both define their actual moment and act in anticipation of novel events" (Hussenot et al., 2020: 56–57). Therefore, the organization is seen as a configuration of events, where actors are constantly involved in reconstructing its trajectory. A temporal trajectory is a pattern, or a patterning, of events that stretch back into time and extends into the future. A temporal trajectory requires work, which consists of articulation performed at various moments and in multiple places. The work of becoming is the work of performing the temporal conditioning of that very same work. Therefore, events are emerging from other events (Cobb, 2007; Hernes, 2014a); there is no spatial or temporal separation between events, and "the structure of events defines the temporality of the organization" (Hussenot & Missonier, 2016: 8). Different alternative event trajectories may reflect a merely limited coping with the present or a creation of a new (Helin et al., 2014). In either way, the organization *is* its becoming, not as an entity, but as a trajectory of events that never really starts or ends.

Through building upon one another (Luhmann, 1995), events connect internally, which enables us to order time (events) into clusters of events (Chia & King, 1998; Cobb, 2007) or patterns or trajectories (Hernes, 2017). There are various events, like natural and social events, personal, family, community, and organizational events, or intentional and accidental events, which in their multiplicity are becoming simultaneously. Building on the idea that at each moment, multiple events are emerging simultaneously with a surplus of possibilities for further connecting (i.e., Fuchs, 2013; Helin et al., 2014; Luhmann, 1995, 2018; Kahneman, 2011), while each new connection is viewed as a possible event, then events could be described "as related in the form of a manifold" (Hernes, 2014b: 95). In this manifold of possible events, every event must struggle for its becoming, for its emergence and endurance (Shotter, 2006), as well as for its direction. To be connected to the manifold means that the specific event may be influenced by the events that took place, not in the immediate past or recent history, but a long time ago. Alternatively, the specific event in its becoming could be influenced by the expected immediate future events or imagined distant future events or by "non-events" from the past.

The possibility of being influenced by events from the distant past (Hatch & Schultz, 2017; Schultz & Hernes, 2013) or future (Slawinski & Bansal, 2012) or unrealized past events (Luhmann, 2018; Valsiner, 2011) increases the unpredictability of current events and adds an element of surprise. At the same time, we can claim that when we experience new events in the perceived passage of time, the relational configuration of events is changing (Oakeshott, 1995). Therefore, the meaning of events is not fixed but open to ongoing re-interpretation and re-evaluation. This re-evaluation always takes place in the present, which is a *locus of action* (Mead, 1932/2002). The past event that had taken place and an anticipated future event are brought into the present to participate in the making of the present event. In other words, the experience from the past and the future anticipation are participating in the present decision-making.

However, in interpreting the present ongoing event and trying to intervene in its evolution, human actors bring to the present event past events that had remained as not realized possibilities together with alternative future possibilities. As a result, the trajectory of the event is far from path-dependent. Although, whatever actors bring to the present moment serves to maintain the perceived continuity of their reality. In other words, they try to maintain the perceived continuity of their time (Zerubavel, 2003), which is not necessarily linear and sequential. Therefore, the present plays a vital role in keeping up the ongoing temporality and shaping the unfolding event trajectories.

Still, no matter if the current event is influenced by the recent or more distant past, the influencing takes place in the present, as the present is the temporal locus of action. Some moments in the present could be more decisive than others. That is, the present could offer an instant moment that could radically change the trajectories of events and may have far-reaching consequences both for better and worse. In other words, some events in the present could be seen as more influential than others, being *those events that mattered* (Hernes et al., 2021: 732) or *watersheds* (Zerubavel, 2003: 84). Those events that matter could represent a *window of opportunity* (Tyre & Orlikowski, 1994) that makes it possible to take a qualitative leap in events trajectory or a *bifurcation point* (Valsiner, 2011) that is a shift in the direction or the course of events trajectory. Alternatively, the meaning of some historical events that lacked public attention at the time they occurred could only retrospectively become defined as significant watershed events. In other words, how they transcend and prehend, that is, how they connect to their predecessors and antecedent events, becomes visible only retrospectively.

Also, events with higher significance could constitute time across different social time layers for different social systems (see the previous chapter) and various social subgroups. That means that events are read and defined differently. For example, a relatively small eruption of the Icelandic volcano Eyjafjallajökull in 2010 had a massive economic impact because of the chaos it created in European air travel for almost a month. More precisely, it kept most European aircraft grounded while creating some troubles in the North Atlantic. I found myself stranded in London for two weeks. In my case, the meaning of the eruption of Eyjafjallajökull was a bus trip from London, UK, to Tallinn, Estonia—a modest 2600 and something kilometres. One American woman who was staying in the

6 Events, Time, and Events-Based Time   263

same hotel found herself out of a job after being fired because, for obvious reasons, she was unable to show up at work in the United States after the official end of her vacation. My family needed to manage my absence back home, and my husband, being home alone with two relatively young children, learned to operate the washing machine. At the same time, for many people, this objective natural event had no meaning other than another headline in the news and therefore remained largely unnoticed as an event (or at least a relevant event).

To illustrate the subjectivity of event-ness, Zerubavel offers the example of the foundation of the Israeli state in 1948. While most Israelis consider it "a virtually indisputable *watershed*," it is ignored and treated as a non-event by Israel's ultraorthodox community, which remains apolitical (Zerubavel, 2003: 95). Therefore, the lack of consensus about the event-ness of an event could be an issue even concerning an objective event like a volcanic eruption or the formation of a state. Even if there is agreement about the event's occurrence, it guarantees neither a shared understanding nor a common meaning of the event nor its significance.

However, seeing events as becoming, an events-based view of time does not ascribe any prior importance to events. The meaning of events evolves together with the events. Therefore, the past, once considered unattractive, might lose its unattractiveness as events evolve (Hernes, 2014a: 165). Similarly, a future once fantasized as the most desirable or most undesirable may be re-evaluated, respectively, in light of new events that have emerged and new experiences that have been acquired (Kahneman, 2011). Some events, viewed as relatively insignificant at the time they occurred, could still play a significant role in connecting events as patterns.

While working together with Tor Hernes on the case of InnoShip, we recognized how a regular customer meeting provided a window of opportunity for a strategic shift for the company. In this meeting, different past events transcended, combined, and formed, what we call, the temporal nexus event. First, there was the idea of the wave-piercing bow that the designer started to toy with in 1997–1998 before joining InnoShip. After joining the company, the new bow idea appeared on the cover of the InnoShip in-house magazine at the end of 2003. Second, in late 2003 or early 2004, one of the CEOs of a client company saw the mock drawing on the magazine cover. As a former sea captain, he intuitively recognized the benefits of the new bow design for mitigating the effects of hitting waves in rough seas.

In addition, he was looking for something special to stand out from his competitors. Therefore, he immediately recognized that the new bow design offered the possibility to stand out. The CEO was accompanied by the technical director of the client company, who confirmed the possible technical feasibility of the design. Third, InnoShip was looking to re-enter the international naval design industry, and therefore, they saw an opportunity to make their breakthrough. Fourth, although a ship with a traditional bow was under construction, both the designer and the InnoShip management knew that despite all the risks, they can handle the change in construction because of the craft their yard had acquired over almost a hundred years in the business (Hernes & Pulk, 2020).

In this specific event, various past events, like the experience of standing on deck in rough seas (the client CEO's experience) and a hundred years of managing changes in orders (InnoShip construction), transcended the current event. Simultaneously, these past events were combined with the expectation of (the client) being able to stand out from their competitors with these new vessels and the anticipation of re-entering the international naval design market (InnoShip). While both the client's CEO and the InnoShip designer sensed the opportunity, the meeting only became *the event that mattered* retrospectively when the design won numerous awards and, after the initial launch of the first NewBow in 2005, served as the basis for other technically novel bow designs. In 2014, the NewStern followed, and in 2016, the Twin NewStern designs (Hernes & Pulk, 2020).

Working from Whitehead's work on temporality, Hernes (2014a) suggests that the present is an open and indeterminate event; its outcome is open until its (provisional) closure. The situation is different when it comes to past and future events, which are closed in the sense that they are seen as having taken place. Even a future event is treated as hypothetically having taken place (Schütz, 1967). When evaluated from the perspective of the present ongoing event, the past and future events are seen as accomplished. However, the past and future events are only provisionally closed (Hernes, 2014a), and their meaning and relation remain open for inquiry and redefinition. Therefore, depending on the chosen time span, the event's meaning and its provisional closure or openness evolve, while this evolution does not necessarily follow a sequential order. In other words, ongoing evolution refers to continuity, but continuity is not necessarily linear and sequential.

For example, in 2018, Estonia celebrated its 100th anniversary as an independent state. However, between 1944 and 1991, Estonia was not an independent state but was occupied by the Soviet Union. Despite almost 50 years of occupation, Estonia considers the establishment of the first Republic of Estonia in 1918 as the beginning of its status as a state. Regaining its independence in 1991 meant that a connection was made with the first Republic of Estonia, which was provisionally ended almost 50 years ago in 1944 by the Soviet occupation. Therefore, the event called an independent state of Estonia, which during the occupation years existed only in some underground personal archives, memories, stories, fantasies, imagination, dreams, and hopes of people continued its becoming. Although 50 years is a relatively short period compared to "eighteen or twenty-five centuries [that] can sometimes be *bracketed off* as a mere interruption of an essentially continuous national project" (Zerubavel, 2003: 54), it does illustrate a similar phenomenon of the non-linear and non-sequential connecting of events.

However, while the event is becoming, even across a longer time span, it stays recognizable to actors as *this event*. An event's ability to extend from the current moment to the past and endure or carry on across and through time is called transcendence. Concerning organizational life, Hernes has pointed out that "the complexity facing organizers may be seen as spatio-temporal tangledness, which includes their immediate environment but transcends organizational boundaries to include happenings in faraway places and different times in history" (2014a: 13). Events from a more distant past that are used to make historical analogies are regarded as "transhistorical, generic symbols" (Zerubavel, 2003: 51). Zerubavel claims that "historical analogies clearly transcend their historical specificity. Therefore, when drawing such analogies, we do not feel constrained by the considerable temporal distance often separating past signifiers from their corresponding present signifiers. Their evocative power is much greater" (Zerubavel, 2003: 50).

Whitehead, viewing events not as discrete units but evolving and durational, calls the internal non-sequential relatedness of events *prehension*. Extending through time, events in their becoming pervade other events by constituting these other events and their pasts and futures (Hernes, 2014a). Explaining the term *prehension*, Hernes states, "one could say that events *grasp* for each other, as prehension relates to the propensity of an event to connect to another event with which it has common aims. However, the commonality of aims is produced by the connecting of events" (Hernes, 2014a: 159). Hussenot and Missonier explain, "Prehension means that actors always define and act in their actual event through the engagement with past, present and anticipated events" (2016: 531). That means that the past, present, and future events in the organization are not distinct elements but are related to one another in indivisible coherence.

Coherence, according to Whitehead (1929/1978: 3) means "that the fundamental ideas, in terms of which the scheme is developed, presuppose each other so that in isolation they are meaningless." Whitehead explains becoming "as the transformation of incoherence into coherence, and in each particular instance ceases with this attainment" (1929/1978: 25). Whitehead sees coherence as an achievement. Like Luhmann's (1995) idea of simplifying decision-making by reducing a range of available alternatives through the pre-selection discussed above, Whitehead points out that "by successive decisions," conditioned alternatives are "reduced to coherence" (1929/1978: 224). In other words, events in their becoming transcend from the current moment to the past and future across and throughout a spatio-temporal context. Through their internal connections, events form temporal trajectories, which enable actors to prehend them in their present ongoing activities. Prehension allows actors to see events in their temporal coherence.

6.4.2 Immanence of Events

An events-based view of time starts with recognizing that an ongoing temporality does not equal a succession of pasts, presents, and futures, such as points along a line (Hernes, 2014a). Instead, the past and future events are immanent in the present, which means that the experienced past events and anticipated future events constitute the present event (Griesbach & Grand, 2013). In other words, the past, present, and future events are internally related. They are co-constituting one another in the current event, in the present, meaning that "distant events are immanent parts of actors' experience of time" (Hernes et al., 2021: 732). Viewing the present as an actuality that draws a difference between the past and future as non-actualities (Luhmann, 2018) means that neither past nor future events can exist as separate, distinct points occupying a fixed position in the timeline. Whitehead states:

> there are no actual occasions in the future, already constituted. Thus there are no actual occasions in the future to exercise efficient causation in the present. What is objective in the present is the necessity of a future of actual occasions, and necessity that these future occasions conform to the conditions inherent in the essence of the present occasion. (1933: 195)

Therefore, as neither the past nor future events can exist outside the present, they are forming a part of the present experience, meaning both the future and the past are immanent in the present occasion, they form an "immanent temporal trajectory" (Hernes et al., 2021: 733).

The distinction between past and future events, as non-actualities, could happen only by means of present experience (Hernes, 2020). On the one hand, the present is what makes the difference and creates the meaning of past and future events and the past realized and unrealized events. On the other hand, both the realized and unrealized past and anticipated future events participate in the present event. Therefore, the ongoing present implies a highly dynamic configuration of events and their meaning, whatever is taking place in one event is experienced immediately in all other events. Whitehead calls this phenomenon *mirroring* (1925 cited in Hernes, 2014a: 215).

Mirroring means that the event taking place in the present affects multiple events in both the past and the future (Hernes, 2014a). Instead of a spatial view of reality, which sees reality as containing events that took place at specific points in time, mirroring assumes a temporal view of reality, which is reality constituted by events in becoming. In other words, every event is mirroring itself to other contemporary events as well as past and future events. Hernes explains that *"Mirroring* is not to be seen as synonymous with becoming identical, but conveys a symmetry of mutual creation. Thus, events are nothing in themselves, nor are they causes of other events. At best events have *anticipation*, making for their own becoming, by creating, or *feeling* another event" (2014a: 215). Therefore, events continuously redefine themselves, and this redefinition includes both past and future events. Through ongoing redefinition, events modify their trajectory, they "bend the trajectory" of the events pattern, and by doing that, they "are revising the design of the past" (Hernes, 2014a: 92). Redefinition presupposes a selection from a "multiplicity of pure potentiality" (Whitehead, 1929/1978: 164) and bending requires work (Hernes, 2014a). Therefore, building up event trajectories is a highly creative activity (Whitehead, 1929/1978).

The immanence of the past and future in present events and the immanence of the present events in the past and future give time its agency (Hernes, 2014a). Alternatively, it could be argued that as "any mention of an event includes a reference to time and vice versa" (Bakken et al., 2013: 18), time as events are enacted, and it is through the enactments that agency is given to time. As Griesbach and Grand stress, "in the enactment of situations, the situation is transcended, thereby influencing other situations beyond the current situation only" (Griesbach & Grand, 2013: 64). The concept of immanence presents events as a dynamic network rather than as pearls on strings. The network of events contains all the possibilities simultaneously, realized and unrealized past and future events. However, this network of events is not fixed, static, and predetermined, but depending on a combination of broader evolvements and more specific selections, realized possibilities, and actualized potentials, new possibilities, and potentialities are emerging while some previous ones vanish in the perishing time. In the words of Hernes (2014a: 98),

> The manifold as described above reflects an event formation as an open, ever-changing, ever-renewed complex of events, which re-generates itself while remaining open to the emergence of novelty. The wholeness of patterns of events enables them to infuse events and bring new events into the

manifold. Events and their connecting into patterns are subject to continuous re-interpretation in the present, at which the event formation may begin to take a new direction.

Instead of seeing events as strings of pearls organized in the sequential order one after the other, the events-based view sees events as forming a dynamic and live field of possibilities. In this field of possibilities, the ongoing process of the realization of possibilities and the actualization of potentialities creates new and maybe unexpected opportunities that redefine the connections between events and form the perceived direction of movement, while previous options left unrealized are vanishing (Hernes, 2014a, 2017, 2020).

6.5 Conclusion

The intimate relations between time, events, and human experience are broadly acknowledged. However, there could be large conceptual differences in how these relations are seen depending on how time and events are defined. The sequential view of time, based on the ontology of time, views time as external and objective, providing a fixed timestamp to events that occur *in* time, while events are seen as *discrete and closed*. This view follows the notion of external, measurable, and homogenous time, which orders discrete events in sequential order like pearls on strings. Therefore, there are two distinctive phenomena, events and time, and *events are in time*. Alternatively, it is claimed that *time is in events* in the sense that *events signify time* by indicating the right time to do something or mark the change in the trajectory or course of events. In either case, the event holds clear a prior meaning and significance. Compared to the sequential view of time, the relationship between events and time is more intuitive and qualitative. However, events are still viewed as concrete and closed. The events-based view of time is based on the ontology of temporality, and it assumes that *events are time*. Events in the ongoing becoming prehend and transcend when constituting new events. Furthermore, events in their ongoing becoming create the temporal reality.

Differences in these different approaches to time, events, and their mutual relations are reflected in different organization theories. Classic theories of organization, which define the organization as a space or entity, operate either with the sequential view of time and events or treating events as signifiers of time. As a space or entity, an organization is in time together with events, events occur in organizations, and mark changing times for organizations. The events-based view of organizations differs from classic theories treating organizations as processes being constituted by events in the becoming. Therefore, instead of viewing the organization as a space or entity, the events-based view sees the organization as a constellation of open-ended events.

The events-based view of time does not preclude the structure/process approach of events/time. Although not identical, these approaches seem to complement one another. The structure/process approach relying on the activities of human actors could be viewed as a narrower event selection model in the events-based view of time(events). Most probably, the temporal structure, whether organized by mechanical clock or sundial, water clock, or an hourglass with running sand, or by the moon, tides, or something else, that is, instrumental time, external to our existential experiences, is important for humans to organize our social life and lived experience of time. Although we need these experiences, the structure alone is not enough. The structure needs to be filled with experiences, with a lived time. As humans' experiences are related to events, events are these temporal elements that are woven together to form our temporal reality, our time across different layers of social time (see the previous chapter).

The events-based time views time as active and enacted in events. The immanence of the past and future in the present relates to events temporally and gives time its agency. Therefore, the events-based view enables us to have a different look at organizations. It invites us to see organizations as formed by events. While recognizing the constraints and far from claiming that everything is possible, the events-based view of organizations assigns to actors significant creative power to create their temporal reality.

References

Adam, B. (1990). *Time and social theory.* Polity Press.
Adam, B. (2004). *Time.* Polity.
Allen, T. D., Freeman, D. M., Reizenstein, R. C., & Rentz, J. O. (1995). Just another transition? Examining survivors' attitudes over time. *Academy of Management Journal,* 78–82.
Ancona, D. G., Okhuysen, G. A., & Perlow, L. A. (2001). Taking time to integrate temporal research. *Academy of Management Review, 26*(4), 512–529.
Anthony, P., & Staberg, J. (2013). *The man who saved the world.* Retrieved August 15, 2021, from https://www.youtube.com/watch?v=8TNdihbV5go
Augustine, G., Soderstrom, S., Milner, D., & Weber, K. (2019). Constructing a distant future: Imaginaries in geoengineering. *Academy of Management Journal, 62*(6), 1930–1960.
Bakken, T., Holt, R., & Zundel, M. (2013). Time and play in management practice: An investigation through the philosophies of McTaggart and Heidegger. *Scandinavian Journal of Management, 29,* 13–22.
Barnett, L. (1949). *The Universe and Dr. Einstein.* Victor Gollancz.
Berger, P., & Luckmann, T. (1991). *The social construction of reality: A treatise in the sociology of knowledge.* Penguin Books.
Bergson, H. (1946). *The creative mind.* Carol Publishing Group.
Blagoev, B., & Schreyögg, G. (2019). Why do extreme work hours persist? Temporal uncoupling as a new way of seeing. *Academy of Management Journal, 62*(6), 1818–1847.
Bluedorn, A. C. (2002). *The human organization of time: Temporal realities and experience.* Stanford University Press.
Bueti, D., & Macaluso, E. (2011). Physiological correlates of subjective time: Evidence for the temporal accumulator hypothesis. *NeuroImage, 57,* 1251–1263.
Callender, C. (2017). *What makes time special?* Oxford University Press.
Chia, R. (1999). A 'rhizomic' model of organizational change and transformation: Perspective from a metaphysics of change. *British Journal of Management, 10,* 209–227.
Chia, R., & King, I. W. (1998). The organizational structuring of novelty. *Organization, 5*(4), 461–478.
Clark, P. (1985). A review of theories of time and structure for organizational sociology. In S. B. Bacharach & S. M. Mitchel (Eds.), *Research in the sociology of organizations* (pp. 35–79). JAI Press.

Cobb, J. B. (2007). Person-in-community: Whiteheadian insights into community and institution. *Organization Studies, 28*, 567–588.

Deroy, X., & Clegg, S. (2011). When events interact with business ethics. *Organization, 18*(5), 637–653.

Emirbayer, M., & Mische, A. (1998). What is agency? *American Journal of Sociology, 103*(4), 962–1023.

Flaherty, M. G. (2020). The lathe of time: Some principles of temporal agency. In M. G. Flaherty, L. Meinert, & A. L. Dalsgård (Eds.), *Time work: Studies of temporal agency* (pp. 13–28). Berghahn Books.

Fuchs, T. (2013). Temporality and psychopathology. *Phenomenology and the Cognitive Sciences, 12*(1), 75–104. https://doi.org/10.1007/s11097-010-9189-4

Gehman, J., Trevino, L. K., & Garud, R. (2013). Values work: A process study of the emergence and performance of organizational values practices. *Academy of Management Journal, 56*(1), 84–112.

Griesbach, D., & Grand, S. (2013). Managing as transcending: An ethnography. *Scandinavian Journal of Management, 29*, 63–77.

Hatch, M. J., & Schultz, M. (2017). Toward a theory of using history authentically: Historicizing in the Carlsberg Group. *Administrative Science Quarterly, 62*, 657–697.

Heidegger, M. (1927/1962). *Being and time*. Blackwell Publishers.

Helin, J., Hernes, T., Hjorth, D., & Holt, R. (2014). Process is how process does. In J. Helin, T. Hernes, D. Hjort, & R. Holt (Eds.), *The Oxford handbook of process philosophy and organization studies* (pp. 1–16). Oxford University Press.

Hernes, T. (2008). *Understanding organization as process: Theory for a tangled world*. Routledge.

Hernes, T. (2014a). *A process theory of organization*. Oxford University Press.

Hernes, T. (2014b). Alfred North Whitehead. In J. Helin, T. Hernes, D. Hjort, & R. Holt (Eds.), *The Oxford handbook of process philosophy and organization studies* (pp. 225–271). Oxford University Press.

Hernes, T. (2017). Process as the becoming of temporal trajectory. In A. Langley & H. Tsoukas (Eds.), *Sage handbook of process organizational studies* (pp. 601–606). SAGE.

Hernes, T. (2020). Events and the becoming of organizational temporality. In J. Reinecke, R. Suddaby, A. Langley, & H. Tsoukas (Eds.), *About time: Temporality and history in organization studies* (pp. 29–43). Oxford University Press. https://doi.org/10.1093/oso/9780198870715.003.0003

Hernes, T., Hussenot, A., & Pulk, K. (2021). Time and temporality of change processes. Applying an event-based view to integrate episodic and continuous change. In M. S. Poole & A. Van de Ven (Eds.), *The Oxford handbook of organizational change and innovation* (2nd ed., pp. 731–750). Oxford University Press. https://doi.org/10.1093/oxfordhb/9780198845973.013.27

Hernes, T., & Pulk, K. (2020). How organizational change emerges from everyday work: The role of temporal nexus August 2020. *Academy of Management Annual Meeting Proceedings, 2020*(1), 15001. https://doi.org/10.5465/AMBPP.2020.15001abstract

Hernes, T., & Schultz, M. (2020). How actors translate between the on-going and the distant: A temporal view of situated activity. *Organization Theory, 1*. https://doi.org/10.1177/2631787719900999

Holt, R., & Mueller, F. (2011). Wittgenstein, Heidegger and drawing lines in organization studies. *Organization Studies, 32*(1), 67–84.

Holt, R., & Sandberg, J. (2011). Phenomenology and organization theory. *Philosophy and Organization Theory, 32*, 215–249. https://doi.org/10.1177/0170840610394299

Hussenot, A., Hernes, T., & Bouty, I. (2020). Studying organization from the perspective of the ontology of temporality: Introducing the event-based approach. In J. Reinecke, R. Suddaby, A. Langley, & H. Tsoukas (Eds.), *About time: Temporality and history in organization studies* (pp. 50–68). Oxford University Press. https://doi.org/10.1093/oso/9780198870715.003.0005

Hussenot, A., & Missonier, S. (2016). Encompassing novelty and stability: An events-based approach. *Organization Studies, 37*(4), 523–546.

Jay, J. (2013). Navigating paradox as a mechanism of change and innovation in hybrid organizations. *Academy of Management Journal, 56*(1), 137–159.

Jones, M. R. (2019). *Time will tell: A theory of dynamic attending*. Oxford University Press.

Kahneman, D. (2011). *Thinking, fast and slow*. Farrar, Straus and Giroux.

Langley, A., Smallman, C., Tsoukas, H., & Van de Ven, A. H. (2013). Process studies of change in organization and management: Unveiling temporality, activity, and flow. *Academy of Management Journal, 56*(1), 1–13.

Levine, R. (2006). *A geography of time: The temporal misadventures of a social psychologist, or how every culture keeps time just a little bit differently*. Oneworld.

Luhmann, N. (1995). *Social systems* (J. Bednarz, Jr. with D. Baecker, Trans.). Stanford University Press.

Luhmann, N. (2018). *Organization and decision* (R. Barrett, Trans.). Cambridge University Press.

Malinowski, B. (1990). Time-reckoning in the Trobriands. In J. Hassard (Ed.), *The sociology of time* (pp. 203–218). Macmillan.

McTaggart, J. (1908). The unreality of time. *Mind, 17*, 457–474.

Mead, G. H. (1932/2002). *The philosophy of the present*. Prometheus.

Merleau-Ponty, M. (2002). *Phenomenology of perception*. Routledge Classics.

Morgeson, F. P., Mitchell, T. R., & Liu, D. (2015). Event system theory: An event oriented approach to the organizational sciences. *Academy of Management Review, 40*(4), 515–537.

Oakeshott, M. (1995). *Experience and its modes*. Cambridge University Press.

Pjatakova, L. (2021). Valedictory address. EBS Graduation Ceremony for the Class of 2021—Master's and Doctoral students June 21, 2021. Retrieved June 22, 2021, from https://www.youtube.com/watch?v=LWrQPi9qQtk [1.03.00:1.10.33]

Polanyi, M. (1967). *The tacit dimension*. Routledge & K. Paul.

Pulk, K. (2016). *Making time while being in time: A study of the temporality of organizational processes*. PhD series, no. 43.2016, Copenhagen Business School [PhD], Frederiksberg.

Puzo, M. (1990). *The fourth K*. Random House.

Reinecke, J., & Ansari, S. (2017). Time, temporality, and process studies. In A. Langley & H. Tsoukas (Eds.), *The Sage handbook of process organization studies*. (pp. 402–416). SAGE.

Schultz, M., & Hernes, T. (2013). A temporal perspective on organizational identity. *Organization Science, 24*(1), 1–21.

Schütz, A. (1967). *The phenomenology of the social world*. Heinemann Educational Books.

Shotter, J. (2006). Understanding process from within: An argument for 'withness'-thinking. *Organization Studies, 27*(4), 585–604.

Slawinski, N., & Bansal, P. (2012). A matter of time: The temporal perspectives of organizational responses to climate change. *Organization Studies, 33*, 1537–1563.

Snowden, D. (2003, April/May). Complex acts of knowing: Paradox and descriptive self-awareness. *Bulletin of the American Society for Information Science and Technology*, 23–28.

Sorokin, P. A., & Merton, R. K. (1937). Social time: A methodological and functional analysis. *American Journal of Sociology, 42*(5), 615–629.

Stake, R. E. (2006). *Multiple case study analysis*. The Guilford Press.

The Future Life Award 2017. Retrieved July 28, 2021, from https://futureoflife. org/future-of-life-award-2017/
The Future Life Award 2018. Retrieved July 28, 2021, from https://futureoflife. org/future-of-life-award-2018/
Tsoukas, H., & Chia, R. (2002). On organizational becoming: Rethinking organizational change. *Organization Science,* 13(5), 567–582. https://doi. org/10.1287/orsc.13.5.567.7810
Tulving, E. (1983). *Elements of episodic memory.* Oxford University Press.
Tyre, M. J., & Orlikowski, W. J. (1994). Windows of opportunity: Temporal patterns of technological adaptation in organizations. *Organization Science,* 5(1), 98–118.
Väänänen, J. (2016). *The smart device.* Vaka Väinämöinen.
Valsiner, J. (2011). Constructing the vanishing present between the future and the past. *Infancia y Aprendizaje, 34*(2), 141–150.
Valsiner, J., & van der Veer, R. (2013). Encountering the border: Vygotsky's zona blizaishego razvitia and its implication for theory of development. In A. Yasnitsky & R. Van der Veer (Eds.), *Handbook of cultural-historical psychology.* Cambridge University Press.
Van de Ven, A. H., & Poole, M. S. (1990). Methods for studying innovation development in the Minnesota innovation research program. *Organization Science,* 1(3), 213–337.
Van Oorschot, K. E., Akkermans, H., Sengupta, K., & Van Wassenhove, L. N. (2013). Anatomy of a decision trap in complex new product development projects. *Academy of Management Journal, 56*(1), 285–307.
Veltri, M. (2017). *The mushin way to peak performance: The productivity, balance, and success.* John Wiley & Sons.
Vooglaid, Ü. (2018). *Sõna on jõud. Raadio ööülikooli loengud 2001–2017.* SE&JS.
Watzlawik, M. (2015). Temporality, lifetime, and the afterdeath: Case studies from hospice patients. In L. M. Simão, D. S. Guimarães, & J. Valsiner (Eds.), *Temporality: Culture in the flow of human experience* (pp. 215–229). Information Age Publishing.
Wearden, J. H. (2005). The wrong tree: Time perception and time experience in the elderly. In J. Duncan, L. Phillips, & P. McLeod (Eds.), Measuring the mind: Speed, control, and age (pp. 137–158). Oxford University Press.
Whitehead, A. N. (1925/1985). *Science and the modern world.* Free Association Books.
Whitehead, A. N. (1929/1978). *Process and reality.* The Free Press.
Whitehead, A. N. (1933). *Adventures of ideas.* The Free Press.

Zerubavel, E. (1982). The standardization of time: A sociohistorical perspective. *American Journal of Sociology*, 1, 1–23.
Zerubavel, E. (2003). *Time maps: Collective memory and the social shape of the past*. University of Chicago Press.

7

Some Challenges Related to Time and Temporality

As both time and temporality are multi-layered concepts, we should be ready to tackle several challenges. However, being prepared to tackle challenges is usually easier when we are aware of the possible challenges that could emerge. This chapter will not point out possible methodological challenges but challenges stemming from our socially and culturally embedded understandings and habitual, common-sense ways of thinking about time. These are some issues highlighted in the literature and some I have encountered on various academic and non-academic occasions. The points covered below do not represent a non-exhaustive list of possible conceptual challenges.

First, challenges arise because "we are always already living in time" (Baars, 2012: 144). As a socio-temporal context, time constitutes the cultural background with its norms, value systems, beliefs, and prejudices (see Chap. 5), which include the notion of time and gives it its socially taken-for-granted meaning. Therefore, to some extent, it could be viewed as a root for other challenges we may encounter in theorizing about time. We have learned to conceptualize time in a particular way. We have learned to associate specific characteristics of time with a specific semiotic meaning and set of time-bounded values established through centuries

© The Author(s), under exclusive license to Springer Nature Switzerland AG 2022
K. Pulk, *Time and Temporality in Organisations*,
https://doi.org/10.1007/978-3-030-90696-2_7

(Elias, 2000). Put differently, as members of a particular society, we have internalized the prevailing temporal norms and values and understanding of time, which are taken for granted (see Chap. 5). Breaking out of this established taken-for-granted common understanding is not necessarily easy, which makes it challenging to get "a clear understanding of time" (Baars, 2012: 144). However, it is possible to extend our understanding of time. Although, it requires a critical analysis of our own internalized knowledge of time, what kind of reality this understanding allows us to create, and how that understanding enables and inhibits us from relating to reality. Notably, breaking free from the taken-for-granted commonsense understanding about time requires us to acknowledge the existence of our taken-for-granted approach and awareness of different options.

To orient ourselves and enhance the field requires a critical analysis of various ways time is defined and conceptualized, the possible consequences of different conceptualizations, and how these differently conceptualized times connect and relate to one another. Considering that "Time is lived, experienced, known, theorised, created, regulated, sold and controlled. It is contextual and historical, embodied and objectified, abstracted and constructed, represented and commodified. In these multiple expressions, time is an inescapable fact of social life and cultural existence" (Adam, 2004: 1); this is quite an ambitious task requiring that theoretical and empirical insights across disciplines are integrated into the unified body of knowledge (Aeon & Aguinis, 2017).

Therefore, stressing the existing dichotomies and praising one type while criticizing the other does not carry us far but limits our understanding of reality. For example, in the literature, clock time is heavily criticized and compared to the cyclical time of nature (Hatch, 2002), often described as unnatural, inhuman, and almost evil (i.e., Adam, 1990, 2004; Reinecke & Ansari, 2015). However, if we think about the working conditions, for example, in Amazon, it is evident that clock time cannot be blamed for the inhuman treatment of the "fulfilment centre" employees. Neither does clock time as such force somebody to use empty bottles instead of going the toilet. There is no evil *Ticktockman* or *Master Timekeeper* (Ellison, 1965) ruling innocent people. Therefore, although targeted by a lot of criticism, clock time is not bad or evil. What is unfortunate is how clock time is used by some people and the attitudes or worldviews associated with that usage. The objective, rational, egocentric, and chronocentric worldview and constant drive for economic efficiency explain the dominance of clock time, but it is not clock time that drives for economic efficiency or holds an objective, egocentric, and chronocentric worldview; the ones who do that are still people.

Oakeshott (2004) explains that their attitudes mediate the human relationship to the world, but attitudes are directly linked to the time-bounded values of society. With the quote below, Oakeshott describes dominant attitude humans have to the world, which may even too easily extend itself to time. Therefore, in the following quote from Oakeshott, I have switched the word *world* (still presented in brackets) to *time*. This slight shift allows us to describe the dominant attitude towards time, see how closely our attitude to time and the world are connected, and explain the dominance of clock time and its less considerable usage.

> The aim in *work* is to change the time [world], to use it, to make something out of it; the aim of explanation is to illuminate it, to see it as it is. The aim of *work* is to exert power over the hostile time [world], to subdue it, and to extract from it what may be useful for satisfying wants; the aim of *understanding* is to discern the intelligibility of the time [world]. The aim of *work* is to impress some temporary human purpose upon some component of the time [world]; the aim of explanation is to reveal the time [world] as it is and not merely in respect of its eligibility to satisfy human wants. (Oakeshott, 2004: 311)

As the slightly modified quote above indicates, the dominant attitude in Western culture is to use time, change it, conquer it, and use our power to extract the aspects that lend themselves to bend according to our purpose and desires. In this instrumental and utilitarian approach to time, attempts to understand and explain it in its entirety are not a priority. As not all aspects of time are necessarily so readily available for instrumental use as clock time, they are ignored. Nevertheless, these less instrumental or maybe even entirely not instrumental aspects of time could expand our understanding of time, the world, and reality. However, as already said, the ultimate instrumentality does not stem from the clock time but from our attitudes toward it, from attempts "to satisfy human wants."

However, attempts "to satisfy human wants" link our perspective on time directly to the question of morality. As Wallace and Rabin (1960: 232) put it, "It follows, therefore, that time perspective involves a moral rather than molecular (or atomistic) approach to the problem of temporal behavior." Put differently, like any behaviour, temporal behaviour is grounded in our internalized value system and institutionalized norms (Granqvist & Gustafsson, 2016). Respectively, the problems related to clock time are not caused by clock time as a measurement tool or structure but by how this tool is used and by the value system associated with its usage.

Therefore, the critical analysis of clock time shows that the suppression of humanity in its different forms or ignoring sustainability is not caused by clock time as such, but by the intentional or unintentional, unbalanced approach to and usage of clock time by humans. Therefore, to analyse clock time, we need to be aware, on the one hand, of the nature of clock time per se and, on the other hand, people's tendency to misuse clock time as a tool for manipulation, suppression, and even dehumanization (Flaherty, 2020; Levine, 2006; Zerubavel, 1982). However, by focusing in their action and analysis on some aspects of time and overemphasizing those while ignoring others does not support a comprehensive understanding of our reality. Most importantly, what we tend to miss is clock time's relationship to other types of times and how all these different times participate in creating our reality.

Therefore, the *distinctions* between the different times, as not precise and objective, could be less important than the *connections* between these different times. Zerubavel's (1991) call to pay close attention to where and how we draw lines in social science and make distinctions is essential. If we choose to draw lines and borders, which from an analytical perspective might be helpful, we need to stay alert about how these borders function. Respectively, what, how, and with what consequences do they separate and with what consequences do they bound together. Even when drawing lines, we should remember their tentative nature and try to avoid an overly narrow focus on one aspect or dimension of time at the expense of others. In other words, it is crucial to prevent the "fallacy of misplaced concreteness" (Whitehead, 1929/1978: 7).

As all the different types of time mentioned in Adam's (2004) quote cited earlier are relevant in different ways, it is essential to articulate our working assumptions when describing, explaining, and analysing time and temporality. Further, because all of the various aspects of time are relevant in different ways in the ongoing creation of reality, instead of pitching one against another, the effort to consolidate multiple aspects of time and temporality (Adam, 1990, 2004) seems to be worthwhile. That means paying attention to mechanisms for handling temporal tensions, like "temporal ambidexterity" (Slawinski & Bansal, 2015) and "ambi-temporality" (Reinecke & Ansari, 2015). Temporal ambidexterity refers to integrating short-term and long-term time perspectives and ambitemporality to integrating seemingly conflicting temporal orientations. In both cases, the authors showed that the ability to move from dualism to duality[1] and find a balance between contradictory orientations resulted in superior results. However, in their review, Putnam et al. (2016: 122) point out that besides dualism as *either-or* and duality as *both-and* approaches, there is also a *more-than* approach.

The either-or approach works as a defence, selection, and separation mechanism. The both-and approach, treating opposites as inseparable and interdependent, stands for paradoxical thinking ("focuses on increasing cognitive abilities to recognize opposites, question and reflect on them, and shift mental sets" (Putnam et al., 2016: 124)), vacillation or spiralling inversion ("focuses on shifting back and forth between the poles at different times or in different contexts" (Ibid)), and integration and balance ("seeks a compromise or a middle-of-the-road approach, sometimes through a forced merger between the opposites" (Ibid)). While a certain exaggeration of one or another type of time has probably been justified to break the taken-for-granted thinking and enhance existing theories, further enhancement of the field seems to benefit from getting over the oppositions, dichotomies, and dualisms in favour of a more-than approach. The more-than approach stands for relational synthesis. According to the review by Putnam et al. (2016), a more-than approach

---

[1] Dualism: "the existence of opposite poles, dichotomies, binary relationships that are able to create tensions, but can be separated" (Putnam et al., 2016: 69).

Duality: "Interdependence of opposites in a both/and relationship that is not mutually exclusive or antagonistic" (Ibid).

includes reframing and transcendence, connecting and dialogue, reflective practice, and serious play. The insightful synthesis of different types of time could be helpful not only for theories but also in organizational practices and everyday life.

Second, as we are part of time and time is part of us, we cannot step out of time to observe or analyse it purely without any subjective or social filter from an external and objective observer position. We cannot define time "in the same way as material objects such as a chair or even abstract objects such as a straight line: it is a fundamental concept like *nature* or *life* in the sense that we are always already part of what we try to understand through these concepts" (Baars, 2012: 144). Therefore, time tends to slip away not only "because we are living (in) it," but also because "we are always already living time" (Ibid). Meaning, as much as we are part of *nature* or *life* or *time*, nature, life, and time are also always part of us. In other words, we are always part of time, and time is always part of us. Our reciprocal relationship to time does not make it easier to analyse it; there is no option to explore it from an entirely detached, objective perspective.

Third, although time is a fundamental concept, not a material object, we are used to thinking about time as an external, distinctive entity like a chair or line. Consequently, there is a common-sense understanding of time as something distinct from events, life, and us. An instrumental approach to time in management and organization studies is so well rooted that it tends to overshadow existential aspects of time and temporality, especially the power of endogenous temporality and becoming. However, different possibilities to view on and theorize about both time and reality are opening up if we put an equation mark between time and life, time and subject, time and events, time and system, time and organization.

Fourth, while the distinction between the ontology of time and the ontology of temporality (Hussenot et al., 2020) is helpful to navigate through existing literature and theories, it is another duality introduced in the realm of time and temporality, which may work against Adam's (1990) call to acquire a better understanding about the relations between different forms of time. Adam claims, "We must be aware, however, that we can grasp time in its complexity only if we seek the relations between time, temporality, tempo, timing, between clock time, chronology, social time and time-consciousness, between motion, process, change, continuity and the temporal modalities of past, present and future, between time as a resource, as ordering principle and as becoming of the possible, or between any combination of these" (1990: 13). When pitching one approach against another, it is easy not to notice that "time represents two different realities at the same time: the lived and the thought," and these two realities "are completely different spheres, but equal in their ontological status" (Klempe, 2015: 20).

Schütz (1962/1982) explains this phenomenon through his analysis of action and act. Action is an intuitive continuing process led by *in-order-to* motives that always plays in the *flowing present* (Schütz, 1962/1982). Action stands for lived reality. In its teleological nature, action is always directed to the future. However, the motives of an act, which Schütz calls *because-of* motives, are always presented in the mode of reflective rationalization, which stands for the thought reality and is retrospective. That is, reflective rationalization is always directed to the past. Schütz (1962/1982) argues that because the meaning ascribed by reflective rationalization is selective, it breaks the unity of the flowing present into partial elements. Therefore, the thought reality is unable to grasp the ongoing unity of the lived reality. Nevertheless, we need them both. Therefore, it is important to be aware of these different realities, of these different ontologies, and our ability to shift our focus between them.

Fifth, many organization and management scholars who are trained to see human actors as having the agency and doing the acting might find it hard to accept the agency of time and recognize how it plays out in social reality. Also, an ultimately egocentric view creates unjustified confidence and critical blind spots—a combination that tends to lead to unpleasant unexpected consequences. Viewing our reality as an outcome of the co-creation of human (temporal) agency and agentic time does not rob human actors of their agency, although it decreases it by giving some agency to time. However, viewing reality as a kind of co-creation hopefully helps to reduce myopic beliefs associated with the superior agentic power of humans while also inhibiting the view of hegemonic time.

Sixth, the tendency of seeing the past as fixed and closed instead of open possibilities means that the future attracts most of the attention.

However, the projected, anticipated, or expected future based on the present or immediate closed past is much more limited than the future enabled by the open past. Understanding the present requires an understanding of the past. To benefit from the open past, we need to pay attention to it, including its unrealized possibilities and unactualized potentialities that are still present in the present. However, the past is not fixed and granted but dynamic. That is to say, the present influences and possibly changes the past(s) because (1) the past is continuously accumulative and (2) we assess and interpret the past through the lens of the current experience.

Seventh, it is hard to avoid a spatial representation of time and temporality. It is hard to visualize time and temporality without the help of any spatial or geometrical forms. Crilly (2017) claims we are almost universally used to thinking in spatial terms, and in our attempts to visualize time, we are forced to spatialize time at least to some extent. Several authors working with concepts like time and temporality stress the shortcomings of spatial metaphors when applied to time and temporality (i.e., Klempe, 2015; Merleau-Ponty, 2002). However, metaphors are powerful tools for shaping our understanding, approaches, and behaviours. For example, much of what clock time is criticized for results from the mechanical machine metaphor. Adam (1990: 158) claims that "Since metaphors play such a central role in our theories, it is pertinent for us to learn to *see* what has thus far been invisible: the design principles of artifacts that guide and structure our understanding. Only once we become fully aware of them can we use the metaphors to our full advantage."

The phrase *fully aware* indicates that when applying metaphors to time and temporality, we should highlight the similarities or analogies between the metaphor and the phenomena and be explicit about the differences as these differences tend to play a significant role. Ignoring differences between phenomena and metaphor could conceal some of the significant differences between the two. Instead of helping us see "what has thus far been invisible," it could cover things up or mislead us. Therefore, thinking about time and temporality in terms of space and using spatial metaphors like a flying arrow, or a flowing river, or a point or line or time travel or ego- or time-moving frames could be misleading due to their inability to grasp the nature of time and temporality and offer inappropriate analogies.

For example, Klempe (2015) argues that thinking of time in geometrical terms is pointless because time cannot be like a line consisting of past, present, and future points. That kind of visualization is inappropriate because all that exists in its actuality is present while both the past and the future do not exist. In Luhmann's expression, the past and the future are non-actualities (Luhmann, 1995). Therefore, as non-existing, the past and future points cannot form any line. At the same time, points are without direction or open to all directions, which does not allow us to draw a line with starting and ending points (Klempe, 2015). Adam (1990) claims that analysing points *in time* that do not extend temporally but are missing their endogenous temporality and future orientation could lead to diachronic or *over time* analysis only. Put differently, instead of following becoming in time we may find ourselves comparing states over time.

The spatial view also influences how we conceptualize the distant past and distant future. Distant past and distant future are almost automatically interpreted based on spatial time, as a chronometric distance from the present. However, as Augustine et al. (2019) and Hernes and Schultz (2020) have highlighted, the distance could be interpreted not as chronometrically remote but as qualitatively different from the present. Again, it is always healthy to remind ourselves that things "could also be otherwise" (Luhmann, 1995: 106). From the perspective of organizational decision-making, Crilly warns that "inappropriate analogies may provide misdirection to corporate decision-making" (2017: 2385) and recommends the use of "time-related metaphors that do not involve space" (2017: 2385–2386). Instead of spatial metaphors, Crilly recommends money-related analogies like *time is money* and *time famine* (2017: 2386). However, these analogies, although not partial, are associated with shortcomings discussed in Chap. 2.

My favourite metaphors about time, which allow a great deal of agency and creativity, are metaphors that present a field of possibilities and the "constant weaving and re-weaving of temporal threads of events" (Hernes,

2014: 186). The combination of the two mentioned metaphors could be compelling. The field of possibilities metaphor underlines the dynamic and undetermined nature of reality where each event or decision could open a door to the realization of different non-actualities. This metaphor stresses the fragility of the current state and highlights the possibility of becoming otherwise by stressing that the distant, as qualitatively different, could be closer than we tend to think, just one step away. Maybe this step is not necessarily one step forward but to the side.

Constant weaving and re-weaving is a metaphor for the active construction of temporal reality. Although a *fabric* as an outcome of *weaving* is not entirely free from spatial features, it allows the expression of a creative agency through combining different pasts and futures or different past and future events and/or possibilities, as dynamic temporal threads, into patterns in the fabric of life. Also, technically speaking, weaving uses two types of threads—ones that give a structure and others that form patterns or the content, an arrangement that is reminiscent of Luhmann's (1995) description of the pre-selection of possibilities (see Sect. 6.1). Therefore, weaving seems to incorporate different types of time, both the external, measurable, and more objective time that gives a structure and the creative material of temporality that enables the creation of patterns. The latter includes temporality as imaginative past and future possibilities connected in the present and the temporality of the *objective* time in the form of frequency, tempo, duration, and so on. These temporalities have their role in creating life patterns and keeping them intact in the fabric, while the external time acts as a structure. For their evolution, patterns follow trajectories. A tiny piece of the fabric, like a snapshot or bracketed-off piece, could reveal only very simple patterns like small polka dots. At the same time, it remains insufficient to reveal more complex and complicated patterns. Importantly, this weaving metaphor allows us to ascribe some agency to human actors and some to time or events. While human actors are active in influencing the connecting of the past and future events into the temporal patterns or event trajectories, the fabric is dynamic due to the continuously emerging and perishing time.

References

Adam, B. (1990). *Time and social theory*. Polity Press.
Adam, B. (2004). *Time*. Polity.
Aeon, B., & Aguinis, H. (2017). It's about time: New perspectives and insights on time management. *Academy of Management Perspectives, 31*(4), 309–330. https://doi.org/10.5465/amp.2016.0166
Augustine, G., Soderstrom, S., Milner, D., & Weber, K. (2019). Constructing a distant future: Imaginaries in geoengineering. *Academy of Management Journal, 62*(6), 1930–1960.
Baars, J. (2012). Critical turns of aging, narrative and time. *International Journal of Ageing and Later Life, 7*(2), 143–165.
Crilly, D. (2017). Time and space in strategy discourse: Implications for intertemporal choice. *Strategic Management Journal, 38*(12), 2370–2389.
Elias, N. (2000). *The civilizing process: Sociogenetic and psychogenetic investigations*. Blackwell Publishing.
Ellison, H. (1965). *"Repent, Harlequin" said the Ticktockman*. Retrieved July 21, 2021, from https://www.d.umn.edu/~tbacig/cst1010/chs/ellison.html or https://libcom.org/files/Repent,%20Harlequin%20said%20the%20 Ticktockman%20-%20Harlan%20Ellison.pdf
Flaherty, M. G. (2020). The lathe of time: Some principles of temporal agency. In M. G. Flaherty, L. Meinert, & A. L. Dalsgård (Eds.), *Time work: Studies of temporal agency* (pp. 13–28). Berghahn Books.
Granqvist, N., & Gustafsson, R. (2016). Temporal institutional work. *Academy of Management Journal, 59*(3), 1009–1035.
Hatch, M. (2002). Essay: Doing time in organization theory. *Organization Studies, 23*(6), 869–875.
Hernes, T. (2014). *A process theory of organization*. Oxford University Press.
Hernes, T., & Schultz, M. (2020). How actors translate between the on-going and the distant: A temporal view of situated activity. *Organization Theory, 1*. https://doi.org/10.1177/2631787719900999
Hussenot, A., Hernes, T., & Bouty, I. (2020). Studying organization from the perspective of the ontology of temporality: Introducing the event-based approach. In J. Reinecke, R. Suddaby, A. Langley, & H. Tsoukas (Eds.), *About time: Temporality and history in organization studies* (pp. 50–68). Oxford University Press. https://doi.org/10.1093/oso/9780198870715.003.0005

Klempe, S. H. (2015). Temporality and the necessity of culture in psychology. In L. M. Simão, D. S. Guimarães, & J. Valsiner (Eds.), *Temporality: Culture in the flow of human experience* (pp. 3–22). Information Age Publishing.

Levine, R. (2006). *A geography of time: The temporal misadventures of a social psychologist, or how every culture keeps time just a little bit differently*. Oneworld.

Luhmann, N. (1995). *Social systems* (J. Bednarz, Jr. with D. Baecker, Trans.). Stanford University Press.

Merleau-Ponty, M. (2002). *Phenomenology of perception*. Routledge Classics.

Oakeshott, M. (2004). *What is history? And other essays*. Imprint Academic.

Putnam, L., Fairhurst, G. T., & Banghart, S. (2016). Contradictions, dialectics, and paradoxes in organizations: A constitutive approach. *The Academy of Management Annals, 10*(1), 65–171. https://doi.org/10.1080/19416520.2016.1162421

Reinecke, J., & Ansari, S. (2015). When times collide: Temporal brokerage at the intersection of markets and developments. *Academy of Management Journal, 58*(2), 618–648.

Schütz, A. (1962/1982). *Collected papers I: The problem of social reality* (M. Natason, Ed.). Martinus Nijhoff Publishers.

Slawinski, N., & Bansal, P. (2015). Short on time: Intertemporal tensions in business sustainability. *Organization Science, 26*(2), 531.

Wallace, M., & Rabin, A. I. (1960). Temporal experience. *Psychological Bulletin, 57*(3), 213–236.

Whitehead, A. N. (1929/1978). *Process and reality*. The Free Press.

Zerubavel, E. (1982). The standardization of time: A sociohistorical perspective. *American Journal of Sociology, 1*, 1–23.

Zerubavel, E. (1991). *The fine line: Making distinctions in every*. University of Chicago Press.

Index[1]

A

Abundance, 99–101, 104, 105, 148
A-causal, 252, 255
Acceleration, 7, 27, 32, 44, 46, 51, 93, 236
Achronal, 253
Act, 20, 25, 36, 91, 100, 138, 148, 149, 169, 190, 194, 195, 212, 238, 257, 260, 266, 283, 286
Action, 7, 18, 25, 26, 32, 37, 45, 52, 53, 70, 85, 86, 91, 99, 103, 105, 106, 118, 119, 123, 132, 133, 143, 148, 150, 151, 154–156, 158, 161, 164, 168–170, 173, 174, 187, 192–199, 202, 210, 214, 217, 218, 223, 239, 252, 259, 261, 262, 280, 283
Activities/activity, 10, 17, 18, 21, 23, 28–32, 34–38, 40–43, 46, 54–56, 69, 71–74, 79, 80, 85, 86, 93, 94, 100, 104, 106, 107, 130, 135, 140, 141, 145, 173–175, 187, 188, 190–201, 209, 212, 215, 219, 224, 234, 237, 238, 245, 246, 249, 251, 252, 255, 266, 268, 270
Actualities/actuality, 146, 147, 149, 152, 154, 157, 169, 222, 267, 285
Actualization potential/potentialities, 9, 145–151, 153, 164, 175, 269
Adam, Barbara, 6, 17, 19, 27, 29, 43, 44, 52, 54, 55, 171, 195, 235, 245, 246, 252, 259, 278, 281, 282, 284, 285

---

[1] Note: Page numbers followed by 'n' refer to notes.

Agency, 8–10, 80, 82, 83, 86, 88, 92–95, 97, 105, 139–151, 153, 155–157, 172–174, 176, 197, 217, 256, 257, 259, 268, 270, 283, 285, 286
  See also Agency of time; Temporal, agency; Temporal, structure of an agency
Agency of time, 10, 105, 143–145, 164, 175, 176, 223, 283
Agentic power, 69, 80, 82, 83, 92, 95, 97, 105, 175, 194, 234, 258, 259, 283
Allocentric, 154
Alzheimer, 125
Amazon, 29, 29n3, 30, 30n4, 44, 278
Anterograde amnesia, 125
Anthropocene, 219, 251
Anticipating, 81, 169, 211
Anticipation, 49, 71, 84, 103, 126, 128, 133, 144, 148, 162, 165, 169, 171, 190, 197, 214, 245–247, 260, 261, 264, 268
Anxiety, 47, 107, 157, 170
Apple, 248
Aristotle, 1, 221
Arkhipov, Vasily, 249, 250, 253, 259
Attention, 3, 4, 6–8, 10, 19, 28, 29, 37, 40, 41, 41n5, 53, 56, 68, 69, 71, 86, 90, 93, 117, 119, 129, 132, 134, 141, 145, 151, 158, 167, 176, 203, 204, 208, 217n4, 234, 236, 242, 247, 249, 254, 262, 280, 281, 283, 284
Awareness, 101, 138, 141, 164, 210, 278

B
Baars, Jan, 19, 54, 55, 117, 123, 124, 140, 164, 167, 170, 171, 186, 277, 278, 282
Backward, 217, 236, 243, 253
Because-of motives, 133, 134, 164, 283
Become otherwise, 12, 148, 149, 164, 216, 248, 260
Becoming, 3, 9–12, 35, 103, 118, 120, 130, 137, 138, 140–142, 144–152, 154, 155, 163, 164, 170, 172, 175, 176, 186, 202, 203, 207, 213, 216, 219, 221, 222, 238, 243, 249, 253, 257–270, 282, 283, 285, 286
Being, x, 4, 9, 20, 24–26, 31, 35–37, 45–47, 51, 55, 69, 70, 72, 73, 78, 80, 88, 92, 93, 99, 102–106, 119, 120, 122, 124, 127, 130, 134, 135, 139–146, 148, 150, 152, 154, 157, 158, 162, 163, 165, 166, 169–172, 175, 176, 188, 191, 192, 194, 195, 197, 198, 201, 202, 205, 206, 209, 211, 214, 216, 219, 221, 222, 224, 236, 236n1, 238, 244, 253, 254, 257–259, 261–264, 270, 277
Being-as-having-been, 162, 163
Being-ready-to-hand, 220
Bergson, Henri, 117, 121–123, 139, 239
Berlin Brandenburg Airport (BBA), 75
Bifurcation point, 153, 262
Blattner, William, 122, 125, 128–130, 132–135, 139, 140

Index

Bluedorn, Allen C., 4, 7, 10, 18, 24, 26–28, 31, 33–35, 38, 42–44, 46, 47, 52, 53, 77, 78, 89–91, 118, 119, 124, 192, 195, 201, 212, 213, 217, 252
Boredom, 50, 69, 70, 99–104, 106
Boundary condition, 201
Bracketing off/out, 257

C

Callender, Craig, 1–4, 6, 68, 69, 71, 77–79, 82, 83, 86, 126, 132, 142n4, 143, 145, 152–158, 165, 201, 207, 238, 240, 242, 253
Causal asymmetry, 156, 158
Causality, 252, 254
Ceteris paribus, 253, 255
Chernobyl, 151
Chronocentric worldview, 51, 279
Chronocentrism, 49, 50, 102
Chronological time, 18–20, 76, 205, 253
Chronological view, 234
Chronometric time, 19, 55, 70, 100, 167, 238
Closed, 96, 157, 165, 198, 199, 251, 264, 269, 283, 284
Co-creation, 176, 283
Cognitive frame(s), 94, 95
Coherent temporality, 130
Common sense, 18, 24, 28, 119, 222, 223, 277, 278, 282
Complexity, 17, 32, 53, 85, 117, 163, 187, 194, 206, 238, 254–256, 265, 282
Concentric, 203, 205, 206, 208
Conscious, 37, 48, 69, 121, 127–130, 132, 137, 138, 142, 145, 168, 175, 209
Consequence(s), 3, 6, 19, 22, 24, 25, 43–52, 73–75, 78–80, 95, 96, 103, 148, 149, 153, 154, 175, 209, 219, 240, 247, 250, 255, 256, 262, 278, 280, 283
Context, 10, 19, 36, 42, 54, 68, 79, 83, 92, 105, 165, 173, 174, 185–224, 235, 241, 242, 254, 266, 277, 281
Contingencies, 9, 105, 144, 147, 173, 190, 244
Continuity, 9, 55, 96, 105, 120, 124–132, 135–138, 141, 144, 145, 159, 169–171, 186, 190, 191, 205, 217, 224, 260, 262, 265, 283
Coordination, 6, 7, 17, 21, 30–44, 52, 55, 191, 193, 197, 203, 206, 207, 211, 212, 223
Coping, 36, 43, 100–102, 108, 152, 209, 260
Corporeal imagination, 222
COVID-19, 55, 105, 106, 235, 237
Creativity, 55, 56, 97, 102, 144, 285
Cuban Missile Crisis, 249
Cues, 74, 86, 106, 167, 168, 245, 256
Cycles, 17, 28, 33–40, 42, 44, 99, 191, 192, 212, 238, 247
Cyclical time, 237, 278

D

Danske Bank, 96
Death, 70, 78, 96, 137, 222

Decision-making, 46, 47, 79, 85, 124, 158, 159, 174, 235, 261, 266, 285
Dementia, 125
Depression, 47, 50, 102, 103, 106, 107, 125
Difference, 5, 6, 8, 22, 68, 71, 81, 81n3, 86, 89–91, 118, 139, 140, 152, 156, 158, 159, 170, 190, 194, 216, 217, 224, 267, 269, 270, 284
Direction, 2, 11, 55, 68, 77–88, 90, 92, 128, 131–133, 136, 137, 144, 155, 158, 163, 164, 173, 193, 200, 239, 245, 256, 261, 262, 269, 285
Disactualisation, 129
Discontinuity, 91, 190, 191, 224, 255
Disentrainment, 38, 39
Disorientation, 125, 129
Distance, 79, 82, 83, 86, 90, 91, 204, 265, 285
Distant, 8, 12, 25, 42, 79, 83, 85, 90, 91, 124, 136, 168, 170, 252, 261, 262, 265, 267, 285, 286
Disturbance, 130, 132
Duration, 5, 8, 18, 19, 26, 32, 42, 54, 67–77, 79, 91, 93, 99, 100, 103, 108, 130, 133, 141, 142, 144, 190, 196, 197, 199, 202, 212, 224, 235, 243, 244, 246, 286

E

Ecological imaginary, 26, 27
Economic imaginary, 26, 27
Effectiveness, 7, 22, 24, 25, 28, 31, 33, 39, 44, 47

Efficiency, 7, 24, 25, 28, 31, 44, 86, 210, 215, 252, 279
Egocentric, 154, 155, 279, 283
Ego-centric view, 163
Ego-moving frame, 81–87
Elapsing present, 124, 153
Emergence, 20, 24, 121, 253, 260, 261, 268
Emergent, 54, 92, 174, 193, 198, 253
Emerging, viii, 50, 120, 126, 127, 143–146, 154, 157, 164, 172, 175, 247, 258, 260, 261, 268, 286
Emotional well-being, 97
Empty, 45, 69, 97, 99, 100, 147, 237, 243, 278
Entity, 9, 39, 118, 120, 127, 139, 141, 142, 175, 205, 252, 255, 258, 260, 270, 282
Entraining, 32, 35, 37, 56, 200
Entrainment (theory), 7, 35, 40–43, 251
Environment, 25, 30, 32, 35–37, 39, 41, 47–51, 53, 81, 85, 92, 95, 101, 106, 150, 174, 196, 203–205, 216, 218, 223, 265
Episodic memory, 121
Eso-time, 186, 201–203, 205, 210–216, 217n4, 220, 221, 238
Estimation, 8, 36, 68, 71, 72, 74, 76
Estonia, 95, 213, 215, 246, 262, 265
Events/event
  actual, 242, 247, 266
  confirming, 240, 241, 243
  deviating, 240, 243
  discrete, 252, 254, 256, 257, 266, 269
  improbable, 240, 241, 243
  probable, 240, 241, 243

time, vii, 5, 11, 40, 41, 192, 194, 237, 245
trajectory, 133, 240, 241, 245–250, 253, 260, 262, 268, 286
Events-based time, 5, 11, 12, 142, 233–270
Everyday coping, 108
Existential, 5, 6, 50, 52, 96, 108, 119, 121, 122, 127, 128, 130, 133, 139, 157, 270
Existentiality, 145
Existential temporality, 108, 121, 176, 282
Expectation, 9, 26, 71, 73, 80, 84, 86, 102, 126, 129–131, 133, 157, 161, 165, 171, 186, 188, 197, 209, 214, 224, 237, 239, 246, 264
Expectational structures, 239–241, 249
Expecting, 71, 122
Experience, 5, 7–9, 12, 18, 45, 48, 51, 56, 67, 69–73, 77, 78, 84, 91, 93, 94, 96, 100, 103, 108, 118–139, 144, 145, 152–155, 161, 164–167, 185, 187–189, 236, 238, 244, 253, 256, 261, 263, 264, 267, 269, 270, 284
Experienced differences, 46
Extended present, 49, 91, 96, 101, 103, 105
Eyjafjallajökull, 262

F

Fallacy, 72–76, 79, 83, 88, 90, 108
Fallacy of misplaced concreteness, 255, 280
Fargo, 154
Fast, 1, 46–48, 50–52, 54, 214, 218

Field of possibilities, 12, 129, 269, 285, 286
50 First Dates, 125
Filling time, 107
Fingerprint, 88, 172, 195, 210, 212
Finitude, 99, 127
Fleeting now, 153
Flow, 40, 77–88, 123, 130, 135, 145, 153, 155, 156, 166, 189, 221, 254, 255, 260
Forgetting, 45, 167, 168, 170
F-Origin, 248
Forward, 76, 79–81, 83, 134, 136, 158, 171, 173, 197, 217, 286
Fragmentation, 4, 129–131, 136
Frame(s), 27, 68, 76, 78, 80–89, 81n3, 94, 95, 108, 125, 127, 128, 154, 205, 208, 209, 211, 217, 237, 285
Fuchs, Thomas, 49, 95, 97, 103, 105, 107, 117, 123, 125, 128–132, 135, 137, 145, 148, 158, 185, 188, 261
Fukushima, 151
Fundamental, 6, 40, 44, 77, 78, 89, 146, 187, 194, 266, 282
Future, 5, 6, 8–10, 18, 19, 25–27, 34, 42, 48–51, 72–74, 77–79, 102–107, 118, 120–125, 156–172, 186, 188, 190–193, 195–200, 209, 233, 242, 244, 246, 252, 253, 283–286

G

Geometrical, 202, 284, 285
Gig economy, 47
Gig-worker, 47
Gurvitch, Georges, 2, 189–191, 194, 201, 210, 211

H

Hegemony, 104
Heidegger, Martin, 117, 118, 120–122, 122n2, 124, 127–129, 132–134, 139, 140, 145–147, 154, 157, 158, 162, 175, 187, 188, 202, 210, 212, 220, 233, 255–257
Hernes, Tor, 3, 6, 9, 12, 20, 42–44, 91, 107, 117, 118, 120, 123, 124, 126, 127, 135, 137, 138, 141, 143–145, 147, 148, 150, 152, 155, 161, 162, 165, 166, 168, 170–173, 175, 187, 188, 194–200, 207, 209, 210, 217, 219, 233–235, 240, 241, 247, 251, 252, 255–269, 285
High temporal uncertainty, 41, 42
Husserl, Edmund, 117, 118, 120, 128, 130, 132, 133, 171

I

Imaginary, 26, 27, 91, 151
Imaginative, 151, 173, 286
Immanence, 10, 168–172, 266–270
Immanent, 12, 267
Immediate, 8, 25, 72, 83, 86, 122–124, 128–130, 135, 150, 155, 165, 166, 170, 203, 204, 208, 252, 261, 265, 284
Infinity, 103, 127
InnoShip, 263, 264
Innovation, 55, 194, 200
In-order-to motives, 133, 134, 283
Instantaneous time, 47, 48, 103
Intensification, 7, 48, 49, 103
Intentional, 10, 36, 45, 86, 127, 158, 193, 211, 220, 261, 280
Intentionality, 137, 157, 158, 166, 169, 174, 187, 233
Intentions, 9, 121, 129, 157, 158, 194, 210
Interactions, 25, 32, 35, 37, 40, 41, 93, 101, 103, 107, 135, 143, 186, 188, 189, 191, 203, 209, 210, 221, 224
Interconnectedness, 88, 205
Interdependency, 32, 49, 52, 74
Interest
　economic, 24
　legal, 24
　political, 24
　social, 24, 53
International Meridian Conference, 22, 24
Interruption, 130, 265
Intersubjective, 5, 10, 185–189, 203, 205, 209–211, 223, 224
Intra-actions, 255
Intrasubjective, 67, 121
Involuntary, 36–38
Irreversibility, 123, 164, 204, 221, 236, 240, 260
Irreversible, 40, 45, 78, 123, 163, 164, 175, 203, 208, 218, 221, 224, 236, 240
Isolation, 55, 99, 100, 102, 106, 186, 218, 237, 252, 266

J

Jazz, 38, 39

K

Killing time, 101, 107
Kodak, 247–249, 254, 259

L

LEGO, 138
Levine, Robert, 2, 5, 69, 125, 126, 195, 202, 212, 213, 245, 252, 280
Life, vii, ix, 2, 7, 10, 18–20, 23, 24, 26–28, 30, 43–47, 50, 52, 53, 55, 56, 68–70, 73, 74, 76, 78, 96, 97, 99, 106, 107, 122, 125, 127, 130, 135, 152, 153, 155, 156, 158, 162, 164, 185–187, 189, 190, 193, 209, 211, 212, 215, 216, 223, 224, 236–239, 243, 244, 246, 257, 259, 265, 270, 278, 282, 286
Life markers, 243, 259
Limited coping, 146, 147
Linear, 189, 194, 252, 253, 262, 265
Lived experience, 8, 9, 118–138, 163, 165, 172, 175, 176, 187, 220, 270
Local time, 18, 20–22, 54
Lockdown, 55, 106, 237
Long-present, 91, 103, 199
Long-term, 26, 27, 84, 85, 94, 125, 194, 198, 219, 281
Luhmann, Niklas, 2, 6, 11, 24, 25, 30, 39, 53, 79, 123–126, 138, 148, 152, 154, 155, 157–159, 162–168, 174, 196, 216, 221, 233–236, 236n1, 238–243, 247, 248, 250, 252–254, 259–261, 266, 267, 285, 286

M

Macro-time, 10, 186, 201–203, 205, 206, 217–219, 250
Making time, 74, 101, 107

Manifold, 121, 253, 261, 268, 269
Manipulation, 53, 280
Mead, George Herbert, 9, 67, 103, 117, 123, 126, 127, 133, 139, 141, 142, 145, 151, 152, 154, 155, 157, 161, 165, 168, 173, 174, 197, 217, 233, 260, 261
Meaning, 5, 10–12, 37, 43, 48, 53, 54, 68, 79, 95, 96, 99, 101, 103, 104, 107, 123, 124, 127, 128, 132, 133, 138, 146, 148, 149, 153, 154, 157, 161, 165, 168–172, 174, 186–192, 195, 196, 209, 210, 212, 215–218, 220, 221, 224, 237, 238, 245, 247, 250, 253, 256, 258, 261–265, 267, 269, 277, 282, 283
Measurement, 18, 19, 44, 52, 54, 70, 212, 237, 238, 280
Memento, 125, 128
Memory/memories, 73, 74, 76, 88, 108, 121, 124–126, 131, 137, 156, 159, 165–168, 171, 186, 199, 209, 218, 233, 256, 265
Memory bias account, 74
Mental disorder, 125
Mental wellbeing, 127
Merleau-Ponty, Maurice, 78–80, 117–122, 124, 126, 127, 134, 139–141, 141n3, 144, 158, 170, 175, 187, 203, 218, 220, 233, 258, 284
Meso-time, 10, 201–203, 205, 208–211, 214, 216, 217, 219, 221, 238
Metaphor, 8, 12, 39, 40, 68, 77–88, 81n3, 121, 202, 205, 210, 212, 284–286

Micro-time, 10, 186, 202–205, 208–214, 217, 219, 221, 224, 250
Moment, 40, 50, 92, 100, 123, 126, 129, 146, 148, 149, 152–155, 159, 162–166, 169, 170, 172–174, 176, 198, 234, 235, 242, 244, 260–262, 265, 266
Monetized time, 7, 28, 30
Monotony, 50, 54, 100, 103, 104
Multidimensional, 121, 174, 187, 188, 194
Multidimensionality, 187, 207
MyDevice, 248
Mythological thinking, 25–27, 56

N

Network of events, 208, 268
Network of intentionalities, 126
Nokia, 247–249, 254, 259
Non-actualities/non-actuality, 148, 152, 165, 169, 242, 253, 267, 285, 286
Non-events, 247, 252, 253, 261, 263
Non-perfect aspect, 132
Now, 1, 3, 50, 51, 82, 120, 123, 130, 131, 142, 151–156, 159, 162, 165, 166, 173, 215, 219, 253, 257

O

Oakeshott, Michael, 159, 161, 168, 171, 213, 218, 257, 261, 279
Objective time, 5, 6, 8, 11, 18, 52, 67–108, 120, 121, 186, 187, 189, 192, 197, 212, 244, 286
One-directional, 143, 204, 210, 218, 256

Ongoing present, 126, 137, 152, 155, 162, 165, 168, 176, 259, 267
Ongoing temporality, 6, 124–126, 155, 165, 166, 216, 221, 224, 242, 262, 266
Ontogenetic, 203, 208, 222
Ontology of temporality, 6, 9, 11, 12, 92, 93, 117, 187, 240, 257, 258, 269, 282
Ontology of time, 6–8, 11, 12, 18, 42, 56, 67, 93, 119, 187, 240, 251, 257, 269, 282
Open, 12, 23–25, 39, 75, 78, 119, 129, 130, 140, 144, 147, 148, 156–159, 161, 163–166, 170, 171, 176, 193, 195, 213, 236, 238, 240, 242, 248, 258, 261, 264, 268, 283–286
Openness, 10, 145, 149, 157, 158, 164, 166, 171, 198, 214, 255, 265
Order of events, 18, 55, 251–255
Organizational temporality, 126, 135, 138
Organizational time, x, 11, 189, 195, 215, 240, 242
Organization meaning structures, 135, 137, 138, 199, 210
Oscillations, 38
Overabundance, 97, 103

P

Pandemic, 105–107, 235
Passage, 18, 69–71, 73–75, 142, 218, 242, 252, 261
Passing, 9, 69, 70, 97, 101, 107, 108, 123, 126, 127, 142, 143, 145, 175

Index

Passing time, 9, 104, 106, 107, 118, 120, 123, 124, 126–132, 139–151, 164, 170, 171, 175, 176, 187
Past
  closed, 251, 283, 284
  encapsulated, 159, 161
  historical, 159, 161, 257
  open, 159, 284
  practical, 159, 161, 213, 218
  recalled, 159, 161
  remembered, 159, 161
  short-term, 198, 199
Pathological time, 49
Perfect aspect, 132–134, 138
Periodicity, 17, 19, 21, 28, 30, 32, 35, 38, 39, 56
Periodic view of time, 251, 255
Perishing, 107, 120, 123, 126, 127, 141, 143–145, 148, 164, 166, 175, 242, 268, 286
Personal time frame, 208
Petrov, Stanislav, 249, 250, 253, 259
Phase, 32, 35, 38, 70, 128, 254
Phenomenological, 26, 94, 118–120, 126, 140, 141, 154, 187, 202, 218, 233
Phenomenology, 9, 92, 120, 122, 125, 128, 187
Phenomenon of retrospective coherence, 253
Physics, ix, 1–4, 7, 18, 19, 152, 153, 155, 207, 255
Planning fallacy, 8, 72–76, 83, 88, 108
Plurality, 10, 53, 54, 187, 189–194, 202, 220, 221, 224, 257
Possibilities, 4, 9, 10, 12, 36, 37, 46, 50, 51, 56, 78, 90, 91, 94, 99, 104, 122, 125, 126, 128–130, 144–153, 156–159, 161–166, 168–170, 172–176, 186, 193, 212–214, 221, 224, 236, 238–242, 247–254, 256, 258, 259, 261, 262, 264, 268, 269, 282–286
Potentialities, 91, 144–151, 153, 156, 157, 162–164, 172, 175, 213, 221, 222, 242, 249, 250, 268, 269, 284
Power, 7, 24, 30, 35, 50, 53, 69, 80, 82, 83, 91, 92, 95, 97, 102, 105, 108, 128, 147, 171–173, 175, 194, 201, 213, 214, 218, 223, 234, 242, 247, 249, 250, 255–259, 265, 270, 279, 282, 283
Prehend, 254, 262, 266, 269
Prehension, 145, 266
Present, 4, 10, 19, 73, 118, 168, 176, 188, 252, 253, 255, 283
Pre-visioning, 129
Prison, 97, 99–103, 105
Probabilities/probability, 73, 76, 124, 129, 148, 157, 158, 173, 222, 240, 249
Process, 5, 9, 11, 28, 30, 32, 35, 36, 38, 41, 47, 48, 56, 74, 91, 101, 119, 122–124, 127–130, 132, 136, 145, 146, 157, 161, 167–169, 172–175, 189, 194, 197, 212, 216, 221, 234–243, 250, 251, 253, 255, 258, 260, 269, 270, 283
  theory, 79, 119, 146, 221, 233, 258
  view, 11, 240
Projecting, 134, 169, 173
Projection, 121, 170, 173, 176

Protention, 103, 128–132
Proximity, 37, 84, 86, 108, 124
Psychology, 2, 3, 8–10, 36, 40, 67, 68, 71, 108, 117, 124–126, 151, 153, 204, 206, 207, 233, 244

Q

Queen Elizabeth, 147

R

Railroads, 21–24, 55
Range of possibilities, 130, 152, 153, 157, 172, 236, 254
Rationality
 formal, 24, 25
 instrumental, 24, 25
 substantive, 24, 25
 value, 24, 25
Realisation of possibilities, 145–151, 175, 269
Realism, 139, 140
Realities/reality, 3, 6–8, 10, 18, 20, 25, 43, 55, 56, 67, 68, 77, 79, 86, 96, 108, 118, 119, 124, 125, 127, 138, 151, 152, 156, 157, 162, 174, 175, 187, 201, 206, 207, 220, 222–224, 238, 242, 258, 262, 267, 269, 270, 278–283, 286
Real time, 43, 140
Reckoning, 18, 21, 22, 24, 25, 54, 55, 187, 189–194, 243, 246, 247, 249
Recollection, 120, 129
Reflection, 4, 20, 23, 55, 129, 130, 138, 173, 222, 223

Relevance, 100, 124, 125, 132–134, 152, 159, 165, 171, 209
Relevant, 4, 22, 102, 132–135, 138, 174, 263, 281
Remembering, 148, 161, 167, 168, 170
Responsibility, 25, 250, 259
Retention, 128–132
Rhythm, 17, 32, 34–42, 54, 99, 100, 105, 106, 185, 186, 192, 203, 208, 211, 236, 246
Risk, 31, 37, 41, 85, 106, 147–150, 243, 264

S

Samsung, 248
Sasson, Steve, 247, 248
Schizophrenia, 125
Schütz, Alfred, 133, 134, 151, 158, 168, 187, 197, 256, 264, 283
Scientific Management, 28, 29
Sequencing, 32, 34, 42
Sequential time, 12, 251–253
Short-term, 25, 47, 83, 85, 86, 88, 94, 125, 171, 194, 198, 199, 281
Short-termism, 7, 25–27, 47, 86, 91, 215
Signifiers, 11, 12, 234, 243–255, 265, 270
Simultaneous/simultaneously, x, 6, 12, 35, 36, 38, 40, 46, 84, 90, 93, 99, 120, 123, 128, 129, 134, 142, 145, 163, 165, 169, 175, 191, 192, 194, 199, 203, 205, 218, 236, 249, 253, 259, 261, 264, 268
Slow Movement, 51, 52

Social
  accomplishment, 20
  imaginary, 26, 27
  power, 24, 30
  structure, 93, 235, 238, 239
Society, 8, 17, 19, 20, 26–28, 43, 46, 48–52, 95, 102, 186, 190, 191, 211, 212, 214–217, 219, 221–223, 239, 243, 246, 247, 251, 278, 279
Sociology of expectations, 214
Soviet Air Defence Forces, 249
Soviet occupation, 95, 214, 215, 265
Soviet Union, 214, 265
Spatial, 8, 12, 49, 53, 68, 77–88, 81n3, 92, 121, 140, 188, 202, 207, 251, 257, 260, 267, 284–286
Speed, 29, 32, 44, 46–48, 51, 52, 54, 219
Standardized clock time, 7, 10, 19–27, 20n2, 54, 55, 185, 223
State-like, 36, 88, 89, 92
Structure, ix, 10, 11, 20, 26, 32, 42, 43, 45, 55, 79, 93, 118, 128, 138, 141, 172–176, 189, 191–194, 196–200, 203, 205, 209, 210, 214, 234–243, 249, 250, 256, 259, 260, 270, 280, 284, 286
Subject, 9, 10, 93, 118, 122, 128, 140, 142, 143, 161, 165, 172, 187, 209, 216, 250, 269, 282
Subjective time, 5, 6, 8, 10, 53, 67–108, 118, 120, 152, 172, 185, 187, 188, 195, 208, 209, 220
Subsidiary awareness, 137

Subsystem, 240, 242, 243
Surplus of possibilities, 236, 261
Survival, 51, 122, 141, 190, 219, 246
Sustainability, 26, 48, 51, 52, 85, 86, 150, 250, 251, 280
Synchronization, 34, 38, 40, 41n5

T
Taken-for-granted, 12, 23, 27, 28, 39, 209, 220, 223, 278, 281
Telic aspect, 132–134, 213
Tempo, 5, 19, 32, 35, 36, 38, 39, 46, 47, 54, 196, 283, 286
Temporal
  agency, 9, 10, 68, 80, 88, 93–108, 144, 157, 163, 172, 173, 176, 195, 256, 283
  agony, 102
  aspect(s), 8, 132–135, 195, 197
  autonomy, 42, 100, 102, 104, 105
  bias, 40
  conditions, 94, 97, 107, 108, 172
  context, 105, 187, 188, 201, 205, 209, 210, 212, 213, 220, 223
  continuity, 9, 96, 105, 125, 130, 135–138, 217
  coordination, 17, 30, 31, 41, 193
  cues, 74
  depth, 8, 68, 88–93, 103, 108, 124, 198, 199, 212, 213n1, 217
  dimensions, 5, 8, 67–108, 119–122, 124, 127, 128, 136, 174, 175, 186, 196, 202, 203, 212, 258

Index

Temporal (cont.)
  distance, 83, 86, 90, 265
  elements, 43, 121, 169, 176, 197, 210, 234, 235, 238, 241, 242, 260, 270
  estimation, 36
  existence, 107, 127, 144, 259
  fit, ix, 41, 42, 195
  focus, 10, 68, 89, 90, 92, 93, 108, 174, 195, 212, 213n1
  frame(s), 68, 89, 154
  framing, 82
  idealism, 9, 118, 139–151, 175, 202, 258
  monotony, 50
  norms, 223, 235, 239, 278
  orientation, 10, 43, 68, 88–93, 108, 172, 174, 176, 187, 194–201, 209, 211, 212, 224, 281
  orientation of activities, 10, 93, 195–201, 224
  patterns, 35, 42, 43, 172, 187, 286
  personality, 88, 91, 172, 210
  positioning, 119
  realism, 18, 43, 56, 139, 140, 187
  reality, 119, 124, 162, 201, 223, 224, 269, 270, 286
  reckoning systems, 55
  reference, 17, 19, 20, 30, 55, 126, 173, 195, 196, 209, 235
  structure of an agency, 10, 118, 172–176
  structures, 10, 20, 42, 43, 55, 93, 118, 172–176, 190–194, 197, 198, 200, 209, 235, 237–239, 270
  structuring, 9, 10, 41, 44, 55, 236
  struggles, 136, 201, 202
  trajectory, 137, 241, 260, 266
  unit(s), 69, 74, 256
  work, 9, 10, 191–194
Temporality
  endogenous temporality, 6, 9, 118–120, 131, 139–151, 164, 175, 186, 187, 196, 197, 241, 256, 258, 282, 285
  exogenous temporality, 119, 120
  explicit temporality, 130, 131, 135–137, 145, 164
  implicit temporality, 129–131, 135, 136, 138, 145, 164, 165
  subjective temporality, 9, 10, 90, 92, 107, 108, 118–138, 141, 175, 176, 185–188, 208
Terminal illness, 95
Time
  bias, 8
  deepening, 45, 46
  famine, 7, 45, 97, 285
  giver, 35–37, 40, 212
  horizon, 26, 49, 90, 154
  management, 2, 27–31, 40, 44, 101, 282
  marking, 100, 103, 104, 258
  orientation, 8, 42, 88, 90, 101, 195–197, 209, 210, 224
  perception, 8, 44, 45, 67–71, 74, 120, 124
  perception bias, 8
  prediction, 72, 76, 77
  pressure, 7, 45–47, 97, 104–106, 236
  reckoning systems, 18, 22–24, 54, 55, 187, 189–194, 221, 224, 245–251, 259
  travel, 121, 285

unit of life, 238, 243
work, 4, 11, 23, 93–108, 215
Time as a context, 185–224, 217n4
Time-centric view, 80–88, 155, 164
Time-moving frame, 80–88, 94, 95
Timetables, 21, 32, 34, 55, 170
Trait-like, 37, 90, 92
Trajectory of events, 134, 241, 245, 260
Transcendence, 259, 265, 282
Two-directional, 256
Typology of social times, 194

U

Uncertainty, 32, 41, 42, 83, 85, 94, 136, 154, 158, 193
Unconscious, 121, 127, 128, 133, 134, 164, 209
Underestimation, 8, 72, 75, 76
Uneventful, 69, 99, 103, 243, 244
Unfolding time, 128
Unintentional, 36, 37, 86, 280
Unplanned, 250
Unpredictable, 41, 157, 192
Unpredicted, 153, 250
Urgency, 32, 45, 46, 84, 95, 105, 192, 250

V

Väänänen, Johannes, 248
Validity of a process, 241
Validity of expectations, 241
Valsiner, Jaan, 117, 123, 124, 126, 153, 156, 157, 162, 206, 253, 260–262

Vico, Giambattista, 221, 222
Virtual, 147, 154, 175, 248
Voluntary, 36, 37, 106

W

Waiting, 54, 69–71, 74, 80, 84, 95, 99, 101, 106, 107, 158, 237, 251
Well-being, 46, 48, 96, 97
Whitehead, Alfred North, 7, 9, 19, 97, 117, 123, 126, 141–143, 145, 146, 157, 169, 170, 233, 234, 255–258, 264, 266–268, 280
Window of opportunity, 153, 200, 262, 263
World, 5, 6, 9, 22, 24–27, 40, 41, 49, 50, 52, 55, 56, 78, 106, 120, 122–124, 127, 128, 140–146, 150, 156, 158, 171, 174, 176, 185–188, 196, 197, 202, 209, 211–216, 220, 221, 233, 250, 252, 253, 255, 256, 279
Worldview, 24, 27, 44, 51, 55, 202, 212, 252, 279

Z

Zeitgeber, 35, 41, 212
Zerubavel, Eviatar, 2, 5, 7, 8, 10, 17, 19–22, 20n1, 27, 28, 32, 42, 43, 52–55, 77, 78, 171, 186, 190, 212, 217n4, 218, 235, 243, 262, 263, 265, 280

CPSIA information can be obtained
at www.ICGtesting.com
Printed in the USA
LVHW082229170222
711449LV00004B/67